# RODIN

# RODIN

BERNARD
CHAMPIGNEULLE

New York and Toronto
OXFORD UNIVERSITY PRESS

TRANSLATED FROM THE FRENCH BY

# J. MAXWELL BROWNJOHN

© 1967 EDITIONS AIMERY SOMOGY S.A., PARIS
THIS EDITION © 1967 THAMES AND HUDSON, LONDON
REPRINTED 1980

**Library of Congress Cataloging in Publication Data**

Champigneulle, Bernard, 1896–
  Rodin
  (The World of Art)
  Bibliography: p.
  Includes index
  1. Rodin, Auguste, 1840–1917. 2. Sculptors—
France—Biography. I. Series: World of Art.
(INB553.R7C43 1980)   730′.92′4 (B) 79–26175
ISBN 0–19–520191–4

*Printed in Spain by*
*Printer Industria Gráfica, s.a.   Provenza, 388   Barcelona*
*D.L.B. 9596-1980*

# Contents

# Foreword

I do not know why I should have been so fascinated by a reproduction found by chance in a heap of old newspapers. I was fourteen or fifteen at the time, and art scarcely figured among the preoccupations of my adolescent world. At school, where we set up our easels in serried ranks, drawing-classes were largely an excuse for noisy horse-play. Rodin, then at the end of his career, meant nothing to me.

Even so, I could not tear my eyes away from that serenely radiant face as it jutted from its rugged and almost uncut block of marble. The caption read : ' Rodin—Bust '. I had never yet lingered over a work of art nor sensed its mysterious appeal, but I read a great deal. Privately, I christened this piece of sculpture ' mind divorced from matter '.

A German art book which I bought not long afterwards informed me that it was *Thought*, one of the illustrious sculptor's best-known works. I had cut the picture out and mounted it above my desk so that, when my mind strayed from the tedium of Latin prose composition, my eyes would meet those of the marble head. It would be dishonest to pretend that *Thought* brought me any intellectual stimulation. It just encouraged my day-dreaming.

While I would not place this sculpture at the peak of Rodin's œuvre, it certainly taught me that works of art can be imbued with a strange power which enables us to exchange what we bestow on them for what they bestow on us.

The marble head spoke to me with mute fervour because it had, after all, been conceived by a great artist. I soon discovered that this artist was regarded as a contemporary genius—a fact which made an even greater impact on me because I had always imagined that a genius had to be a historical figure.

An ordinary photograph is hard put to it to reveal the art of the sculptor, with its countless interactions between light and matter. Nevertheless, this one introduced me to an unknown world—the world of art, which has constantly whetted my curiosity and has led me to devote the greater part of my life to its study.

Now, after more than half a century, I have been presented with an opportunity to express my gratitude to Rodin. He has been an unfailing source of joy to me. May his shade forgive me if, in my eternal inability to stifle the spirit of criticism, I have sometimes treated him with reserve or severity.

B. C.

# CHAPTER ONE

## The silent schoolboy

Neighbourhoods are like human beings. They are born, grow up, become handsome or ugly, change their outward appearance, and age without forfeiting their personality. The same spirit lives on in them. Rodin first saw the light of day in Mouffetard, a motley quarter prone to public tumult and rooted in the early history of Paris. Its backbone, the long and narrow Rue Mouffetard, which runs from the Place de la Contrescarpe to Saint-Médard, was the old route from Italy, the Roman road to Lutetia, traversed by marching legions and the patrician builders of the Montagne Sainte-Geneviève. The Faubourg Saint-Médard was more than a village. It was the most extensive parish on the outskirts of Paris, and noted for its abundance of street markets. It lived on the daily bustle and tramp of the army of housewives which formed the liveliest and most effervescent feature of the Parisian streets. The tradition has survived. Where cobbler and inn-keeper, cook-shop and pork-butcher once plied their trades side by side, stalls alive with noise and colour overflow into the street.

Auguste Rodin was born near by, in the Rue de l'Arbalète, on 14 November 1840; but it is no use looking for a plaque on the wall. The house has gone. [1]

One of the witnesses present when the child's birth was registered at the local town hall was an architect, the other a baker. Two months later, the baptismal register in the church of Saint-Médard was signed by an errand-boy and a housemaid.

Auguste Rodin's father, Jean-Baptiste, had come to Paris with the swarms of provincials who were attracted there in about 1830 by the first wave of industrialization. Born at Yvetot, he came of a family of cotton-merchants who, at a period when people travelled little, toured the district offering their wares for sale. He spent several years with the Brotherhood of the Christian Doctrine and even became a lay brother—that is to say, non-teaching and dedicated to practical tasks—before coming to Paris and obtaining a subordinate post at the Prefecture of Police.

Jean-Baptiste, whose sole ambition was to lead a respectable and uneventful family life, worked at the Prefecture for the rest of his days. Clotilde, the daughter of his first marriage, disgraced herself in some way. His second wife, whom he married at the age of thirty-four, was a girl from the other side of France. She bore a good Lorrainese name—Cheffer—and came of an old family of Moselle farmers. She was born at Laundorff, in German-speaking Lorraine, where the countryfolk spoke a Germanic patois. Marie Cheffer was a devout and dutiful woman, but dour and somewhat sour-faced. Her first child by Jean-Baptiste, named Maria, was followed two years later by Auguste.

The ties between the two families were close, which was why nephews from Lorraine lodged with the Rodins when they came to seek their fortune in Paris. One of them, Auguste Cheffer, married his first cousin, Anna Rodin, and became a heraldic engraver. Another became a typographer and a third an industrial draughtsman.

Socially, the Rodin family fell mid-way between the proletariat and the *petite bourgeoisie*—a fairly widespread intermediate class in the mid-nineteenth century. Office workers like Jean-Baptiste Rodin toiled for ten hours a day. Manual labourers worked from dawn to dusk. Meals, which consisted principally of bread, were frugal, and men alone were entitled to a bottle of wine. Rent accounted for between a hundred and a hundred and fifty francs a year.

Rodin *père* had to support himself and his wife and two children on an annual salary of eighteen hundred francs. The family's staple form of recreation was a weekly promenade to the neighbouring Jardin des Plantes. In summer, armed with a picnic, they would take the train to the Bois de Meudon.

Families of modest means welcomed the humble pleasures of existence as though they were great joys, and there were few who did not placidly accept their lot. People were still ignorant of advertisements which foster a corrosive sense of inferiority among the underprivileged. They did not strive to follow fashion, emulate their idols, go places, or surround themselves with useless objects. Human desires had still to be multiplied by material progress, and creature comforts had changed little since the Middle Ages. The conjugal bed, beds for the children, the dining-table and sideboard, father's arm-chair—these were enough for most men.

No one quibbled about morals and religion in a social environment which, like this one, had been moulded by centuries of Christianity. Evening prayers were a communal affair, and the entire Rodin family trooped off to mass at Saint-Médard every Sunday. As for Clotilde, the daughter of the first marriage, her name was never mentioned once her misdemeanours became known. Was she a prostitute ? Possibly, but a single youthful indiscretion would have been quite enough to bar her from the family fold for ever.

Unlike his elder sister Maria, who showed considerable promise, young Auguste was no great source of satisfaction to his parents. He attended the Écoles Chrétiennes in the Rue du Val-de-Grâce but had great difficulty in learning to read and write despite the ' Brothers' ' noted achievements in the field of primary education. At the age of nine he was packed off to his paternal uncle Alexandre, the intellectual of the family, who ran a boys' boarding school at Beauvais.

There Auguste became acquainted with a discipline verging on that of the prison or barrack-room. Reared in these poor but respectable surroundings—which he later described as 'eighteenth-century'—he acquired a habitual politeness, gentleness and courtesy which never deserted him. The coarseness of his fellow-pupils offended his sensibilities. He loitered in the corner of the play-ground, a silent and solitary figure, and dreaded the dormitory's lack of privacy. As for his studies, he seemed to be genuinely retarded. His dictation was riddled with crass spelling-mistakes. He never succeeded in learning Latin like the others, and his mathematics were non-existent. He drove his teachers to despair, since the only thing that appealed to him was drawing, and he spent most of his time recording in pencil what he saw around him.

The boy had been drawing for as long as he could remember. The grocer patronized by Madame Rodin used to wrap his prunes in paper cornets made out of pages from illustrated magazines. These were Auguste's first models.

When he was thirteen, his uncle decided that there was nothing more to be done with him and sent him back to Paris. He was overjoyed to return to his family and especially to his beloved Maria, the gay and affectionate sister who brightened the Rodin home and helped him forget the awful times at Beauvais.

A corpulent frock-coated figure, silver beard superbly frizzled, majestic as an Olympian god, surrounded by a bevy of pupils, secretaries, eminent friends and elegant mistresses, glamorous stars of society or stage—such is the image of Rodin bequeathed to us by photographs taken at the beginning of this century. What a contrast with the carrot-haired, thick-set, pig-headed, ill-dressed urchin whose muscles seemed to have developed at the expense of his intellect and who left school virtually uneducated!

His father, an unimaginative but practical man, realized that Auguste would never be able to go into an office like himself. There was no prospect of turning him into a civil servant. The boy could hardly write, let alone juggle with figures. Butcher, baker, candlestick-maker—whatever he became, it was high time for him to stop being a burden on the family exchequer and learn to support himself. He had reached the age when he must embark on an apprenticeship of some kind. It seemed a pity the girl was doing so well at school since she would only marry and have a husband to support her.

Auguste had one admirable failing, however. He was incredibly stubborn. He had his own idea of what to do and he stuck to it. He wanted to draw because drawing was the only thing that interested him.

His suggestion met with scorn and disapproval. What sort of profession was that, and what future did it hold? Financial instability, bohemianism—in a word, perdition.

The boy found an ally in his sixteen-year-old sister, who was now earning her own living and carried some weight in the family circle. Maria argued that his one pleasure at school had been to copy engravings or draw his fellow-pupils. His Cheffer cousins were studying drawing with their parents' approval and intended to make a career of it. The elder Rodin turned the matter over in his mind. Perhaps it was wrong to thwart such a definite vocation. If the boy were pitch-forked into a career against his will he might well abandon it immediately.

There was no harm in trying. Like other cities, Paris boasted an ' École gratuite de dessin '. This had occupied the handsome premises of the former School of Surgery at 5 Rue de l'École-de-Médecine since the reign of Louis XVI, its founder (and remained there until replaced in 1875 by the École des Arts Décoratifs, now Rue d'Ulm). Its fifteen hundred pupils underwent a training whose merits were universally recognized and could lead to steady and lucrative employment. Jean-Baptiste Rodin gave in.

Young Auguste was thoroughly overawed by his first sight of the domed rotunda where the first-year students were assembled. He felt awkward, rubbing shoulders with boys of whom many were brighter and the majority better educated than himself. What was more, he felt ashamed of his coarse grey linen jacket.

Weeks were devoted to the ABC of drawing—the interminable copying of works by old masters. Teaching methods had changed little since the school's foundation. The teachers distributed prints of eighteenth-century paintings and corrected their pupils' efforts. Later, the students graduated to plaster busts, capitals and ornaments in the classical style.

Most of the pupils in this establishment, which was called the Petite École to distinguish it from the ' Grande ' École des Beaux-Arts, went there to acquire a training which would enable them to enter the service of ornamental engravers, commercial artists, goldsmiths, jewellers, textile manufacturers, embroiderers, lace-makers, and so on.   There was also a studio where pupils practised wood-carving for furniture and the interior decoration of country houses or churches, as well as stone-carving destined for the decoration of public monuments or private premises.   Like the rest, the sculpture class began with drawing, which they had to master perfectly before passing on to modelling.

One day, while exploring the building, Auguste opened a door and came upon pupils modelling in clay, constructing moulds and making plaster casts.   He drew closer and watched.

It was a revelation.   ' I saw clay for the first time, ' he wrote later, ' and I felt as if I were ascending into heaven.   I made separate pieces—arms, heads, feet—then tackled an entire figure. I grasped the whole thing in a flash, and I did so with as much facility as I do today.   I was in transports. '

That settled it.   He was going to be a sculptor, and life held no other meaning for him from then on.

He was always to work with the same passionate enthusiasm. At daybreak he used to visit Lauset, an elderly painter to whom he had been introduced by his mother.   From Lauset he learnt the rudiments of painting in oils by copying pictures under his guidance.   Next came a headlong dash to the École, which opened at 8 a.m. in summer, 9 a.m. in winter.   Classes were over by midday. Then, munching the hunk of bread and lump of sugar which his mother had slipped into his jacket pocket, he crossed the Pont des Arts and made for the doors of the Louvre—admission free.   He examined everything, took an intense interest in everything he saw, and filled his sketch-book with drawings.   He lingered in front of sculptures ancient and modern, concentrating particularly on the works of Bouchardon, Houdon and Clodion.   Sometimes he went off to the print room of the Bibliothèque Impériale and immersed himself in folios of engravings—those, at least, which a shabbily dressed youngster could be trusted with. Then, striding out briskly, he would walk all the way across Paris to the Gobelins Manufactory, whose courses included life classes. Sixty students assembled there every evening.

Hard work and long walks across town—there was no question of taking a bus—did nothing to quench his ardour. Deaf to his mother's entreaties, he spent long evenings at home drawing from memory by lamp-light, an exercize recommended by his teachers.

As for the latter, he was lucky enough to be instructed by Horace Lecoq de Boisbaudran, an exceptional teacher who was destined to become head of the Petite École ten years later. Lecoq recognized the boy's promise, and Rodin remained grateful to him for the rest of his days. In 1913, when a new edition of Lecoq's *L'Éducation de la mémoire pittoresque* was due to appear, he sent a prefatory letter at the request of the publisher in which he recorded his debt to Lecoq, both as a boy and throughout his career:

' Despite the originality of his teaching, he was an upholder of tradition, and his atelier might be called an atelier of the eighteenth century.

' At the time, neither Legros nor I nor the other youngsters realized, as I realize now, how fortunate we were to fall into the hands of such a teacher. Most of what he taught me remains with me still. '

The Petite École enjoyed an excellent reputation. It employed distinguished artists who were more in sympathy with its methods than with those of academic education. Carpeaux had applied for and secured an assistant's post there after his stay in Rome, which was how he came to supervise the work of pupils in Rodin's class. [2] It was a great source of regret and self-reproach to Rodin in later years that he never exploited this boon to the full nor appreciated the true value of the young teacher's tuition. He had no inkling that Carpeaux was the only contemporary sculptor whose mastery he would genuinely acknowledge.

Many of the artists of Rodin's generation received their training at the Petite École. Among them were Dalou, a one-time friend who later begrudged his success and quarrelled with him, the engraver Alphonse Legros, a loyal and devoted friend and fellow-student who made a portrait of him at the age of forty-two, and the painters Lhermitte, Cazin, and Fantin-Latour.

With his years at the Petite École behind him, Rodin looked forward to continuing his studies. All he had done so far was to learn the rudiments of his profession. Only the École des Beaux-Arts—or so he believed—could teach him the great laws of composition.

His father was worried. He had hoped that drawing classes would equip the boy for a career, yet here he was, after three whole years, eager to embark on an even longer and more arduous road leading to a very uncertain career.

Many fathers tend to minimize the talents or qualities of their children. Jean-Baptiste Rodin, who kept his feet planted firmly on the ground, unfavourably compared his son's roseate dreams with his daughter's solid achievements.

Once again, Maria interceded with her customary gentleness and discernment. Auguste was a tireless worker with a passion for art and a probable talent for it as well. Plenty of sculptors succeeded. Even if he never aspired to the Olympian heights of Hippolyte Maindron, who secured fat commissions and was the current darling of the Salons, there was no reason why her brother's firm vocation should not help him to make a respectable career as a sculptor.

Madame Rodin approved the plan and her husband began to waver, but he refused to take such a momentous decision without first consulting an authority on the subject. A letter went off to the uncle in Beauvais, the family's few important contacts were tapped for information, and Maria pulled strings. It was finally arranged that the boy should be interviewed by an acknowledged master—none other than Maindron himself.

Having loaded what he considered to be his best sketches and plasters on one of the hand-carts which could be hired on every Parisian street-corner, Rodin hauled them to the sculptor's door. A man-servant showed him into a vast studio. The author of *La Velléda* in the Luxembourg, then sixty-six and at the height of his

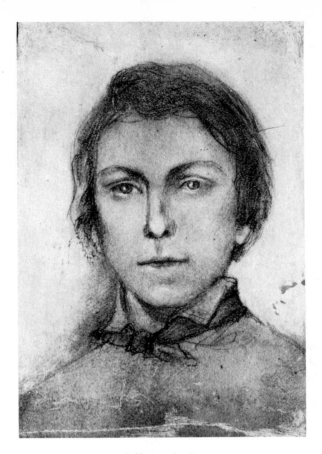

1 *Self-portrait* 1859

career, was an open-minded man with a streak of romanticism. It did not take him long to reach a verdict on Rodin's efforts. He told him that he had talent—the sort of talent which ought to be cultivated at the École des Beaux-Arts.

The young artist walked home on air. He saw his future taking shape. What with his teachers' encouragement, the esteem of his fellow-students, who envied his skill, and his own self-assurance, now fortified by Maindron's expert opinion, he approached the École des Beaux-Arts in high hopes. He was at the top of his form when he entered the lists.

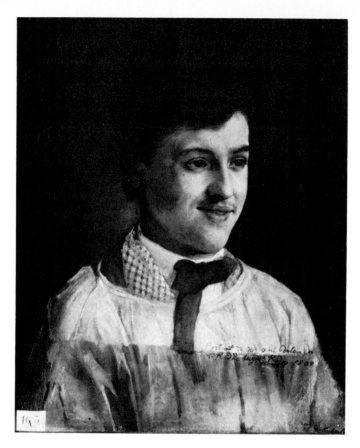

2 *Portrait of Abel Poulain* 1862

To everyone's surprise, the examiners rejected him. He went back to work with even greater fervour, only to meet with another setback. At his third attempt he failed yet again. He did not understand why, but he realized that the doors of the École were closed to him for ever.

Preserved in the museums in Philadelphia and the Rue de Varenne are drawings—nude studies—dating from this period. Faced by such evidence, we can only marvel that examiners with any insight at all should have blundered to the extent they did. Their decision merely exemplified the decadence and lack of discernment of an institution whose role was, precisely, to discern.

In retrospect, it is possible to account for this unlikely series of failures. The Grande École was the guardian of an academic tradition which went back to David's artistic supremacy. There was a deep gulf between Rodin's 'naturalism' and the principles which the École believed that it had inherited, via that revered master, from the world of Graeco-Roman antiquity. These were what it felt bound to perpetuate. To academics who imagined themselves in possession of the Tables of the Law, Rodin's drawing and modelling did not display the requisite conformism. It would, perhaps, be crediting these pedagogues with too much intelligence to suppose that they recognized these test-pieces as the work of someone who was destined to raise the banner of rebellion against academicism and its mummified, hidebound representatives. What they did immediately recognize was that Rodin was not one of their own.

Far from succumbing to these failures, which he knew to be quite unmerited, Rodin seemed to become even more grimly determined. There was no question of abandoning the struggle. Calmly accepting the likelihood that even harder times lay ahead, he faced them with the dogged determination which remained with him always. Since his father had neither the means nor the inclination to support him, the first essential was to earn his own keep.

Auguste Rodin spent twenty years touting for work, twenty years of financial uncertainty, of ups and downs, of undistinguished and unprofitable toil. Sometimes paid by the week, sometimes unemployed, he drifted from one employer and studio to the next. He was always on the verge of penury, but his work was an unfailing source of joy. Inspired by a half-unconscious faith in his own artistry, he never complained. He was not ambitious, far less envious, and could never have pictured the blaze of glory that was to surround him in later years. Neither temperament nor training inclined him towards the rosy dreams of the future which haunt the young. He believed in his profession and its supreme importance. Even at the height of his success, he always repeated that ' one should not seek for effect but strive conscientiously to do well '.

For the time being, he slaved for decorators and public works contractors. He acted as sculptor's assistant and caster in turn, according to demand. He worked in every corner of Paris, always on the look-out for something new to learn, always profiting by contact with skilled workmates or veteran craftsmen who could teach him new tricks of the trade. He turned out standardized ornaments, repaired public monuments and performed insipid tasks without flagging, confident that he was acquiring a technique which would later enable him to tackle anything with ease.

His parents had left the Rue de l'Arbalète for an old house in the Rue des Fossés-Saint-Jacques, just off the Place de l'Estrapade. Rodin, who was still no bookworm but had rubbed shoulders with young men brighter than himself, recognized the gaps in his education. He learnt to read, or, rather, began to absorb what he read. He borrowed books and frequented public libraries, discovering a whole new world whose existence he had never suspected. He made straight for the poets—great poets like Hugo and Lamartine. Michelet, the poet of history, opened his eyes to the world and remained one of his idols.

He neglected no opportunity to learn. Having made the acquaintance of Barye's son, he was able to attend the master's courses—if that was the right word for them—at the Museum. Barye was an advocate of ' silent instruction '. Here is what Rodin said on the subject when recalling memories of his youth:

' We felt ill at ease surrounded by amateurs and women. I think we were unnerved by the polished parquet of the library where the course was held. After carefully exploring the Jardin des Plantes, we unearthed a sort of cave in the basement. The walls streamed with damp, but we moved in there with delight. A plank supported by a post driven into the ground served as our modelling stand. It did not rotate. Instead, we rotated round our stand and whatever we were copying. They were good enough to let us stay there and borrow animal specimens

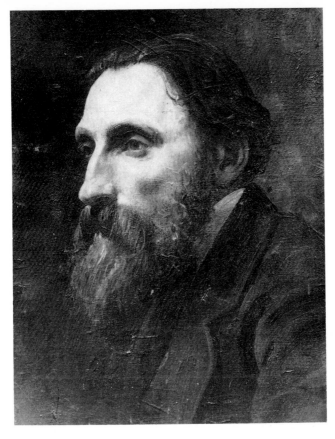

3  Jean-Paul Laurens. *Portrait of Jean-Baptiste Rodin* 1860

from the lecture-rooms, lions' paws and the like... We worked
like men possessed and looked like wild beasts ourselves. The
great Barye used to come and visit us. He inspected what we
had done and usually departed without uttering a word.'[3]

Official gallery catalogues long persisted in calling Rodin
' a pupil of Barye and Carrier-Belleuse '. There was no foundation
in this where Barye was concerned. Rodin was no more influenced than the rest by his negative tuition, and it was not until long
afterwards that he testified to his admiration for the noted animal
sculptor. As for Carrier-Belleuse, more will be said of him later.

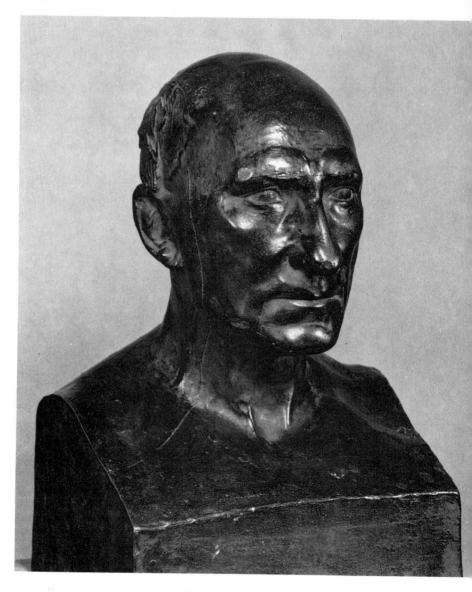

*4 Bust of Jean-Baptiste Rodin* 1859

Despite his jobbing activities, Rodin always found time for free-style work. He drew plants, trees and horses. An early bust of his father in the classical manner shows that, for all his nineteen years and immature technique, Rodin was already capable of producing a fine portrait of someone dear to him.

It was at this period that Rodin's life became scarred by an event which affected him so deeply that he did not recover from it for a long time to come. The mainstay of his early years in the austere family circle had been the warmth and affection of his sister Maria. She was a gentle and intelligent girl, and not lacking in character. Her grave features were lit up by a pair of clear blue eyes shining with candour and melancholy. Impressed by her hard work and mature intelligence, the family had allowed her a measure of freedom, even in her teens. She earned her keep by working in a shop which sold devotional articles. The Sisters of the Doctrine, who had educated her from an early age, followed their gifted pupil's progress with interest, hoping some day to make a teacher of her.

Maria's story followed a classic pattern. One of Auguste's young painter friends started visiting the house, and painted the portraits of Auguste and Maria. We shall never know what passed between him and Maria or what went on inside that reserved but warm-hearted girl. All that is certain is that the young man's visits became less frequent and eventually ceased altogether, and that one fine day he announced his engagement to someone else.

For Maria, this was the end. All her plans and hopes, all her nebulous dreams of the future had been cruelly dashed. The family feared for her sanity, but the Sisters of the Doctrine were there to receive her and God to console her. After a two-year novitiate she underwent an unsuccessful operation for peritonitis and came home to die.

Her brother, who helped to nurse her during her last days, was completely shattered. Dazed with grief, he stayed shut up in the darkened house. The tools which he had always wielded so tirelessly fell from his hands, and his half-completed works remained untouched.

Rodin was twenty-two, an age when the tide of human will-power flows too strongly to be curbed, but he had fallen into an abyss from which no words of advice or comfort could extricate him. He closeted himself with his grief, desperate enough to commit any act of folly.

Having exhausted his stock of Christian consolation, the priest of Saint-Jacques decided to put Rodin in touch with Father Eymard, a man who had a reputation for saving lost souls.

In order to pursue his missionary activities in the quarter, Father Eymard had several months earlier acquired 68 Rue du Faubourg Saint-Jacques. This old and dilapidated house near the intersection with the Boulevard Arago had been purchased with an unsecured loan advanced by a family given to charitable works. It contained a well-furnished chapel—a prime requirement for Father Eymard and the small religious community which he had founded, the ' Pères du Très-Saint-Sacrement ', a group of priests devoted to perpetual adoration, that is to say, to praying in round-the-clock shifts.

Father Eymard had taken it upon himself to catechize the gangs of ragged and rowdy street Arabs who roamed the quarter outside working hours. In this fringe district of Paris, workshops were multiplying, together with the horrible slums of the Butte-aux-Cailles and the Fosse-aux-Lions inhabited by working families. It must have seemed a hopeless task to woo these youngsters, few of whom had ever been to school or heard of morality, let alone religion, and most of whom regarded the cassock as an object of derision. Nevertheless, Eymard's strong and kindly personality, coupled with his rugged physique, enabled him to win over and later educate even the most hardened cases.

Such was the man who now entered Rodin's life. We do not know what led up to this unexpected spiritual development. Both Rodin and Eymard are silent on the subject, but the fact remains that, a few weeks after their first encounter, the young man joined the community as a novice under the name of Brother Augustin.

Thus, brother and sister each passed through the same cycle within a short space of time: despair induced by an emotional shock followed by a withdrawal into religion.

24

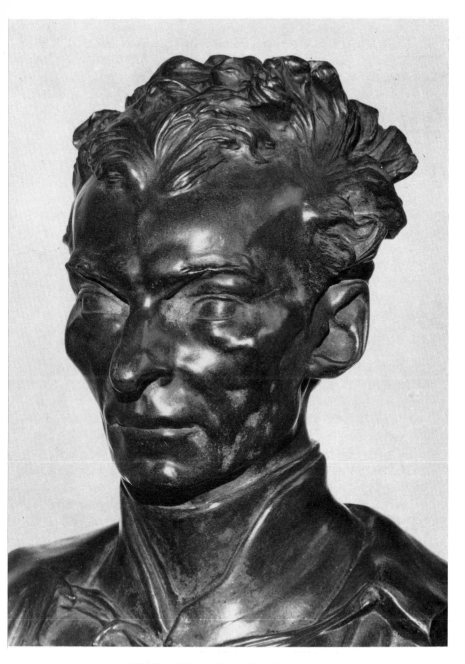

5  *The Blessed Father Pierre-Julien Eymard* 1863

The small but growing community of the Pères du Très-Saint-Sacrement still numbered only half a dozen members. (There are now about sixteen hundred scattered across the globe.) Contact with them and with the spiritual effulgence of the monastic community as a whole restored Rodin's spirit and will to work. He was assigned a shed at the bottom of the small garden where he could retire to sculpt during the periods of leisure prescribed by the rules. Father Eymard had noted his novice's enthusiasm. He may also have recognized his talent, though this is less certain. As an experienced priest, he knew that acts born of despair do not always amount to a firm vocation. Rodin's request for permission to make a bust of him gave Eymard an opportunity to have long talks with the young man. He suggested that Rodin might not necessarily be destined for monastic life, and that his true vocation lay in the artistic activities which he pursued with such fervour. Less than two years after entering the community, Rodin left it for good.

One record of this period of his life survives: the bust of Father Eymard, Rodin's first major work, solid, vital, and expressive of the enduring respect which the novice felt for a superior who had shown him the light when he was lost in darkness.

Having saved Rodin from spiritual shipwreck, Father Eymard helped him to rediscover the life of a man totally dedicated to sculpture. ' I entered sculpture as one enters a religion, ' declared Marcel Gimond, and his words might equally have applied to Rodin.

Before we bid farewell to what was more than just an episode in the sculptor's life, it is worth recalling that Father Eymard was beatified by Pius XI and canonized by John XXIII in 1962.

# CHAPTER TWO

## Hard times

Rodin resumed his craftsman's existence. It is difficult to identify his anonymous works, many of which no longer survive. Their author, who was not over-proud of them, never waxed talkative on the subject. We do know, however, that he worked on the foyer of the Gaîté theatre and also on the Théâtre des Gobelins. The latter, though now converted into a cinema, still boasts a narrow façade decorated with flying goddesses done in a wholly banal Napoleon III style.

It was while working on the decoration of this small local theatre that Rodin met a young girl employed by a neighbouring dress-shop. One look at her fresh face and the sweet simplicity of her answering gaze, and he felt his shyness melt away. It was love, some say his first love, and it lasted fifty-two years.

Rose Beuret, then aged twenty, was born in a small village on the banks of the Marne near Joinville. She came of farming stock and had only just arrived in Paris. The two young people fell in love. Their flirtation developed into an affair and they pooled their slender resources to set up house together.

A son was born a year later, but Rodin was reluctant to legitimize him. Rose, ever amenable to the artist's wishes, does not seem to have pressed the point, so the child took the name Beuret —Auguste Beuret, since the least his father could do for him was give him his own Christian name.

Young Auguste Beuret had to be introduced to the family, who had no idea what was going on. Aunt Thérèse Cheffer, a

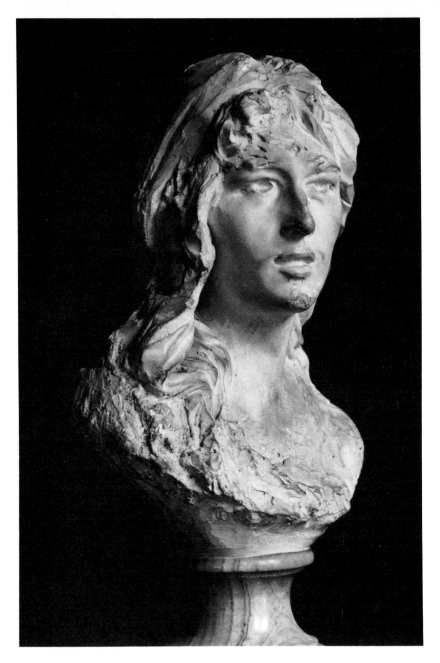

6 *Mignon* 1870

broad-minded woman, agreed 'to prepare the ground. Rose being a deferential, hard-working and respectable-looking girl, the situation seems to have been accepted without undue demur, though the illicit relationship and its bastard offspring remained a gross affront to the family code. Rodin's mother was failing and his father going blind, and he continued to visit them at least once a week. To the end of his days, Rodin remembered his father with respect and affection.

Concentrating on one's work while sharing cramped quarters with a wife and child presents considerable difficulties, especially to a sculptor. Rodin's acquisition of a cheap studio—a stable, to be more precise—came as a great relief. ' Ah, I shall never forget my first studio! I spent some hard times there. Since my finances precluded me from finding anything better, I rented a stable in the Rue Lebrun, near the Gobelins. It seemed to be sufficiently well lit and to provide me with the requisite space to step back and compare my clay with the original—an essential principle which I have always adhered to and never departed from. Air seeped in from all sides through the ill-fitting windows and warped wooden doors. The slates on the roof, whether worn by time or displaced by the wind, admitted a permanent draught. It was freezing cold, and a brimming well sunk in one corner maintained a penetrating humidity all the year round. Even now, I wonder how I stood it! '

We are well acquainted with Rose's face and body because she regularly posed for her companion, at least during their early years together. She was a handsome peasant type with a strength and vigour of feature which makes one wonder why Rodin, after completing his first bust of her, should have entitled it *Mignon*. The treatment approximated to that of Carpeaux, but Carpeaux without the smile. Rodin's faces never smiled. *Young Woman in a Flowered Hat,* after the same model, possesses a charm which owes much to its decorative elegance.

Then there was Rose's body... And here we come to the story of *The Bacchante,* which was accidentally smashed during a move to a new studio. Rodin never got over its destruction. The following description of what went into its making was written fifty years later:

' There was not much movement in it, but that was of little importance to me. On the one hand, I did not want to tire my companion by arranging her in a pose which it would have been difficult to hold for any length of time; on the other, I was convinced that to work well one had to work " faithfully ". In my desire to get as close to the life as possible, to the exclusion of modelling and embellishments devised by my own imagination, I deliberately selected a simple pose which the model would easily be able to resume after her spells of relaxation, thus enabling me to make the comparisons indispensable to good and genuine execution.

' I spent almost two years on this figure. I was twenty-four at the time, and already a good sculptor. I saw and reproduced the direct radiation of form, as I do today. I was absolutely scrupulous about drawing outlines. How long I took to see and reproduce them! I made ten new starts, fifteen if necessary. I was never satisfied with an approximation. I pass over all the material difficulties I met—any artist who has been poor will understand.

' The exigencies of every-day life obliged me to work on other people's premises, so we set about our task at dawn and did not resume it until I returned at nightfall.

' Sunday was our day off. After a long morning sitting, we used to make up for the hardships of the week by going for walks across the fields and woods on the outskirts of Paris. '

In reality, Rose had been the victim of her lover's temperament ever since their first encounter. With an artist's egoism, he now saw her only as his model, and the hours he spent with her were devoted to sculpture, not love. Rodin hated emotional outbursts, and the humble peasant-girl, anxious not to annoy him and terrified of being abandoned with the child whose screams disturbed his work, held her tears in check.

Rodin was moderately satisfied with a bust he had made of a local lay-about nicknamed Bibi. His friends declared that there was an element of classical beauty in this strange head, with its broken nose, vigorous modelling, and air of dignified suffering. Why not submit it to the Salon ?  Then, one day when the temperature in the stable-studio fell below zero, the bust cracked. Only the mask survived, but Legros assured Rodin that this only made its expression more moving.

The jury did not agree, and *The Man with the Broken Nose* was rejected.

There is little point in dwelling on the young sculptor's fresh defeat by the potentates of academicism.  He believed, not unjustly, that the piece he had submitted possessed an affinity with classical works.  It was not their brand of classicism, and that was all there was to it.  *The Man with the Broken Nose,* which was later translated into marble and cast in bronze, already reflects the major quality which struck such terror into the jury: a potent personality.

1864, the year of Rodin's meeting with Rose, was also the year of his first encounter with Carrier-Belleuse.

Dalou once said of Rodin, not without a touch of envy, that he had been ' lucky enough not to get into the École des Beaux-Arts '.  It is unlikely that the École's teaching methods would have stunted his genius or stifled his individuality, which was too strong not to have cut loose.  The clearest evidence of this is his close association with Carrier-Belleuse, which lasted for five years.  Everything argued against the wisdom of collaboration between a successful artist and an alert and receptive pupil sixteen years his junior, yet Rodin survived the test.

Carrier-Belleuse was an artist of good taste and staggering virtuosity.  He practised his profession like a man conducting a business-affair and extracted the maximum profit from his talents. A distinguished former pupil of David d'Angers, he had made his mark in a certain artistic circle with a *Bacchante* which was notable for its morbid charm.  Some critics called him a latter-day Clodion.  His quick hand and shrewd commercial sense enabled him to run his studio in the Rue de la Tour d'Auvergne on the lines of a factory.  Realizing that commercialized art was his

31

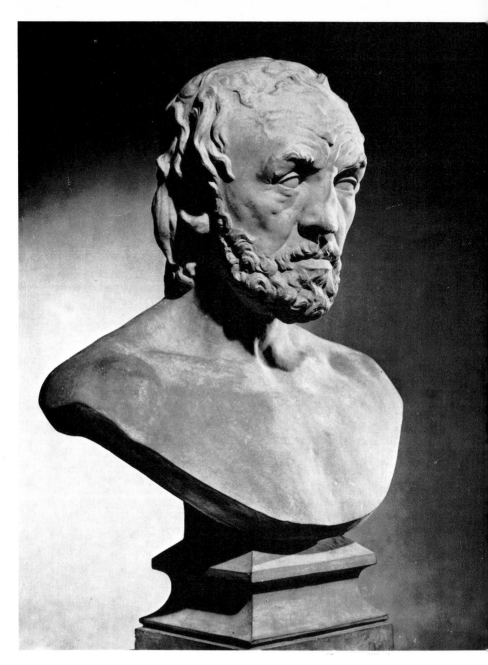

7 *The Man With the Broken Nose* 1872

true vocation, he employed a score of craftsmen to copy his models down to the last detail. He was much sought after by wealthy bourgeois as a supplier of statuettes, vases, epergnes, candelabra, and ornamental clocks. At the same time, he accepted special commissions of every description—devotional works such as the *Messiah* in the church of Saint-Vincent-de-Paul, mythological works such as *Jupiter and Hebe,* military works such as *The Death of Desaix,* and busts of current celebrities ranging from George Sand and Renan to Hortense Schneider and Napoleon III.

This jack-of-all-trades cultivated the ' arty ' side of his appearance. His flowing locks, broad-brimmed felt hat, buckled shoes and black cape with huge silver clip made him the exact opposite of Rodin, but he quickly recognized the young craftsman's exceptional ability and turned it to good account. After only a few weeks Rodin was producing models in the master's style and bearing the master's signature.

He soon secured a more permanent and better-paid position in the studio. [4] It was to him that Carrier-Belleuse entrusted the most delicate ornamental motifs, decorative figures for the doorways of opulent mansions, medallions for the adornment of elaborate staircases. We know nothing of the anonymous works which he was so loath to talk about except the decorative motifs on the roof of the very ornate Hôtel de Paiva at 25 Avenue des Champs-Elysées, where Dalou, under his own name, sculpted a fireplace flanked by satyrs which was much admired at the time.

Though hardly profitable to Rodin himself, these routine exercizes cannot be said to have prejudiced the future flow of his inspiration. On the frequent occasions when he became short of money after leaving his employer, he continued to turn out statuettes *à la* Clodion on his own account. Not bearing the magic name of Carrier-Belleuse, however, they failed to find a ready market.

Perhaps the most extraordinary feature of Rodin's career is that it should have begun with extravagant fripperies of this kind and culminated in the fearsome anthropomorphic crag which we know as *Balzac.*

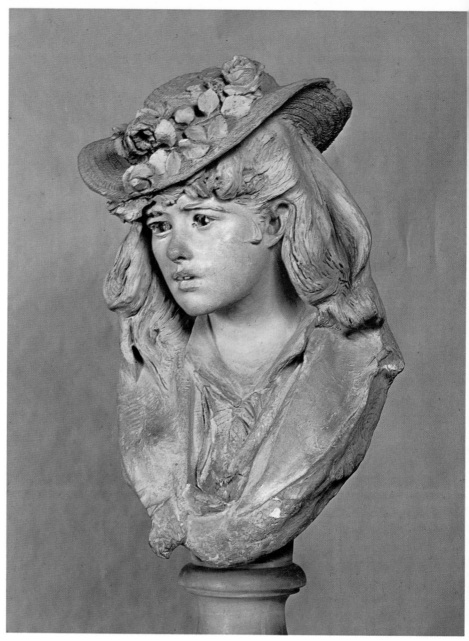

8  *Young Woman in a Flowered Hat* 1865-70

To be nearer Carrier-Belleuse's studio, Rodin moved first to Clignancourt and then to the top of Butte-Montmartre, where he found accommodation in the countrified Rue des Saules, later painted by Cézanne, Van Gogh and Utrillo. We may take it for granted that he never patronized the neighbouring *Cabaret des Assassins,* a Bohemian rendez-vous which became celebrated ten years later under the name *Lapin à Gill.* He worked twelve hours a day, seldom drank and never smoked.

Then it was 1870, and the Franco-Prussian War broke out. Rodin was now thirty years old.

Drafted into a regiment of the Garde Nationale, he soon earned his corporal's stripes but was discharged by a medical board on the grounds of his weak eye-sight. It should not be imagined that he welcomed his discharge. He was patriotic to the core, and France's defeats affected him deeply. Besides, there was no more work to be had. To a sculptor, the war meant unemployment and poverty. Carrier-Belleuse had departed for Belgium, leaving Rodin with little prospect of supporting himself and his mistress and their child. Rose had found work at a military clothing factory, and his father, now totally blind and confined to a wheel-chair, was living on an annual pension of nine hundred francs. It was a grim winter, the winter of the siege, and the poor suffered terribly from privation.

Rodin wrote to inform Carrier-Belleuse that he was now exempt from military service and without means. The post arrived from Brussels with an answer to all his problems. Carrier-Belleuse had been commissioned to decorate the Brussels Bourse, a major project for which he had recruited a whole team of Belgian sculptors. He invited Rodin to join them.

Leaving Rose and his son behind in Paris, Rodin set off for Brussels. He had no very clear idea of what he was going to do except earn a living. He said *au revoir* to his family as though they would be reunited within a few weeks, but fate decreed otherwise.

The capital of Belgium, now in its fortieth year of independence, was in the throes of transformation. Large and luxurious mansions and public buildings, the latter exemplified by the

Babylonian Palais de Justice, which covered an area of more than 200,000 square feet, were springing up cheek by jowl with old districts which preserved the style and popular tastes of bygone days. Enough funds were made available for the construction of the Bourse du Commerce, designed by the architect Léon Suys, to make its extensive and elaborate decoration a symbol of national prosperity. It was conceived in accordance with the ornate and ponderous classicism which then reigned supreme in all major cities throughout the world. Its sculptural decoration required a large and disciplined labour force. Very little was left to individual initiative, needless to say, and the decorative schemes embodied nothing which could possibly stimulate the imagination.

Carrier-Belleuse had been put in charge of the team of ornamentalists. He had left Paris because the war had put a stop to artistic activity and because he had been lucky enough to secure this temporary but important assignment abroad. Apart from recruiting local sculptors, he had brought along his assistant Van Rasbourg, whom Rodin had got to know well during his days at the Paris studio.

Rodin's life in Brussels was another unending round of toil. The whole day was spent in the studio or on the scaffolding. At night, back in his room, he modelled statuettes which his employer signed and sold to dealers in bronzes.

He had taken lodgings at an *estaminet* in an old street in the Bourse quarter, cutting his expenditure to the bone in the hope of sending a little money to his family. He wondered how Rose and his parents were faring in the eye of the new storm that had burst upon the French capital. Reports of the siege were confused but invariably alarming in tone. Then came the Commune and its repressive measures. Paris went up in flames, blood flowed, and men were shot in hundreds. The city was cut off from fresh supplies. There were stories of endless queues outside bakery doors and shops looted by the starving populace.

The postal service ceased to operate. At last, relayed by Aunt Thérèse, news arrived. They were all safe—Rose, the child, and his parents. Rose was still working, but food was hard to find.

Summoning up his shaky syntax, Rodin replied. He described his financial situation—in other words, his complete lack of money. He hoped things would change for the better but remained vague on the subject. 'My little angel,' he wrote, 'I am happy that you are both safe and sound. The only thing is, I am greedy for news and you don't say much. You don't answer all my questions. Give me some details of what you have been doing during these dismal days. Let me cheer you up in advance by telling you that I shall be sending some money in a few days' time, because I shall be getting paid soon. I think my affairs are going to take a turn for the better, so keep hoping, my angel. If I decide to stay in Brussels I shall send for you. I miss you. You don't mention M. Garnier or M. Bernard, to whom I shall be sending money. Go and see him soon, also the studio. Is anything broken? I wrote you a long letter in reply to the one you sent me a month ago. Didn't you get it? I asked you about the house, the studio, everything. What have you received in the way of letters? I have had plenty of worries, Rose darling, as you can imagine. Almost three months without work, so you can understand what a hard time I've had. We had a row with M. Carrier, but things will sort themselves out. You'll have to wait a little longer, Rose —I haven't a sou at the moment. A chemist and one of my work-mates have helped me out, fortunately for me. I don't know what I should have done without them. I asked you in the letter I sent you to pawn my trousers at the Mont-de-Piété. That would be money for nothing. What about M. Tyrode? Please tell him I shall send him some money as soon as I can. I don't see how we can go on affording such an expensive place. However, I ought to know in a month's time whether I shall be staying on in Belgium or coming home...'

He wrote again to say that he would be sending money to other people. Meanwhile, he had fallen out with his employer, and we know why. Producing statuettes for Carrier-Belleuse every evening after work, he was struck with the idea of signing one of them with his own name and offering it to the dealer direct. His reasoning was so ingenuous that one is tempted to pardon the indiscretion. Rodin argued that ' M. Carrier ' was the real forger because he signed pieces which were not only produced by someone else but so perfectly imitative of his own style that they required no retouching. The inevitable happened.

Although the statuette was offered at half price (twenty-five francs instead of fifty), the dealer jibbed and informed Carrier-Belleuse, his usual supplier. Carrier-Belleuse flew into a rage and sacked his assistant on the spot. Hence the picture of an unemployed and penniless craftsman thrown on the mercy of a charitable workmate and a local chemist.

Luckily for Rodin, events intervened. Peace descended on Paris, and Carrier-Belleuse at once broke his contract with the Belgian government to return to his family and enviable clientele.

Van Rasbourg took over the completion of work in hand. It was then that the two sculptors evolved the idea of a partnership. They had worked together for several years and knew each other's abilities, so they decided to rent a studio in Ixelles. Their deed of partnership stipulated that Van Rasbourg would sign any works sold in Belgium and Rodin any sold in France. It was a perfect arrangement in theory, but Rodin soon found himself on the losing end of the deal. Van Rasbourg could drum up business on the spot, whereas he, working at a distance, secured no commissions from France. As a result, Van Rasbourg built up a reputation on the strength of his partner's work.

This makes it hard to distinguish what should properly be attributed to Rodin. He has been credited with *Africa* and *Asia,* the main groups on the façade of the Bourse, as well as some caryatids and bas-reliefs inside the building. In later years, Rodin himself laid claim to some decorative figures on the Palais des Académies and a number of caryatids adorning the exterior of several houses in the Boulevard Anspach. All were signed by Van Rasbourg.

For as long as Rose remained in Paris, Rodin bombarded her with instructions about the sculptures left behind in his studio. In every one of his letters he reverted to his ' clays ', which had to be kept permanently draped in damp cloths—a duty which Rose

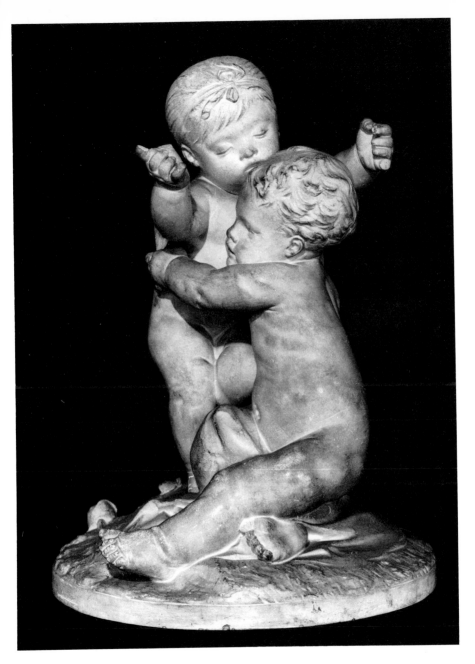

9 *The Idyll of Ixelles* 1876

discharged in a touchingly-faithful and conscientious manner. He drew particular attention to the casts of Father Eymard and Bibi *(The Man with the Broken Nose)*, and, above all, to *The Alsatian Woman,* a rugged and tragic bust of Rose executed during the siege of Paris. And, ever and always, there came the same painful allusions to money: ' My poor darling, I haven't been able to send you any money, but you know how many expenses I have... ' —or again : ' write me a long letter by return. I should have liked to send you a five-franc piece so that you could have invited Mme and M. Pouillebœuf to a little dinner, but it will have to wait. Even so, I should like you to do this when I send the wherewithal. ' One day he sent Rose sixty-five francs: ' thirty for the big Italian [5] who came to see you about me, thirty for my parents, and five for you, for clothes. I'm sending them to you to save Mother a trip. ' He never mentioned his son. Smallpox was raging in Paris, and his mother fell gravely ill. She died as unostentatiously as she had lived. Since there was no money in the house, she was buried in a communal grave—no one knows where.

Rodin, who was now making a reasonable income out of his association with Van Rasbourg, summoned Rose to join him. He continued to produce statuettes in the style of Carrier-Belleuse and sold his models to bronze-founders at prices of up to eighty francs. In addition, he perfected his technique by doing busts of friends or people he was indebted to, generously presenting them with the finished results.

The couple moved into a large room in Ixelles, near the studio. They continued to lead the same modest and hard-working existence, mixing exclusively with the ordinary people of the neighbourhood. Time passed relatively smoothly in a country where food and accommodation were cheap. Whenever Rodin had a moment to spare he plunged into his books. Although he sensed that he was gaining an ever-increasing mastery of his profession, he felt an urge to broaden his horizons and explore the world of general ideas which had for so long been closed to him. He paid lengthy visits to museums, both in Brussels itself and in Antwerp, where he spent several weeks working on a special commission.

Rembrandt made a strong impression on him. Figures gilded with sunlight and looming out of chasms of darkness—what were they, he asked himself, if not sculpture? Whenever he had a free day he would take his paint-box and head for the Forêt de Soignes or the surrounding country-side.

Back in Paris, his father and son had been taken in by the worthy Aunt Thérèse, who had turned washerwoman in order to support the entire family.

We come now to 1875 and an incident which, though minor in itself, proved to be a milestone in the sculptor's life. Having always cherished an understandable predilection for *The Man with the Broken Nose,* he made a marble bust of it and sent it to the Paris Salon. This time it was accepted.

Books and museums filled him with a mounting and increasingly imperious desire to get to know Italy—Rome in particular. His reading had left him with a vivid picture of a city of age-old stone, a fountainhead of greatness and corruption stained with fire and blood. He mustered his meagre savings, instructed Rose to renew the damp cloths on the sculptures in his studio regularly, and set off.

It was a long journey, undertaken partly by train and partly on foot. (He only had seven hundred francs with him.) Passing through Rheims, Pontarlier and Savoy, he crossed the Mont-Cenis and Appenines and trudged on towards Pisa, where he wrote to Rose: ' Rain... I must tell you that I don't always eat regularly, and that I only treat my belly when there's nothing left to see... Dinant is picturesque. As for Rheims, the cathedral possesses a beauty which I have yet to meet here in Italy. '

At Florence: ' None of the photographs or casts I have seen gives any idea of the Sacristy of San Lorenzo. These tombs have to be seen in profile and three-quarter-face. I have been in Florence five whole days, and only saw the Sacristy this morning. Well, those five days left me cold. My three lasting impressions to date are of Rheims, the ramparts of the Alps, and the Sacristy. It isn't possible to analyse what one sees straight away. You won't be surprised to learn that I have been making a study of Michelangelo ever since my arrival in Florence, and I believe that the great magician is revealing a few of his secrets to me... I have been making sketches in my room in the evenings, not of his works but of all the structures and systems which I devise in my imagination in order to understand him... '

Rodin made straight for the heights—Rheims and Michelangelo. He visited the tombs of young Giuliano and Lorenzo de' Medici, living bodies, tragic and grandiose, vibrant with energy and controlled strength, whereas the accompanying figures known as *Day* and *Night, Dawn* and *Evening,* were weighed down and over-whelmed by death.

The female figures were finished, the male figures only rough-hewn. It was these which fascinated him most. He sensed the exertions of the sculptor who had conjured these figures out of raw marble, the work that had never been brought to a conclusion, the inability of the world's most potent sculptor to complete the tomb of Lorenzo the Magnificent, the man who had given him so many tokens of friendship and esteem.

Something of importance did escape him, however. This was the extraordinary cohesion of the Medici chapel and its intimate relationship between sculpture and architecture, the synthesis in which light and shade were distributed so as to govern the rhythm of an enclosed space in which a cornice could assume the same importance as sarcophagi or figures designed according to the same laws. Rodin fathomed the secrets of Michelangelo the sculptor without grasping those of Michelangelo the architect.

He saw the Raphaels in Rome and decided that the Parisian pain-ters who considered themselves his heirs were completely out of touch. Moses and the frescoes in the Sistine Chapel claimed Rodin's fullest attention and convinced him that, even in painting, the colossus called Michelangelo remained a sculptor.

Rodin's trip to Italy had a profound and lasting effect on him. It not only confirmed and strengthened him in his ideas and methods but taught him a great deal that was new. Above all, the contact with great masters enabled him to glimpse that he, too, could and must become a master in his own right.

42

# CHAPTER THREE

# Art and craftsmanship

Ought Rodin to have regretted sacrificing his youth to menial tasks ?  Certainly, he never ceased to express his gratitude to his teachers at the Petite École and to the conscientious and experienced craftsmen who had taught him the tricks of the trade when he was a craftsman himself.

We must divest ourselves of all prevailing and preconceived ideas if we are to arrive at a sound assessment of the position of professional artists at the period when Rodin was merely one anonymous craftsman among many.  The ' age of genius ' has dawned since his day.  Craftsmanship may be a technical asset but it is no longer a criterion of value.  It has been abandoned in favour of gimmicks and novelties born of an urge for originality at any price and nurtured by a mutual conspiracy on the part of critics and commentators who use a specialized and esoteric language to hint at an artist's underlying motivation.

As one whose upbringing and training made him heir to the Ancien Régime, a fact which he often stressed himself, Rodin spent the earlier part of his life in close proximity to the period when there were guilds of ' master painters and sculptors ' whose professional skills enabled them to decorate ceilings, cupboards, pilasters, capitals and façades, or to paint columns, amatory pictures, devotional works, and perfect likenesses.  The artist was, by definition, one who plied his trade in just the same way as a cabinet-maker or craftsman in wrought-iron, and the best-trained practitioner, if not the most gifted, could bank on securing the best clientele in the country. The guild system insisted on an apprenticeship. It also demanded some talent. It was strict, finical and exclusive, but it did not prevent a man like Watteau, when painting a shop-sign to order, from producing a work like the *Enseigne de Gersaint*.

The Revolution toppled this edifice by decreeing that artists must cease to be ' servile '. Then, with guilds banned, force of circumstance dictated the formation of cells of craftsmen who became wage-earners dependent upon a commercial employer. They had to work long hours for lower wages. On the other hand, any sculptor worth his salt could easily find work and make a living. Quantitatively speaking, the second half of the nineteenth century was an exceptional period. Public monuments were loaded —indeed, overloaded—with sculpture. The plethora of ornamentation on the exterior of apartment houses was indicative of the social status to which owner and tenant alike aspired, and disbursements on decoration, both exterior and interior, were reflected in rents. Private mansions and wealthy middle-class homes were adorned with cornices, moulded string courses, pilasters, ornate window and door frames—even caryatids. Monuments broke out in a rash of bas-relief or modelling in the round, as though plain surfaces might be construed as a symptom of poverty. France became dotted with town and country houses of vaguely Renaissance aspect, prefectures and theatres in a hybrid style, churches obedient to the canons of Gothic, chambers of commerce, banks, savings banks, grand hotels, and casinos, all of which vied with each other in decorative splendour.

Sculpture had punctuated architecture with comparative restraint at the beginning of the nineteenth century. During the Second Empire it invaded everything. Architecture was so weak and mediocre that it tried to boost its prestige by self-adornment, but the mish-mash of archaeological pastiches with which it bedecked itself only accentuated its formal decay and made it look like an aging woman in fake jewellery.

The neglect and destruction of historic buildings during the Revolution and thereafter was succeeded by a period of restoration and, in many cases, complete reconstruction, and new sculptural decoration was invariably more elaborate than the original. (Rodin's condemnation of these restorers' excesses was not only rare for the period but extremely well founded, as we shall see later.)   Viollet-le-Duc and his emulators employed hundreds of sculptors to execute statuary and ornaments for which they provided the models.   The halls of the new Louvre were adorned with escutcheons and caryatids and surmounted by exuberant pediments and groups of colossal proportions.   Eighty-six statues of famous men were arrayed on the porticos and sixty-three allegorical groups at roof-level.   The frontage of the Rue de Rivoli was so pock-marked with niches that not all of them could be filled.   There were also consoles, capitals, plaques, friezes and vermiculations whose chief function seemed to be to prevent bare stone from showing through.   The exterior of the new Hôtel de Ville in Paris was furnished with 110 statues of eminent Parisians (one of them justly accorded to Rodin himself), and the reception rooms were enriched with assorted allegorical figures. In public squares and gardens, both in Paris and the provinces, the Third Republic lavishly erected effigies of personalities from the world of politics, literature and art, effigies whose authors are now as obscure as most of the names they sought to immortalize.

All this may well have imparted a bitter tinge to the ambitious dreams of contemporary sculptors who never even got a chance to do busts of company chairmen—a commonplace and remunerative form of employment at this period.

In total contrast to the modern artists who exhaust themselves in a quest for original formulae and end by applying the term ' sculpture ' to objects in which sculpture plays no part whatsoever, Rodin devoted his youth and a proportion of his maturity to the traditional pursuits of the architectural sculptor.   These consisted in reproducing and interpreting models, and, more rarely, in conceiving new ones with a natural regard for the lessons of the past.   He belonged to the then large and important body of craftsmen known as ' *sculpteurs ornemanistes* ', and he was one of the best of their number.

Qualified, skilled, and in some cases extremely talented, these craftsmen gradually disappeared for the very good reason that less and less ornamentation was required. The origins of this decline went back a long way, and Rodin stigmatized them in his own day. ' The old-fashioned apprenticeship, whereby long years of study enabled a man to learn every aspect of his profession and demonstrate its resources, equipped those who were strong enough to conceive; it transformed humble craftsmen into genuine and useful collaborators. All this has been destroyed. The decline of apprenticeship inaugurated the destruction of craftsmanship. It was thought that apprenticeship could be replaced by academic training, but the student attending our present-day schools is not an apprentice. He is not compelled to exert himself, he works when he pleases, he is already an artist-to-be, not a craftsman; too often, he is already a " Monsieur ". By carrying out a multitude of simple tasks, the apprentice used to absorb the spirit of the studio and learn obedience. He then got to grips with his craft, trained his hand while learning its first principles, and made fresh progress each day. After that, he worked on compositions by his older colleagues, daily contact with whom moulded his youthful intelligence, before being allowed to proceed with trial efforts of his own. In short, before starting to produce, he had time to yearn to produce. ' Comparing this with modern methods, Rodin declared that classes at which a teacher devoted the odd two minutes to each pupil were no training at all.

Rodin, who congratulated himself on having spent so long as an apprentice, reverted to the subject of apprenticeship throughout his life. He remained an apprentice until the age of forty—indeed, he may be said to have remained one until his death, constantly seeking instruction from nature, from cathedrals, and from the classical sculptures with which he surrounded himself in the hope that they would impart their eternal lessons to him.

After his return from Italy Rodin set to work on a decisive project, fortified by his new convictions. He had left behind in his studio a rough model of a young man with a superb physique. The subject was a Belgian soldier, selected by Rodin because he disliked working with professionals who were inured to the dummy-like poses required of them by art schools. He worked on the figure for eighteen months.

It would be tempting to suppose that Rodin's debut as a creative artist was determined by the enthusiasm which Michelangelo's statues had recently aroused in him during his visits to Florence and Rome. In fact, there was no hint of any influence on the part of the author of the tombs of San Lorenzo. Michelangelo's expressive genius manifested itself in a balanced amplification of musculature achieved by the direct hewing of marble, whereas Rodin modelled small luminous surfaces, trickles of shadow and reflected light which irradiated the youthful body and seemed to make the flesh pulsate with life.

Before showing the statue in Paris he sent it to an exhibition held by the ' Cercle artistique belge ', calling it *The Vanquished* as a tribute to the French soldiers of 1870. It aroused a peculiar mixture of admiration and reserve. Critics spoke of its intense vitality but remarked on its strangeness. Then came the insidious question: in view of its high quality, how much of the statue was attributable to casting from the life ?

Rodin almost choked with indignation that such a charge should have been levelled at him, a man who had worked from models for so long, and who, unlike his contemporaries, had always regarded casting from the life as a shameful practice. He countered the libel by offering to introduce his model to an expert so as to establish ' how far removed an artistic interpretation must be from a slavish copy '. Dodging the issue, the newspaper in question pointed out that the subject had merely been raised and that no offence was intended.

Rodin dispatched his statue to Paris and went on ahead to meet it. He removed the javelin on which the despairing figure had previously leant, and the disappearance of this useless accessory changed its character. Having debated the merits of several titles, including *The Awakening of Spring, The Awakening of Humanity,* and *Primeval Man,* he eventually sent it to the Salon under the title *The Bronze Age.*

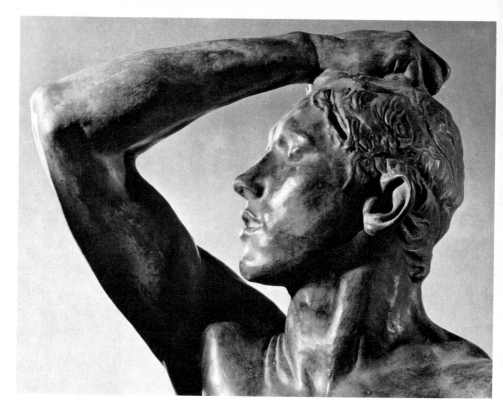

10 *The Bronze Age. Detail* 1877

*The Bronze Age* is neither academic nor naturalistic. It would be vain to scan it for signs of a classical pastiche or, equally, of a desire for originality. There is little to distinguish it from a thousand other nude studies, but the little there is embraces everything. It is life itself, vibrant and luminous, close to nature yet transfiguring it.

Nothing could have been stranger than the confusion into which the sculptor members of the Paris jury were thrown by this nude figure—so simple, so true, but so radiant that it differed utterly from what they were accustomed to seeing and judging by their routine standards. There was something almost impertinent about it, but they accepted it just the same.

11 *The Bronze Age. Detail* 1877  ▶

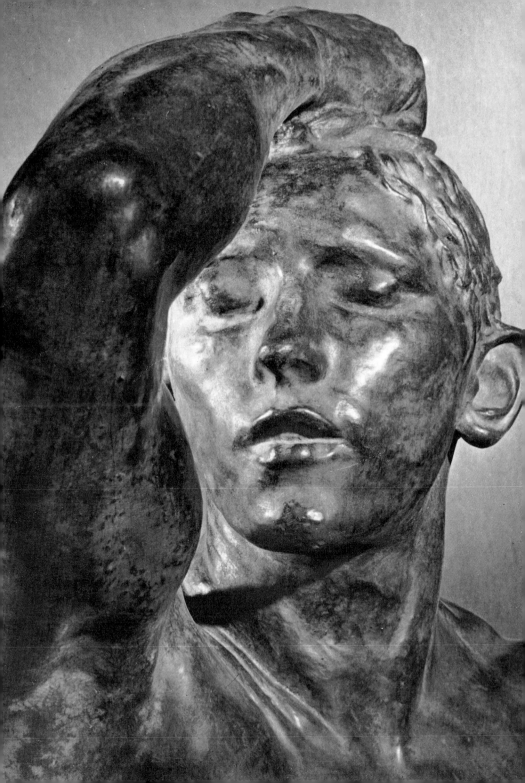

Unfortunately, the Brussels gossip was relayed to France—with the best of intentions, no doubt—and eagerly circulated by a number of not so well-meaning sculptors. The accusations of casting from the life were made again, even more loudly. It was the first time a jury had raised the subject—the practice of partial casting from the life was fairly widespread, even among jury members—and the fact that this spirited work by an unknown artist attracted every gaze helped to propagate the rumour still further.

Rodin had become an object of public scandal and was to remain so, to a greater or lesser extent, for the rest of his life. Genius, as Rilke once said, inspires fear.

He defended himself stoutly but inexpertly. The young model from Brussels agreed to testify on his behalf, even to the extent of stripping in front of the jury if need be, but the Belgian military authorities refused him permission to cross the frontier. This provoked derision in Paris, and there was talk of withdrawing the statue from the Salon. One member of the Institut asserted that it had been cast from a corpse.

Deeply hurt, Rodin wrote to the Under-Secretary of State at the Ministry of Fine Arts, who responded by appointing the usual board of inquiry.

Rodin's plan was to produce photographs of his model for comparison with his statue. Fortunately, some of the more eminent members of the Salon committee rallied to his defence. Foremost among them was Falguière, an admirer of *The Bronze Age,* and further authoritative support came from Guillaume, whom he knew personally, Alfred Boucher, Henri-Antoine Chapu, and Paul Dubois. They were joined by Belgian artists who had watched Rodin at work and, finally, by Carrier-Belleuse, who forgot their quarrel in the face of such a ridiculous allegation.

The battle was won, and the unlikely story only focussed public attention all the more on the talents of the man who had involuntarily provoked it.

Three years later a bronze cast of *The Bronze Age* was purchased by the state and erected in the Jardin du Luxembourg. Since

Rodin had just won a third-class medal with *St John the Baptist,* then on show at the Salon, some committee members grumbled that it was too much of an honour to bestow on the winner of a junior award.

One can only marvel that professional sculptors should have been so mistaken—or ostensibly so—about Rodin's working methods. Perhaps they were unaware that he always used a model and, failing this, sculpted from memory. One glance should have taught them not to confuse casting with an act of creation. How could a caster have obtained such muscular movement, such pulsating skin, and, above and beyond this epidermal quality, a harmony of proportion and vibrancy of modelling which precluded not only casting but the mere imitation of nature? Life-like representation never depends on skin-deep accuracy.

Although dwarfed by the tall houses of Auteuil, the statue still occupies the centre of the square which bears its author's name, its aura of intense life a permanent reproach to the misjudgement of those who once condemned it.

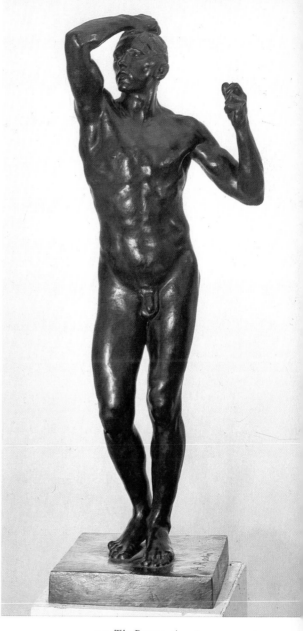

12 *The Bronze Age* 1877

It was now time for Rodin to secure his means of livelihood. The expense of transporting his statue to Paris had not been offset by any sales at the Salon. The Exposition Universelle of 1878 was due to be installed the following year on the Champ-de-Mars and the slopes of Chaillot, where the architects Davioud and Bourdais were completing the Palais du Trocadéro in a Romano-Hispano-Moorish style. By contrast, the ' Palais de l'Industrie ' on the Champ-de-Mars, a structure of cast iron and glass, heralded the advent of a new age.

Seven years after her defeat, downfall and humiliation, France was planning to reassert her place in the world. All the major nations except Germany were represented at this first international exhibition organized by the MacMahon Republic. Rodin was invited to participate, but still as an anonymous craftsman. The creator of *The Bronze Age* was hired by a sculptor named Laouste, himself overwhelmed with work.

This time, Rodin was in Paris and Rose in Belgium. Spurred on by her lover's imperious letters, Rose struggled hard to raise money, sold furniture, and paid the cost of transporting to London a design for a monument which Disraeli proposed to erect in honour of Byron. (Thirty-seven entries were submitted, and Rodin's, for all his high hopes, had little chance of acceptance.)

Since his work would be keeping him in Paris from now on, he went to fetch Rose from Brussels. There was no point in continuing his partnership with Van Rasbourg, so he dissolved it in an amicable manner. Rose and he found accommodation in the Rue Saint-Jacques, on the corner of the Rue Royer-Collard, and took their son and Rodin's father to live with them. Rodin moved twice more in the next six years [6] but never strayed far from his birthplace in the Rue de l'Arbalète.

Family life was not pleasant under such cramped conditions. Rodin's father had lost his reason as well as his sight. He refused to budge from his bed and spent the whole time making irritable and disjointed remarks. Young Auguste was a nice enough boy but showed signs of turning into a mental defective. With the egocentricity of an artist to whom nothing matters but his art,

13 *The Bronze Age. Detail* 1877 ▶

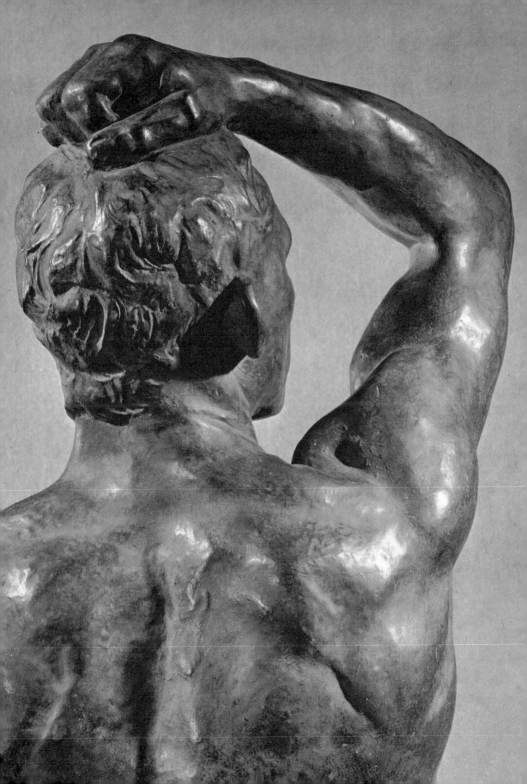

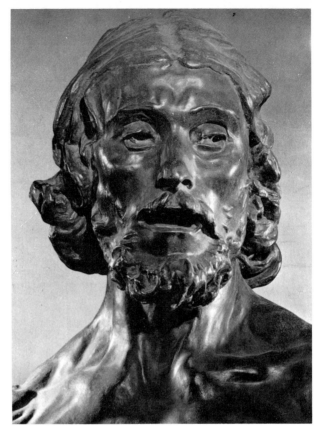

14 *St John the Baptist.  Detail* 1878

Rodin departed for his studio in the morning and only returned at nightfall, leaving poor Rose to cope with the responsabilities of the home.

A sculptor friend named Fourquet had found him a studio near his own in the Rue des Fourneaux. [7] Rodin retained enchanted memories of this quarter, which teemed with sculptors and skilled craftsmen.  As ever, he worked with great intensity, practising all sorts of techniques and perfecting his skill.  ' The need to survive made me learn every aspect of my profession, ' he wrote in later years.  ' I undoubtedly spent too much time on

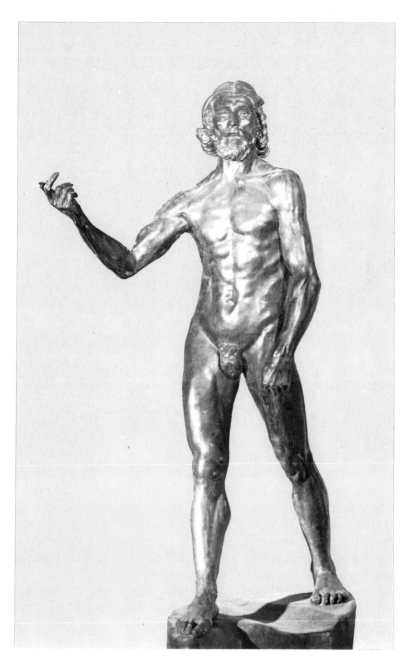

15  *St John the Baptist* 1878

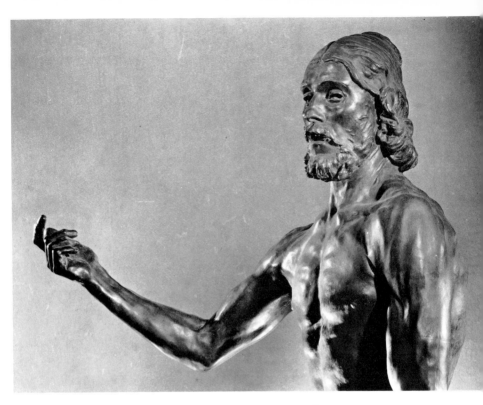

16 *St John the Baptist.* *Detail* 1878

finishing off, on rough-hewing marble, on monuments, ornaments and jewellery, but it stood me in good stead. ' He might have added that he also worked at this period for a cabinet-maker in the Faubourg Saint-Antoine, for whom he carved walnut chests.

While devoting himself to this form of work, which he performed with routine brilliance, he surrendered himself to his dreams. He had been tempered in the furnace of Michelangelo, and Victor Hugo stirred his imagination. At the first opportunity, he would get out his sketch-book and start to draw.

Although he was not unduly proud of the plaster statuettes which it was Rose's job to dispose of through a dealer in the Passage des Panoramas, there was an incomplete work for which he felt a special regard. To quote his own account of its history:

17 *The Walking Man* 1877 ▶

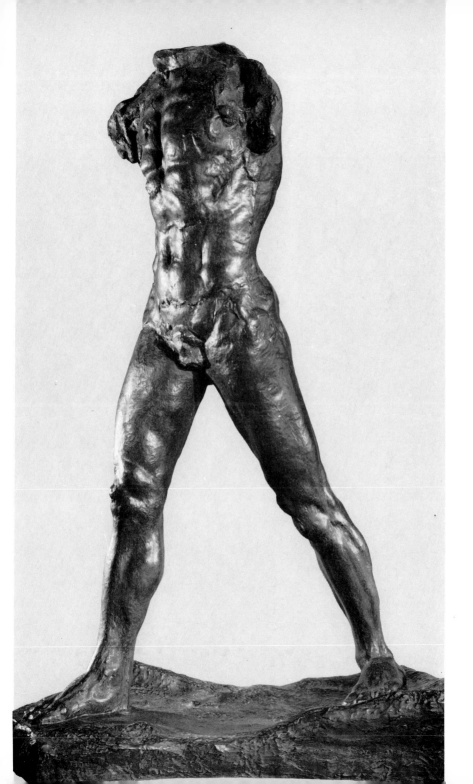

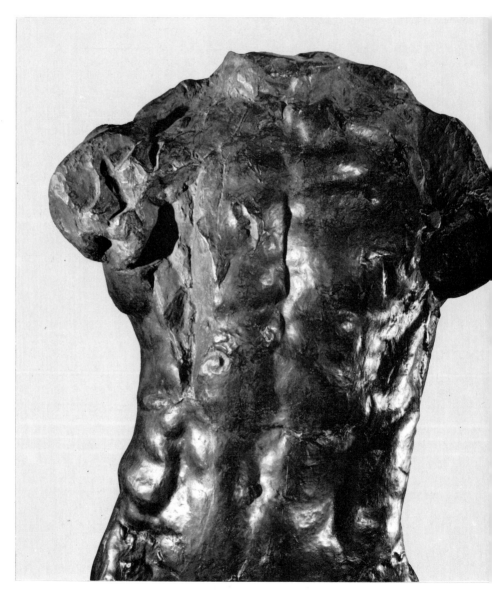

18 *The Walking Man.* *Detail* 1877

'One morning there was a knock at the studio door and I saw an Italian come in, accompanied by one of his compatriots, who had already posed for me. It was a peasant from the Abruzzi who had arrived from his native land the day before and had come to offer his services as a model. Seeing him, I was struck with admiration. The appearance, features and physical strength of this uncouth and hirsute man expressed all the violence but also all the mysticism of his race.

'I at once thought of a St John the Baptist, in other words, of a child of nature, an inspired figure, a believer, a Precursor come to proclaim One greater than himself. The peasant undressed and climbed on to the revolving stand as if he had never posed before. He took up his stance with head raised, body erect, and weight supported on both legs, which were opened like compasses. The pose was so right, so distinctive and so true that I cried out: " But it's a man walking! " I at once decided to make what I had seen. It was the prevailing custom, when inspecting a model, to tell him to " walk ", that is to say, to balance the entire weight of his body on one leg alone. This was supposed to help one to find more elegant and harmonious poses and to give what was termed " shape ". The mere idea of balancing a figure on two legs seemed tasteless, an affront to tradition—almost a heresy. I was already wilful and obstinate then. My only thought was to do something good at all costs, for if I failed to convey my impression exactly as I had received it my statue would be ridiculous and everyone would laugh at me. I promised myself that I would model it with all the application at my command. That was how I came, in turn, to produce *The Walking Man* and *St John the Baptist*. All I did was to copy the model chance had sent me.' [8]

Rodin was referring to the remarkable figure of *St John the Baptist Preaching,* for which *The Walking Man* (without head and arms) was the preliminary study. As we have seen, this piece only won its author a third-class medal at the Salon.

Meanwhile, Rodin doggedly submitted test pieces for every competition that came to his notice: a monument to Diderot for

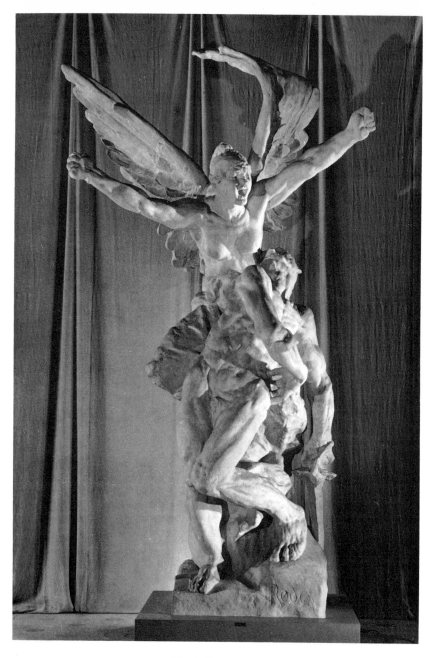

19 *The Call to Arms* 1878

the Boulevard Saint-Germain, a Jean-Jacques Rousseau, a General Margueritte, a Lazare Carnot, etc. His entries were consistently rejected. The monument into which he undoubtedly put most of himself was *La Défense,* dedicated to the glory of the defenders of Paris during the Franco-Prussian War. [9] This was the group which we know as *The Call to Arms.* The spirit of war, a female figure, flings wide its clenched fists and unfurls its wings, one of which has been injured in battle. Its whole face, contorted with pain and defiance, is an eloquent and stirring appeal for help. Below, a naked and reeling warrior with tortured muscles (possibly inspired by one of Michelangelo's *Slaves*) seems to be mustering his strength for a return to the fray. It may have been too animated for a public monument, bit it possessed enough vigour and heroic vitality to have flattened the rest of the sixty-odd entries. Rodin did not even reach the short list.

The sculptor received only one commission from the Fine Arts authorities in Paris. This was a *d'Alembert* for the exterior of the new Hôtel de Ville, an impersonal statue like all the rest and one which nobody has ever bothered to examine closely. [10]

Thanks to a personal favour, however, Rodin managed to stabilize his financial position. Carrier-Belleuse, who had soon dismissed the petty quarrel which had estranged them in Brussels, was now director of the Sèvres Manufactory. Better acquainted than anyone—and for excellent reasons—with the expert craftsmanship of his former assistant, he invited him to join the staff on a non-permanent basis. This brought Rodin a monthly salary of 170 francs in addition to his hourly rate of pay. With his usual generosity, he repaid his benefactor by doing a bust of him.

The Manufactory was currently administered by a chemist named Lauth, who regarded artists with suspicion and hostility. Although he styled himself art director, Carrier-Belleuse quickly discovered that he had nothing to direct. New models were merely stowed away in the dusty store-rooms. The running of the establishment had changed considerably since Madame de Pompadour's day. Its main function was to supply the Presidency of the Republic and government ministers with frightful objets d'art.

It also turned out Sèvres vases destined for presentation to winners of competitions and lotteries—celebrated articles whose identical design and distinctive shade of deep blue constituted a guarantee of origin.

Rodin produced some small decorative figures and a large epergne based on drawings by Carrier-Belleuse and entitled *Les Chasses*.

The Sèvres authorities regarded him with a jaundiced eye. He alleged that his works were deliberately neglected, and some of his pieces were broken. Truth to tell, little enough survives of his output during the three years he worked for Sèvres. His vocation lay elsewhere and his thoughts were devoted to sculptures which would express his personality to the full. When he finally left the Manufactory he got himself replaced by a friend named Jules Desbois, a modest, likable and impecunious young man whose life and undoubted talents were spent in the service of others.

Profitable commissions summoned Rodin away from Paris. He went to Nice and then Strasbourg for some time, still engaged on anonymous decorative projects which involved the elaborate and ostentatious adornment of façades for clients who had been enriched by commercial and financial success.

Meanwhile, political developments were under way. Gambetta's clamorous campaigns had contributed to the election of a Republican Chamber and the formation of a ' centre-left ' government. The Commune exiles were granted amnesty. Among them was Dalou, who, having been appointed to the administration of the Louvre by the Commune and subsequently convicted of ' usurpation of office ', had been living in exile in England.

The two friends celebrated an emotional reunion, but their relationship quickly cooled again. Returning home in triumph, Dalou was irked by the panegyrics which colleagues and critics were now lavishing on his old friend, and became envious of his budding reputation.

One of Dalou's friends was Léon Cladel, a popular novelist who shared his political beliefs and enjoyed a wide readership.

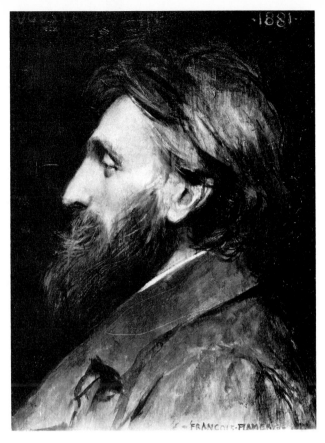

20 François Flameng. *Rodin* 1881

Rodin was thus acquainted with Cladel's circle, which readily embraced writers and artists alike. Among those who frequented his home were the elder Rosny, Rollinat, Séverine, Paul and Victor Margueritte, Mallarmé, a group of Belgian authors and poets which included Verhaeren, Lemonnier, Rodenbach and Georges Eckhoud, all attracted by the aura of Symbolism, and artists such as Van Rysselberghe and Constantin Meunier.

Rodin was vigorously supported by avant-garde writers and critics, the best-known being Octave Mirbeau and Gustave Geffroy. They were later joined by Roger Marx, an authoritative figure despite his youth, and by Camille Mauclair, the pugnacious champion of the Impressionists.

Rodin spoke little at these social gatherings. His voice was shy and diffident, but his work was already gaining him a name. Apart from that, he had the knack of spotting people who could be useful to him. His contacts soon extended to the political sphere, though he took little interest in politics himself. His letters, writings and collected remarks are exclusively concerned with his art. Chance, coupled perhaps with a certain intuition, brought him into contact with men who were travelling the road to power. Having known rebels, he was destined to know ministers.

Nevertheless, his career differed entirely from that of Dalou, who actively engaged in politics. He was never—happily for him—commissioned to edify the great paraphernalia of state and nation. He certainly exploited his contacts and solicited official support, but always with the sole and undivided aim of fulfilling his personal destiny.

His friend Legros did a portrait of him at this period, a strong enough picture in itself but mainly of documentary interest today. The dense masses of beard and hair, with their tawny lights, just reveal a straight nose which exactly follows the line of the forehead, and the arch of the brows is heavily accentuated. Although the profile gives an impression of stubborn and self-assertive power, the eye beneath the heavy and inflamed lid is not only penetrating but strangely gentle.

Rodin was introduced to the salon of Juliette Adam, a favourite haunt of personalities in the public eye. Founder of the *Nouvelle Revue* and author of short stories and essays in which she expounded her philosophical, political and social views with an authority rarely found in other women of her day, Juliette Adam was a very live wire indeed.

Gambetta was to be seen at her soirées, parading his sonorous eloquence before a circle of admirers. Rodin, whose name naturally meant nothing to him, was duly introduced. Whatever it was that impressed the politician—the big red beard or the diffident air—he recommended the sculptor to Antonin Proust, a journalist and parliamentarian who had been a member of his personal staff and was now his Minister of Fine Arts. Proust acquired Rodin's most important bronze, *St John the Baptist,* for the state. Madame Adam's circle also included Waldeck-Rousseau, Spuller, and Castagnary, an art critic who, as Under-Secretary at the Ministry of Fine Arts, consistently helped Rodin to the best of his ability.

Edmond Turquet, a lawyer on whom politics temporarily bestowed the same post as Castagnary, took a particular interest in Rodin because he was recommended by sculptors who, though far inferior as artists, were fortunate enough to carry weight in government circles. These included Boucher, Dubois, Falguière, Chapu, and several other current stars of the Salon, all of whom used their influence on his behalf in the salons.

The chance of an important commission came Rodin's way. The burning of the Cour des Comptes by the Commune had created a ruined site, overrun with bushes and brambles, which remained untouched for twenty-seven years and became known to Parisians as ' the virgin forest '. The plan was to use this site for a Museum of Decorative Art whose function would be proclaimed by a monumental doorway in richly decorated bronze. [11]

This was how Rodin came to tackle *The Gates of Hell,* the huge work which unleashed his visionary power, was enlivened by the whole afflatus of his genius and absorbed his thoughts for twenty years—the work which exercized his powers of imagination in so tumultuous a way that it eventually transcended them altogether and had to be left incomplete, despite the ardent and unfailing breath of inspiration.

Although still the bugbear of academic sculptors, Rodin now embarked on the road to fame. His work, as fiercely controversial as ever and despised by the bureaucrats of the Hôtel de Ville, was lucky enough to benefit by the infatuation of a high society which could make reputations or break them. At a period when all forms of art were in a state of violent flux, he was the only French artist who blithely infringed every current convention and still managed to win the esteem—cautious at first but increasingly assured—of certain members of the establishment.

Painting was in a ferment at the time of his first successes in the 1880s. The Impressionists had organized their first group exhibition at Nadar's in 1874. Among the artists represented were Manet, Monet, Sisley, Renoir, Pissarro, Berthe Morisot and Caillebotte. Traditional canons of painting were now overturned by the incandescent works of men like Cézanne, Gauguin and Van Gogh. The campaign waged so boldly by Durand-Ruel had still to be crowned with success and the public were not yet in step, but the doctrinal importance of the movement grew from day to day, attended by the incomprehension or hostility of the majority and the enthusiasm of a few.

With a spontaneity and sincerity which only the foolish or ignorant called in question, the Impressionists discovered a new vision of nature and its vibrant response to light. To art historians of the future, the sites of their discoveries and personal adventures were destined to ring out like battle-names: Argenteuil, Pontoise, Giverny, le Pouldu, l'Estaque, Saint-Rémy, Auvers-sur-Oise, Tahiti. They spurred each other on, conscious that they were in possession of a rock-like truth on which official taste and the academic powers-that-be would ultimately founder. Painting would never be the same after them, and their painting would come into its own.

In the field of sculpture, this subversive pioneering campaign was conducted by one man alone. It might be argued, in retrospect, that Daumier and Degas also produced sculpture. However, sculptures by painters were commonly regarded as trivia in those days, both by the general public and by the experts.

Cast an eye over old photographs which show gentlemen in top-hats levelling their canes at chilly nudities, genre scenes of the 'Breton bagpiper' variety, or insipid busts produced to order... You are looking at the Salon jury in action. Even in the most remote provincial backwoods, the development of photography enabled people to admire the dexterity with which winners of the 'grands prix de Rome' and other equally acclaimed uncompetitive awards managed to reproduce men, women and children in flesh and bone, cunningly tracing the course of each vein from temple to ankle. Soapy nudes and histrionic gestures reigned supreme in public buildings and public squares.

Rodin's appearance in the artistic firmament illuminated this pretentious and poverty-stricken gloom like a shaft of sunlight. Carpeaux had known how to invest the human form with life, but Carpeaux died in 1875 at the age of forty-eight. Nothing that had happened in sculpture since then—neither the neo-Grecian scholasticism of Chapu, Gérôme and Barrias nor the mannered, so-called Florentine charm of Paul Dubois and his imitators—amounted to more than a technical expertise which was totally incapable of filling a spiritual void.

Things were no better outside France. In Brussels, Rodin had known Constantin Meunier, an artist who enjoyed a brief hour of glory because his preoccupation with social justice prompted him to abandon academicism in favour of popular and contemporary themes which he tried to reproduce with scrupulous realism. However, there is no possible comparison between the Belgian artist's miners and dockers—who are simply miners and dockers—and Rodin's grandiose figures, which transcend naturalism and bring us face to face with eternal man.

Sculpture had sunk so low in every country that it would be difficult to quote the name of a single memorable sculptor.

Although Rodin was taught by Carpeaux for a brief while during his youth, nothing entitles one to compare the ease and sunny charm of *The Dance* with the impassioned vehemence of the man who could instil so much fecund strength into the creatures which he fashioned with his hands. What is even more remarkable is that, unlike the exponents of modern painting, he succeeded in impressing his genius on the less obtuse traditionalists and on certain official circles. Indeed, he succeeded to such an extent that, despite incessant conspiracies on the part of his natural foes, he became the sort of figure whose primacy in his own field wins general acceptance. At the time of his apotheosis, most of the Impressionists were still regarded with indifference.

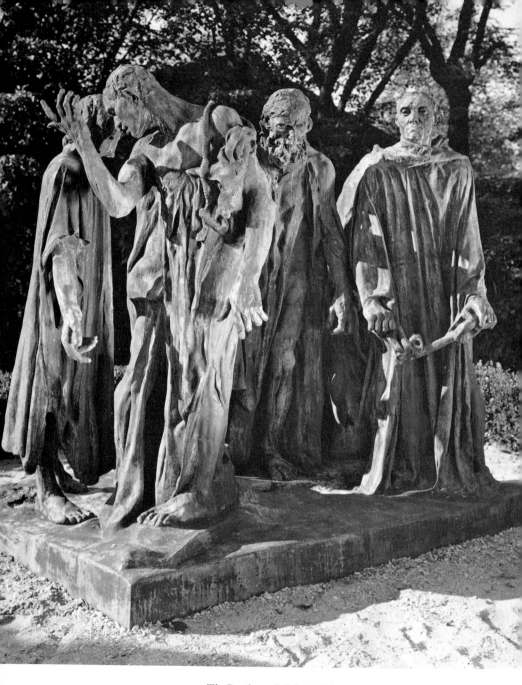

21 *The Burghers of Calais* 1886-88

CHAPTER FOUR

# The Burghers of Calais

The commission for *The Gates of Hell* sent Rodin into a strange fever of excitement. He worked without stop. Sketch-books, exercize-books and loose sheets became filled with tormented drawings, lightning pencil-sketches and wash-drawings in which strange beings took shape, leaping, writhing or embracing in the tempestuous blast of his imagination. He was like a man in the throes of delirium. Even at table he would reach abruptly for his sketch-book in an effort to capture and crystallize the hallucinatory images which flashed through his mind.

He was not delirious, merely inspired by memories of Dante's *Inferno*. What guided his pencil-point was eternal humanity, its hopes, sufferings and passions, its groans of love and cries of fear.

The studio in the Rue des Fourneaux was too small to house this monumental work, which was to be at least twenty feet high and inhabited by a host of figures symbolizing the passions of mankind. The state put two studios at Rodin's disposal in the Dépôt des Marbres, a building at the far end of the Rue de l'Université, not far from the Champ-de-Mars. Here, bordering a large courtyard strewn with raw or rough-hewn blocks of marble, were twelve studios reserved for sculptors or painters engaged on projects of exceptional size. Rodin kept his studios in the Dépôt des Marbres even when he acquired still larger premises—at Meudon or the Hôtel Biron, for instance. 183 Rue de l'Université was the address on his notepaper and the place where he received most of his admiring visitors.

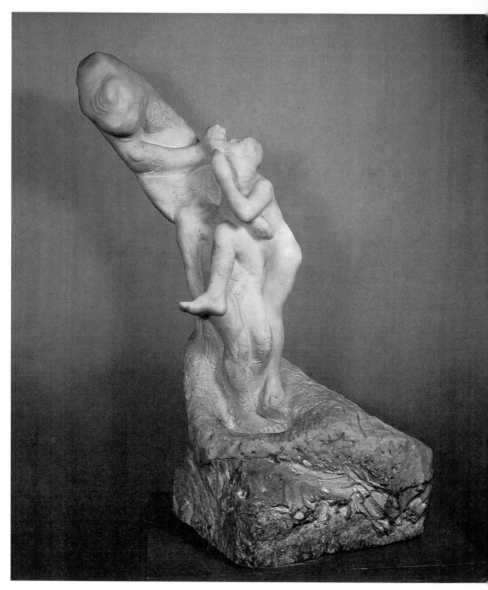

22 *The Creation of Woman* 1905

His first pencil-sketches of *The Gates* as a whole were clearly influenced by the compartmented design of Ghiberti's doors for the Baptistry in Florence, but this was only a passing phase. His maquettes for the souls in torment were modelled at such a frenetic and free rhythm that they soon overflowed their frames. The host of figures which took shape under his hands in a continuous process of development or destruction not only varied in relief but differed in dimensions. The plaster maquette of *The Gates* gradually developed into a fulgurating, voluptuous and terrifying universe which subsided into chaos at the foot of the gates.

The fee fixed for the commission was 30,000 francs, of which Rodin received instalments totalling 27,500 francs over a period of seven years. In addition, the state purchased bronzes of *Adam* and *Eve,* the admirable statues with which he planned to flank *The Gates*.

Parsimonious as he was in his daily life, Rodin never haggled over professional expenses. Sessions with the models without whom he found it impossible

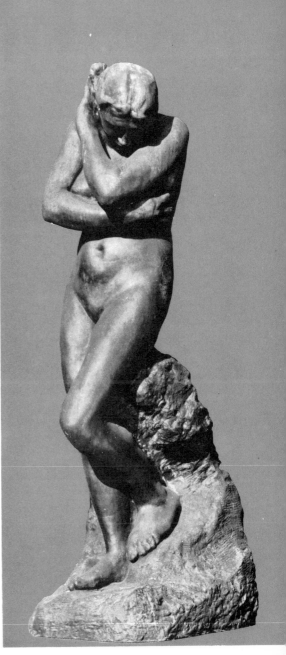

23 *Eve* 1881

to work, innumerable casts of his maquettes, which were repeatedly modified or destroyed, bronze casts, patinas, mouldings—all these were paid for without demur.

Rodin took advantage of his unexpected good fortune and growing influx of commissions to rent some new studios in the suburbs. One of them, a large and lofty room overlooking a garden, was at 117 Boulevard de Vaugirard. At 68 Boulevard de l'Italie, half-obscured by the undergrowth of a neglected garden, he discovered an eighteenth-century mansion with a colonnaded porch and pedimented corner-pavilions. The house, which had once been occupied by Corvisart and also, so it was said, by Musset, was mutilated and partly ruined, but the ground floor lent itself to use as a studio or storage space and some of the rooms were habitable. In fact, Rodin seldom visited the place except for secret assignations. The building was doomed to destruction, and he later watched the demolition of this handsome piece of architecture with a scandalized regret which prompted him to acquire some of the carved stonework that had once adorned its exterior.

Rodin had a taste for mysterious retreats whose existence was unknown to Rose. Judith Cladel tells us of her own surprise on being informed by the caretaker of the Château de Nemours that the ancient tower was let to 'an artist from Paris—a Monsieur Rodin'. When she questioned him about it his only response was 'the silent, mocking laugh with which he derided his little extravagances'.

Rodin was incredibly prolific at this period. In addition to subjects destined for his *Gates of Hell,* some of which were enlarged and became celebrated bronzes and marbles in their own right, he made busts of his friends : Legros, then teaching in London; Jean-Paul Laurens and Eugène Guillaume, his studio neighbours at the Depôt des Marbres; Dalou; and Maurice Haquette, brother-in-law of Edmond Turquet, whom he had got to know at the Sèvres Manufactory.

His bust of Victor Hugo represented a triumph in the face of difficult conditions. The poet was so overburdened with honours that he declined to sit. With the connivance of Juliette Drouet,

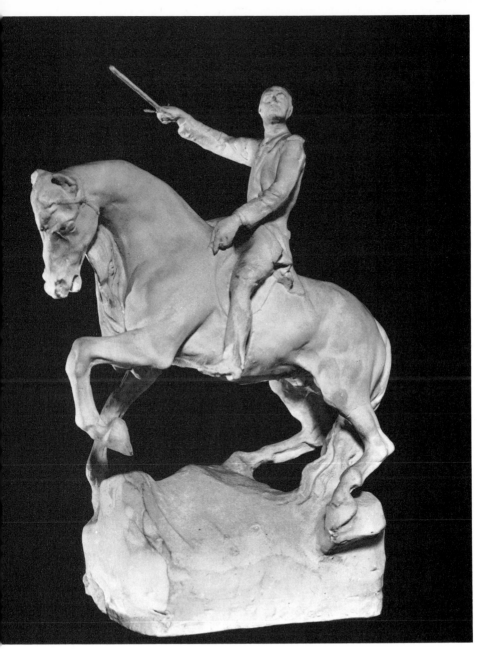

24 *Equestrian statue of General Lynch* 1886

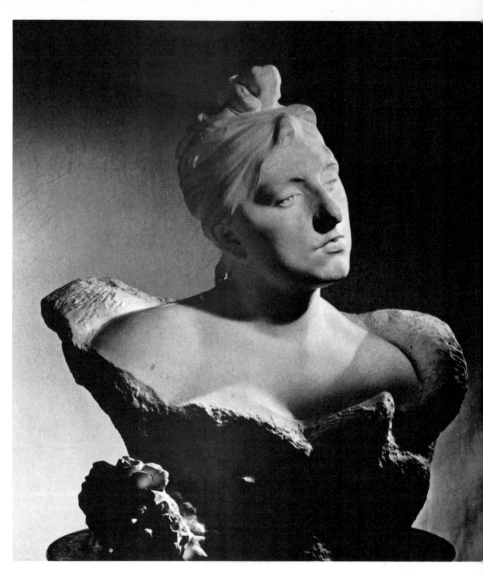

25 *Madame Vicuña* 1884

however, Rodin obtained permission to install a modelling stand in a gallery in the house in the Avenue d'Eylau and make sketches of the master at work in his study, receiving visitors or dining at table. This may have been a blessing in disguise, because it enabled Rodin to adhere to his basic principle, which was to record all the outlines he wanted and capture animated expressions rather than a face wearied by the act of posing.

Another great triumph was his bust of Señora Vicuña, wife of the Chilean minister in Paris. The latter commissioned Rodin to produce two statues for his native land, one of his father, President Vicuña, and the other of General Lynch, the national liberator. Rodin portrayed the President receiving a palm-branch from his grateful country. The other subject afforded scope for an equestrian statue, one of the sculptor's long-standing ambitions. The two maquettes were dispatched by ship but arrived in the middle of one of the revolutions endemic to the countries of Latin America. Whether stolen or smashed, they were never seen again.

As for the bust of young Señora Vicuña, shown at the Salon of 1888, it possesses a miraculous charm compounded of outward ingenuousness and an aura of latent sensuality. The lips are on the verge of parting, the eyelids and nostrils seem to tremble with desire. The bare throat, rounded shoulders and burgeoning breasts convey the nudity of the entire body. Everything about the bust down to the knotted ribbon in the hair—a detail which might have seemed comical if placed there by anyone else—contributes to its aura of femininity.

Rodin was a power-house of talent. In 1884, the very year when this young woman posed for him so assiduously (some said too assiduously!), he embarked on studies for *The Burghers of Calais*—if not his greatest masterpiece, certainly the most successful of his major works.

Reviving an old idea entertained by their predecessors, the mayor and councillors of Calais had resolved to erect a monument in honour of the heroes who offered to sacrifice their lives to save the city from destruction in the fourteenth century. In their view, no municipal authority could have devised a nobler or more fitting plan than to present the citizens of Calais with a token of this milestone in their history and to perpetuate the memory of the sublime act which ensured their city's survival.

Approaches had formerly been made to distinguished sculptors of earlier date, to David d'Angers in the reign of Louis-Philippe and Clésinger during the Second Empire, but the council had never managed to raise sufficient funds. Now, in 1884, at the instigation of a shrewd mayor named Dewavrin, it was decided to launch a national subscription drive which would make it possible to fulfil the ambition so dear to the mayor's heart. Through the good offices of a mutual friend, he got in touch with Rodin.

Only a study of the sculptor's voluminous correspondence with the mayor, his numerous letters with their naive turns of phrase and clumsy penmanship, can convey Rodin's line of thought and the importance which he immediately attached to this project. The proposed theme was one which stirred him deeply. He would be renewing his links with the great traditions of the Middle Ages, with the world of cathedrals to which he always felt so close and that he could never enter without a thrill of excitement. He would be trying to shoulder the burden and express the humanity of a spiritual tradition whose mysteries he had penetrated more deeply than any man of his time.

Monsieur Dewavrin visited Rodin at his studio and went away satisfied that the choice of artist was a wise one. Shortly afterwards, Rodin wrote to him: ' I have been fortunate enough to hit on an idea which appeals to me and would be original if carried out. I have never seen an arrangement better suited to its subject or more utterly original. What makes it even better is that all towns usually have the same monument, barring a few minor details... '

A fortnight later he announced that the casting of his first clay model was complete, and gave details of his plans:

' I find the idea completely original from the architectural and sculptural point of view. Furthermore, the subject itself is heroic and requires heroic treatment, and the group of six figures sacrificing themselves is imbued with expression and emotion. The base must be triumphal, so as to support human patriotism, self-sacrifice and virtue rather than a quadriga... I have seldom produced a sketch with as much verve and restraint. Eustache de Saint-Pierre, alone, by his dignity of gesture, leads and convinces his friends and relations... I am also sending you a drawing today—another idea—but I prefer the plaster model... All I have given you is a rough indication of my ideas, also of the arrangement, which took my fancy at once as I know all the sculptural clichés ordinarily employed in monuments to great men. '

Rodin pleaded his case vigorously. He stressed the originality of his six-figure group and pointed out how different it would be from other public monuments because he knew, only too well, what an artist exposed himself to by violating conventions.

Before setting to work, he carefully read Froissart's account of the incident which it was his task to commemorate. The vision of a whole group of expiatory victims coming forward to sacrifice themselves to their conqueror became so firmly rooted in his mind that it refused to leave him.

Consternation ensued. The city fathers wanted a statue, and a statue was a single figure in stone or bronze, supplemented by an allegorical figure if need be, or supported by a plinth adorned with a narrative bas-relief. What Rodin was proposing was not one statue but six. They did not discuss the merits of the idea; they merely asserted—as Rodin had foreseen they would—that his jumble of figures was not a genuine monument.

Hitherto, the plan had been to symbolize the heroism of the hostages by portraying the lone figure of Eustache de Saint-Pierre, the wealthiest of their number and the one who had inspired the rest by convincing them of the value of their self-sacrifice. Besides, the distinguished sculptors previously consulted about the monument had never conceived of it except in terms of a single symbolic figure.

The committee's reservations were apparent from the first, but Rodin was supported by two former fellow-pupils, his friend Legros, who came over from London, and Jean-Charles Cazin, a native of the Pas-de-Calais and now a celebrated painter. The

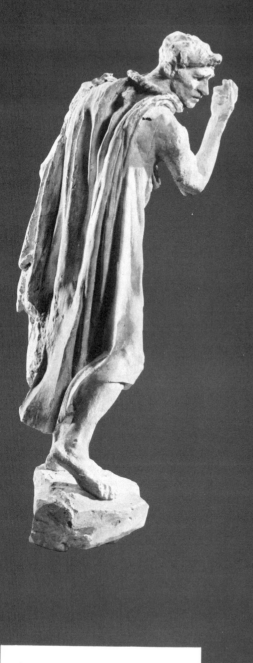
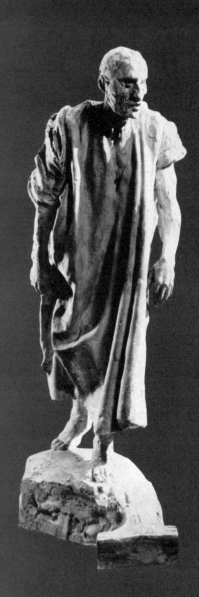

26 *Studies for The Burghers of Calais*
1886-88

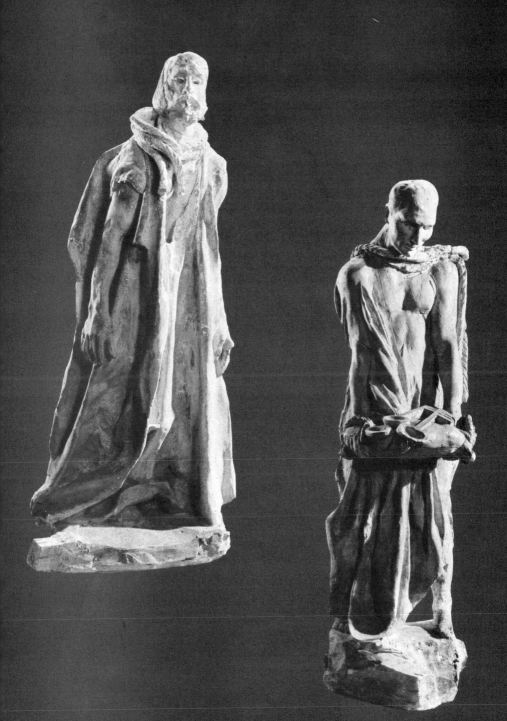

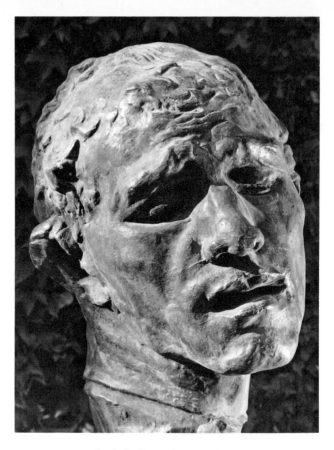

27 *Study for Pierre de Wissant* 1886-88

mayor asked Rodin to visit Calais and submit his scheme to the committee in person.

He did so with all the eloquence at his command. His refusal to compromise and complete inflexibility made a deep impression on those who interviewed him, and the battle seemed won.

A new and enlarged maquette was to be submitted. Rodin quoted a fee in the region of 35,000 francs. 'It isn't expensive,' he wrote. 'The foundry will charge me twelve or fifteen thousand francs at most, and another five thousand must be spent on hard local stone for the base...'

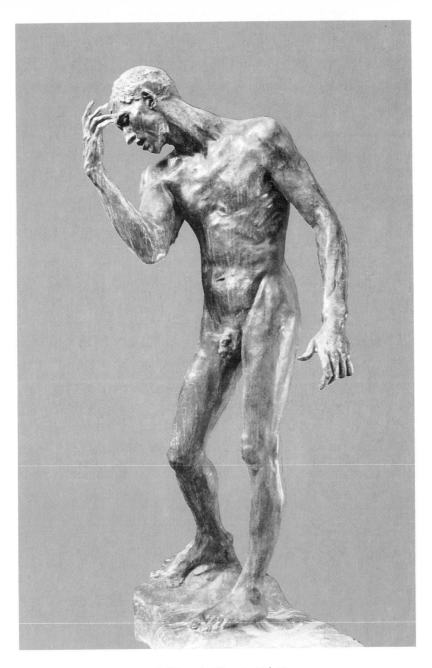

28 *Pierre de Wissant* 1886-88

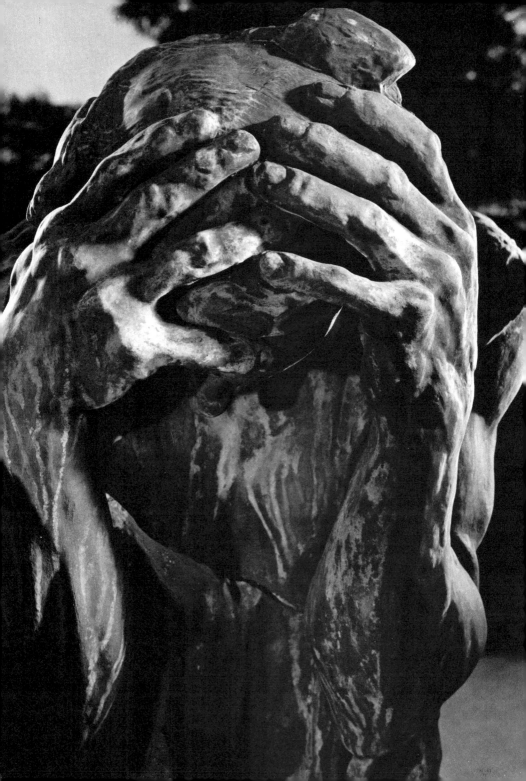

The committee did not argue about money matters but reverted to the basic design of the monument. ' This is not how we visualized our illustrious fellow-citizens. Their dejected attitude militates against our beliefs... The group's silhouette leaves much to be desired in the way of elegance. The sculptor could lend greater variety to the ground which supports his six figures and even break the monotony and baldness of the outlines by varying the stature of his six subjects... We note that Eustache de Saint-Pierre is clothed in a richly draped material which does not accord with the light garment ascribed to him by history... We feel bound to insist that M. Rodin shall undertake to modify his figures' poses and the silhouette of his group as a whole. '

Stung by these criticisms, the sculptor rebutted them in a long letter which, though disjointed, acquired the force of a manifesto. He took issue not with the members of the committee but with the false principles of which they were the unwitting champions. They failed to grasp that by insisting on alterations they would be ' emasculating ' his work. They also failed to grasp that he had already started work on the nude studies, a considerable labour and, from his point of view, absolutely essential.

' In Paris, in spite of the battle I wage against the École's style of sculpture, I am free to work on my *Gates* as I wish. I should be happy to be entrusted with the Saint-Pierre. '

Thanks to Jean-Paul Laurens, Mayor Dewavrin was finally persuaded to take the bait, though not without difficulty.

Rodin pressed on with the work in his studio in the Boulevard de Vaugirard while simultaneously proceeding with maquettes for his *Gates* at the Dépôt des Marbres. Actually, it was the latter which aroused most comment and interest in the Paris art world. Those who visited the sculptor in his studio each Saturday used to see, spread out at the foot of the full-size architectural frame for *The Gates,* a host of maquettes—many of them amorphous masses but all charged with dynamism and vitality of the most arresting kind.

Meanwhile, at the Boulevard de Vaugirard, Rodin continued to wrestle with the nudes for his *Burghers,* repeatedly modifying them, abandoning them and taking them up again. His series of

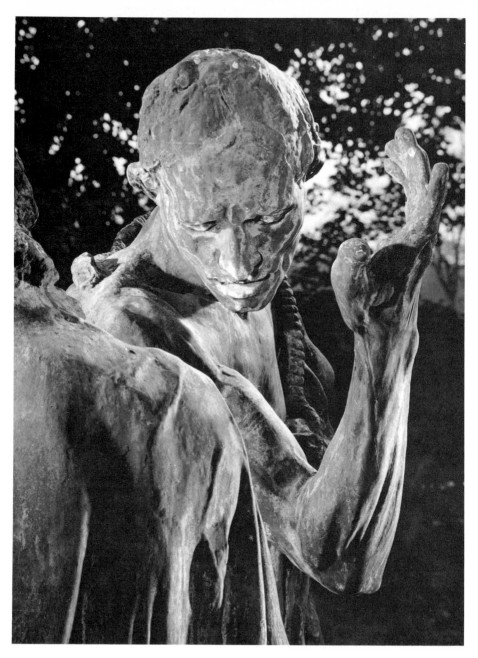

30 *The Burghers of Calais.   Detail* 1886-88

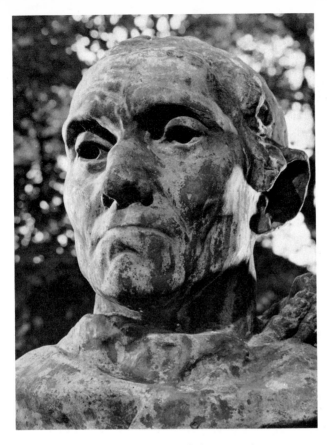

31 *Head of the Burgher with the Key* 1886-88

maquettes for the entire group (now displayed at the Villa des Brillants) shows that he had considerable difficulty in arranging the six figures. His first essays were not particularly meaningful or coherent, and success only came after lengthy experiments which resulted in the transformation of attitudes and expressions. The actual construction of his figures, for which the contract stipulated a height of at least two metres, was a very gradual process.

More than a year had elapsed since the placing of the order, and there was still no sign of a monument... The Mayor of Calais, who bore full responsibility for the project, grew uneasy. Rodin's

85

explanations were hardly designed to reassure him. ' Things are proceeding slowly, but the quality will be good. I sent one of the *Burghers* to Brussels, where it had a great success. I shall probably send it to the Exposition Universelle, but the whole monument won't be ready until the end of the year. Not enough time is allowed for any of the monuments commissioned these days, and they're all bad without exception. Many people cast from the life, which means substituting a photograph for a work of art. It may be quick, but it isn't art. Let's hope you give me enough time. '

The next party to default was the municipality, whose finances were in a shaky condition. (The sculptor had only received a few modest sums on account.) The group, still in plaster, was almost finished. Until times changed for the better, Rodin stored it in a rented stable in the Rue Saint-Jacques. It remained there for seven years. *The Burghers of Calais* caused a sensation when shown in 1889, and even Rodin's opponents called to congratulate him. There were a few criticisms, but, in general, astonishment yielded to admiration. Calais organized a lottery which yielded very meagre results, and the Ministry of Fine Arts responded to pressure on the part of Rodin's friends by making a grant of 5,350 francs.

The monument was finally unveiled in 1895, ten years after the scheme had first been launched. The government was represented by Chautemps, Minister for the Colonies. Poincaré's representative was Roger Marx, Inspector of Fine Arts, who delivered a stirring address.

Rodin's victory was not complete, however. His original plan had been to mount the group on a tall pylon so that his figures would be silhouetted against the sky, but strong opposition compelled him to abandon the idea. He then found himself attracted to the opposite extreme, and asked that the monument should be placed on a low plinth in the centre of the city, almost on a level with passers-by.

The councillors of Calais proved equally unamenable to this suggestion, which struck them as ridiculous, if not outrageous.

86

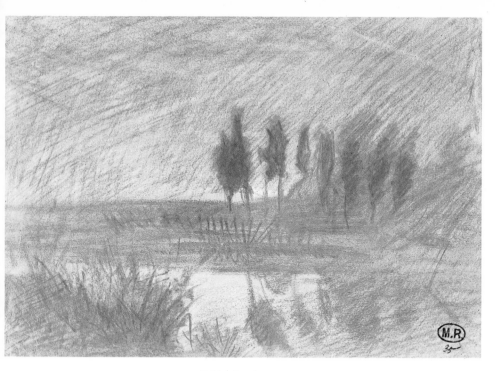

32 *Belgian Landscape*

They decided on a base of conventional size, enclosed—just to add insult to injury—by a paltry and superfluous set of railings.

It is strange that the ideas of an artist who astounded everyone by his rapidity of execution should have been so slow to prevail. Not until 1924, twenty-nine years later, were *The Burghers of Calais* transferred to the Place d'Armes and erected at ground-level, as though mingling with their fellow-citizens. Rodin's wish had finally been fulfilled. [12]

How did the artist manage to create a spectacle which transcended mere narrative and acquired a sort of tragic grandeur whose timeless power related it in spirit to the drama of the ancient world? Having begun by merging his six subjects in a compact but somewhat confused group, each figure made heroic by its proud demeanour, he realized that this was a mistake. The burghers were individuals who differed in temperament, disposition and will-power. Rodin tried to visualize what sort of people Eustache de Saint-Pierre, Jean d'Aire, Jacques and Pierre de Wissant and their two companions could have been. Their postures, features, hands, feet and general physique are keenly descriptive of their personalities. We know nothing about the models except that Auguste Beuret, the sculptor's son, posed for the face of *The Burgher with the Key*. There is probably no other work by Rodin in which imagination played such an important part.

The six men are seen on the verge of departing for the English king's camp, where their fate is to be decided. Everything points to their imminent death, and there is no hint that the queen will be moved to tears and plead for their lives. The eye is drawn first to the central figure of Eustache de Saint-Pierre, a tired old man with drooping shoulders and large swollen hands. The halter round his neck might have been put there in readiness for the hangman. His battered countenance betrays fatigue and determination, resignation and courage, and his pensive gaze seems to be focussed on an unseen world. Pierre de Wissant, with his half-closed eyes and furrowed brow, wears an expression of sorrow and apprehension. Young and handsome, another man has halted in his tracks and turned to make a gesture of farewell, perhaps to the town, perhaps to a grieving wife. It is a strange, possibly instinctive gesture. The half-raised arm and outspread fingers are expressive less of despair than of straightforward submission to fate. The fourth figure, whose feet are planted firmly on the uneven ground, clasps the huge key of the city in both hands. A sturdy young man with piercing eyes, a firm jaw, aquiline profile and taut body, he seems to be a personification of courage. Another man, younger still, brings up the rear of this melancholy procession, head in hands, aghast at the prospect of death.

' This is not how we visualized our illustrious fellow-citizens, ' declared the members of the committee.

In arranging his figures, Rodin had avoided a bunched, pyramidal composition, He isolated and divided them into two irregular groups, maintaining a constant height throughout.

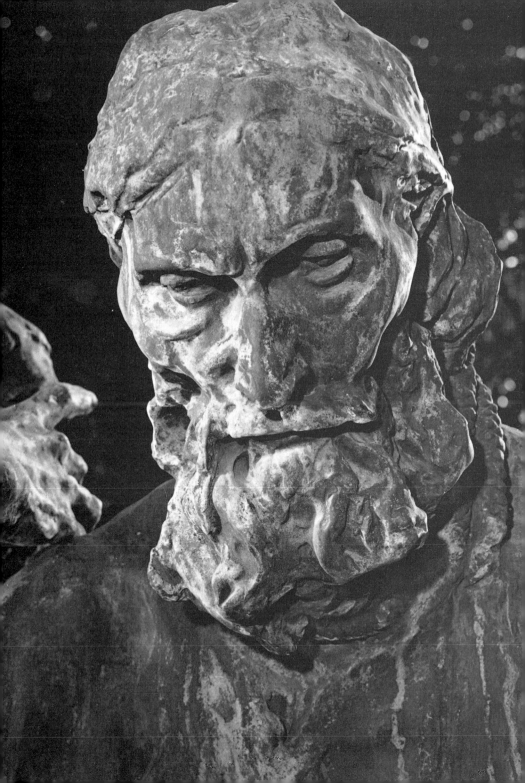

It is true that the beholder cannot gain an over-all view of the group from any angle, but Rodin achieved more than this. He welded his figures together with invisible bonds which derived from their equal plastic impact and brought their entire spatial environment to life.

'The sculptor could... break the monotony and baldness of the outlines by varying the stature of his six subjects...' declared the committee.

The unity of the group is assured by deep vertical folds in the thick homespun smocks, which only part here and there to reveal the musculature of a leg.

The committee members also remarked on the 'richly draped material which does not accord with the light garment ascribed to him (Eustache de Saint-Pierre) by history'.

Rodin transformed all the features which were regarded as faults in need of correction into elements of greatness. He shunned sweeping gestures and high-flown rhetoric in order to convey inward and otherworldly states of mind.

People have sought to compare this art with that of medieval stonemasons, of Sluter or the sculptors of Crucifixion scenes. They are mistaken. It is all new and all Rodin's. Unlike Last Suppers, Descents from the Cross and Entombments, which consist of assorted figures ranged round the central figure of Christ, this group has no focal point. The figures are wretched hostages, expressive of suffering humanity and borne along by an invisible force. The thing that motivates them and commands their obedience is public spirit itself.

'Rodin transformed and ennobled his subject,' wrote Gustave Geffroy. 'Never has his art been more complete. So painstaking was his approach to these works that he sculpted the nudes before giving a thought to the arrangement of drapery, underpinning the latter with human frames, nervous systems, and all the vital organs proper to creatures of flesh and blood. He inscribed his work with the characters indispensable to its purpose. Having done that, he moved on—as always—to the creation of lasting expression, to symbolism and synthesis.' As for Mirbeau, he saw fit to deliver the greatest tribute that any contemporary sculptor could have received: ' His genius consists not only in having given us immortal masterpieces, but, as a sculptor, in having given us sculpture; that is to say, in having rediscovered an admirable and forgotten art. '

Rodin clearly needed to feel inundated with work. Many sculptors like to leave their works to cool off for months or even years before going back to them. This was so in the case of Despiau, who continued to make imperceptible corrections to his *Apollo* almost every day for fifteen years until his death. It also applied to painters like Bonnard, a perfectionist who retouched or almost entirely re-worked pictures after twenty years.

Some people regarded Rodin's abundance of studios as a quirk, a mark of extravagance or vanity. In fact, they were more a necessity than anything else. His increasing output of rough models, coupled with the full-size maquettes of his monumental projects and casts of statues and fragments, created a congestion which grew as his work gained pace.

As we have already said, Rodin worked simultaneously on *The Burghers of Calais* and the never-ending *Gates of Hell*. While still in the throes of this personal drama he tapped an entirely different source of inspiration in order to produce minor but highly sensitive works such as *Eternal Spring, Daphnis and Lycenium, Pomona, Psyche,* and the famous and extremely popular group known as *The Kiss,* which conveys physical love with such tenderness and brilliance that present-day photographers readily use it to illustrate books on sex and invest them with the authority of great art. Still in the same year, 1886, he was commissioned to produce a monument to Victor Hugo. This was to be erected in the Panthéon, where the poet's funeral had taken place the year before. Political commitment allied with literary genius had given Hugo the status of a demi-god and brought him unprecedented renown, both popular and official. No one seemed better qualified to immortalize him than Rodin, who not only admired Hugo but had just done a very fine bust of him. What was more, the writer's verbal tumult found innumerable echoes in the sculptor's work.

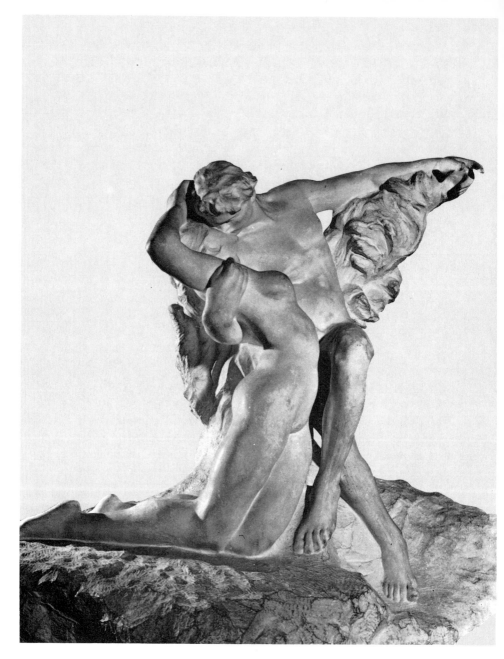

34 *Eternal Spring* 1884

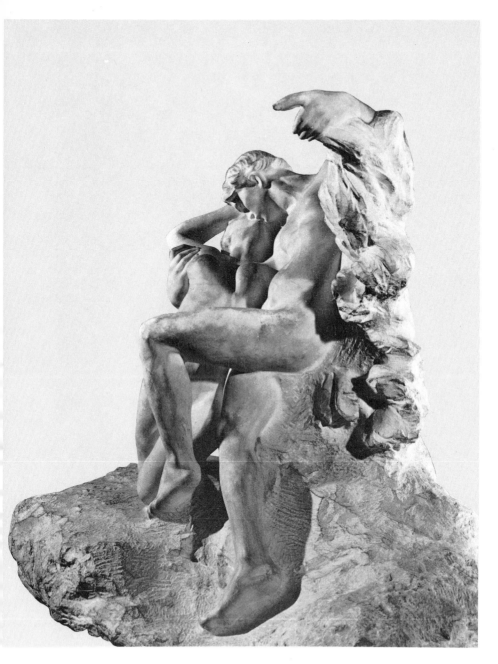

35  *Eternal Spring* 1884

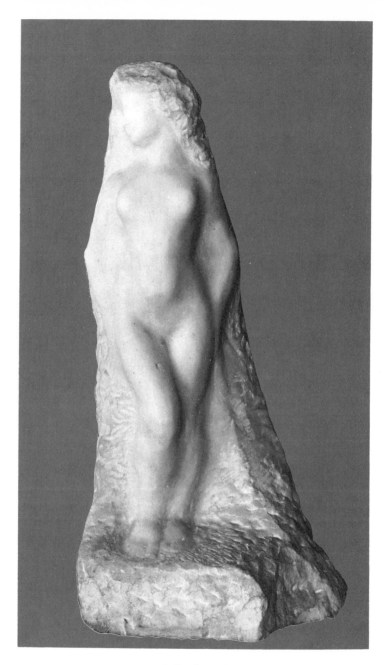

36  *Psyche* 1886

The choice was an undoubted honour. A tribute to Victor Hugo could only have been entrusted to a sculptor worthy of his genius. Dalou, that licensed singer of the Republic's praises, brought about a final break with Rodin by entering the lists against him. He submitted an ambitious model flanked by convoluted allegorical figures which claimed to be an interpretation of the writer's multiform œuvre. The Fine Arts Committee took an intense dislike to Dalou's design and rejected it point-blank.

Rodin dropped his other work and plunged into the new project without delay. Mental pictures summoned up by Hugo's books flooded his brain so impetuously that he had considerable difficulty in finding a formula which would enable him to express himself in sculptural terms. Projected designs accumulated— a dozen or so of them. He felt overwhelmed and incapable of making the necessary eliminations and syntheses. The author of *La Légende des siècles* and god of poetry had to be portrayed in the nude—that much was certain. Rodin pictured him leaning against the rock of exile facing an invisible sea, with a string of muses descending from Olympus to infuse him with the music of his lyricism.

Rodin was not the man for this form of allegory. His muses remained sturdily feminine and stubbornly defied arrangement despite innumerable experiments in pencil and clay. In the end he cut them down to two, *The Muse of Tragedy* and *The Inner Voice* (now *Meditation*), both of them brilliantly expressive but neither firmly integrated in the rhythm of the monument.

Having met Hugo during his lifetime, the members of the Fine Arts Committee were shocked to see the old man stripped of all his clothes. Why was the figure seated when it was intended as a companion-piece for the statue of Mirabeau, which was—needless to say—a standing figure ? Rodin had lost sight of the fact that this was not an open-air monument. It was destined for a church which, though secularized, imposed certain rules and limitations in regard to over-all decoration. The design was unanimously rejected.

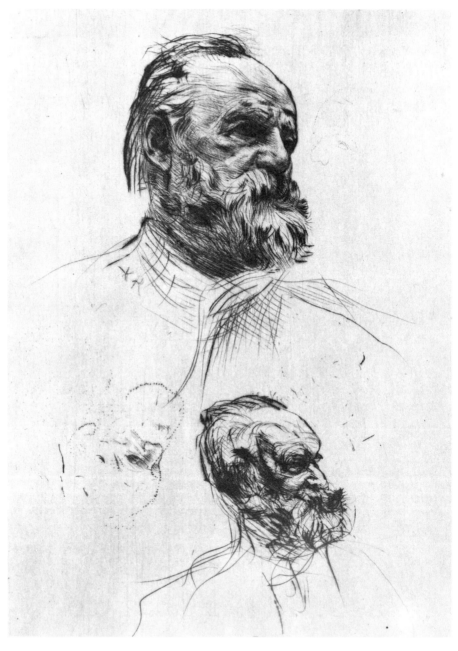

37  *Portrait of Victor Hugo c. 1885*

38  *Study for the monument to Victor Hugo* 1886-90  ▶

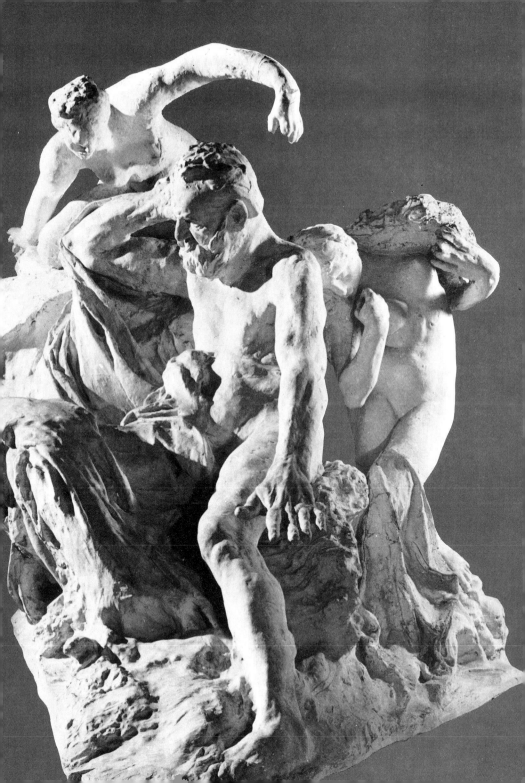

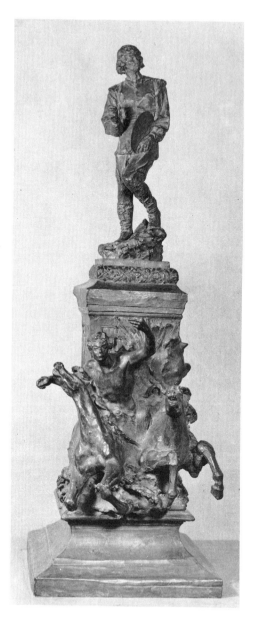

Keen though the sculptor's disappointment undoubtedly was, he had other projects to occupy him. All the visions which haunted his mind would some day find expression and take their place in *The Gates of Hell*.

His young friend, the critic Roger Marx, himself a native of Nancy, informed him that a competition had been organized with a view to erecting a monument to Claude Lorrain in the Lorrainese capital. Although Claude had spent the bulk of his life in Rome and his painting was Italian, he was born near Charmes in the Vosges and his campatriots were determined to commemorate his fame.

The idea for the work came to Rodin in a flash. He went to Desbois' studio, seized some clay, and set to work without even pausing to remove his hat. Three-quarters of an hour later he had completed a rough model two feet high and asked his colleague to execute it in twice the size. Claude was portrayed walking lightly along, palette in hand, towards the landscape of his choice. The features were fine-drawn and intelligent. The curved base was intended to harmonize with the style of the Stanislas palaces. On it, in bas-relief, Apollo's horses could be seen bounding into the light.

The fact that parts of the work bear the imprint of genius only renders it more disappointing as a whole. Apollo's team had to be retouched because the jury found the sculpture 'clumsy', which did not help. The painter, shod with musketeers' boots and mounted on a base of disproportionate height, looks like an undersized refugee from the world of costume drama. In short, everything is out of scale.

The design missed being rejected by only two votes, not because of the defects mentioned above but for reasons relating to the conventions of nineteenth-century statuary. However, Roger Marx had found a persuasive ally at Nancy in the person of Gallé, the Art Nouveau pioneer whose coloured glass was beginning to arouse interest at this time.

The monument stands on a large expanse of grass in the Jardin de la Pépinière, where its qualities cannot be properly appreciated. The sculptor himself was never very satisfied with it. Though fully aware of his own merits, he differed from many artists in his capacity for self-criticism. He disowned or destroyed anything he considered unworthy of him. If the statue of Claude Lorrain had not been cast in bronze, and if it had remained in his possession, it would probably have suffered the same fate.

In 1889, when Monet organized a fund with the object of presenting the state with Manet's *Olympia,* a picture notorious for the scorn and vituperation which had greeted it at the Salon the year before, Rodin contributed to it in company with Renoir, Pissarro, Puvis de Chavannes, Degas, Fantin-Latour, Toulouse-Lautrec, and other painters. Few sculptors subscribed. Rodin did so not only in response to Manet's friendly appeal but also as a token of anti-academic solidarity. He contributed only twenty-five of the enormous sum of twenty thousand francs which the fund ultimately raised, pleading that it was just to get his name on the list and that he was in such financial straits that he couldn't afford more.

Financial straits! The Rodin household, which subsisted as frugally as ever, continued to labour under financial difficulties for several years to come.   Rodin's earnings went on renting studios, paying casters and assistants (he always employed the best), and purchasing materials (his blocks of marble were always of the highest quality).   He was monopolized by his sculpture, knew no other form of distraction and felt no desire whatsoever to go looking for one.   He was not one for chatting in cafés.   He undoubtedly showed a susceptibility to certain worldly pleasures when success finally arrived, but he regarded these as a necessary adjunct to his professional career.

Sculptors have greater difficulty in placing their work than painters.   They have to solicit custom direct.   If their clientele consists almost exclusively of government bodies and public organizations today, the same was largely true at the close of the last century.   Unlike painters, sculptors had no dealers to take an interest in them.   Though waging a war of liberation analogous to that of the Impressionists, Rodin never benefited from the assistance of a fervent propagandist like Durand-Ruel, who arranged exhibitions of pictures at his own expense—some of them as far afield as the United States—and hardly ever made anything out of them.   He had to rely on himself and his friends to find outlets.

Rodin and Monet were born within two days of each other. Both men were of humble origin, and both had to endure years of poverty during which their efforts went unrewarded.   However, while Rodin went his way with patient resignation, Monet flared up and exploded at each setback without losing his fundamental gaiety.   Though dissimilar in temperament, they had the same enthusiasm for their art and the same aversion to conformism. Nothing ever dimmed the friendship which grew up between them.

Almost all the artists who fanned the flames of revolution at this period were of middle-class or, like Manet and Degas, of upper middle-class origin.   (At least one—Count Henri de Toulouse-Lautrec Monfa—was an aristocrat.)   Monet, who had continued his studies with the aid of a bursary, was a man of the people like Renoir, and Rodin, for all their differences in temperament, felt a deep affinity with him.

Monet had moved to Giverny in 1883. It was there that Rodin met Renoir, who used to come over from his little house in La Roche-Guyon—Renoir, a dreamy, quiet man who only abandoned his reserve to utter the occasional witticism with a malicious gleam in his little eyes. Clemenceau, who greatly admired Monet and devoted one of his books to him, liked to desert the political fray and relax among these feasts of colour and the unsophisticated men who created them. One day, Cézanne visited Giverny. Paralysed with shyness, he confided to Geffroy: ' Monsieur Rodin isn't proud. He shook my hand—a man who has been decorated! '

In 1889 a joint exhibition of works by Rodin and Monet was held at the Georges Petit gallery, the smartest of its kind in Paris. It was a great occasion . Public figures and prominent socialites visited the exhibition, this time without turning up their noses at what they saw. Rodin showed thirty-six pieces dominated by *The Burghers of Calais,* which made a deep impact. Monet, who contributed seventy paintings, was the first Impressionist ever to receive such public recognition.

The foreword to the catalogue was supplied by the two artists' most distinguished acolytes, Mirbeau and Geffroy, and Mirbeau's review in *L'Écho de Paris* included the words: ' It is they who, in the present century, most gloriously and definitively embody the two arts of painting and sculpture '.

Without overstressing the affinity between Monet and Rodin, we might say that Rodin belonged to the Impressionist movement in spirit. Above all else, he sought to capture light. The Impressionists tried to reconstitute natural light by breaking it down into component colours; Rodin tried to achieve the same result by breaking up surfaces. He was concerned less with anatomical accuracy than with distributing subtle projections and recesses so as to catch the vibrations of light. What was heralded by the undulations which lightly traversed the nude figure of *The Bronze Age* recurred with even greater force and amplitude in *Balzac.* Each sculpture owes its vitality to the irradiation of light. This is why Rodin's works withstand open-air exhibition so well.   Indeed, the sculptor liked to expose them to the elements in order to see how they reacted.

The Italian sculptor Medardo Rosso was one of the few who treid to translate the discoveries of Impressionism into sculpture. His work greatly interested Rodin, who threatened to resign the chairmanship of a jury which proposed to bar Rosso from exhibiting at the Salon de la Nationale in Paris.   Some people maliciously accused Rodin of borrowing from the Italian, although the latter strove to reproduce his impressions from a privileged angle.   (This is discernible in photographs of his sculptures, which resemble pictures.)   Rodin did precisely the opposite.

To sum up, it was not in Rodin's nature to apply theories, Impressionist or otherwise.   What impelled him towards the vital art into which he infused so much new life was the spontaneous revelation of his own temperament.

# CHAPTER FIVE

# 'I produce slowly'

Most great artists have sought to shroud their creative activity in some degree of mystery. Whether from modesty or a wish to set themselves above or apart from the common herd, they are quite content to foster a belief that the outpourings of their genius are animated by some breath of preternatural inspiration. Not so Rodin, who, while re-inventing the art of sculpture, explained his mode of procedure in very simple terms. It was almost as though he wanted to demonstrate that there was nothing indecipherable or inaccessible about the accomplishment of a task which transcended the ordinary, nor about the conditions that enabled him to carry it out.

We know from remarks recorded by his admirers that he expressed himself with absolute simplicity. He never used long words nor indulged in oracular allusions, never resorted to the flights of fancy with which representatives of every realm of ideas customarily embellish whatever strikes them as a mark of exceptional greatness. If we are to believe Rodin, his sublime masterpieces were attributable to nothing more than well-assimilated formulae and useful tricks of the sculptor's trade. Everything was commonplace and common-sensical to him, and everything seemed correspondingly easy.

Let us, therefore, examine the methods which he described in such prosaic terms. Let us trace the creative process from fertilization and embryo to final thumb-print. Rodin recounted it all in detail with the down-to-earth simplicity of a bricklayer explaining the construction of a wall.

He was no talker, and his observations were polished and paraphrased by those who heard them. If they are of fundamental importance, it is because they convey the ideas of an artist of exceptional stature and because we know that his methods gave birth to masterpieces. What they would have engendered *per se,* if divorced from his own person, is of course another matter.

Having chosen from his rough models one which, to him, was ' true ', he began by building a ' core ', that is to say, a clay skeleton which was allowed to dry and harden. This rudimentary framework provided him with a basis for modelling in clay, which was always carefully moistened between sittings. The superimposition of clay pellets, applied with a dexterity and speed astonishing to those who watched him at work, was a task which he found intensely stimulating. It overjoyed him to invest surfaces with animation and produce an interplay of light and shade which would create a reflection of life itself. His preliminary studies were a quest for the movement which, to him, was the essence of sculpture. Final expression was obtained by modelling. In his opinion, movement and modelling were the soul and life-blood of any great work. On one occasion, when questioned about his religious views, he replied that he believed in God because God had invented modelling.

Rodin used the enlargement method. That is to say, rapid sketches were succeeded by a detailed one-third maquette which he employed an assistant to copy full-size. After a series of retouchings, the piece was entrusted to a specialist to finish off.

' I just copy the model, ' was Rodin's disconcerting response to those who hoped to discover his non-existent secret. ' Always keep in touch with nature, always try to get close to your model ' —another of his favourite maxims—was not simply a way of evading persistent questions.

' In front of a model, I work with as great a wish to reproduce the truth as if I were making a portrait. I do not correct nature but incorporate myself in it. It guides me. I can only work with a model. The sight of the human form sustains and stimulates me. I have a boundless admiration for the naked body—I

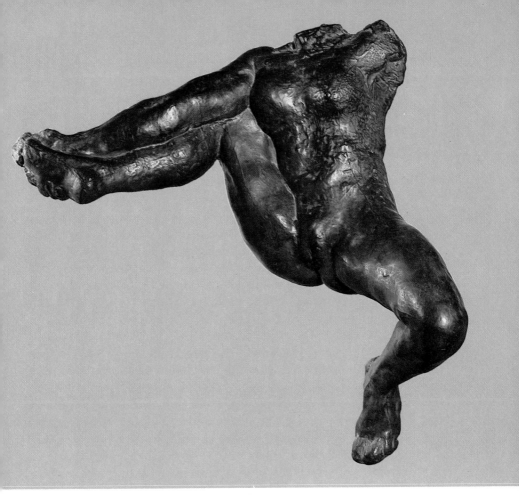

40 *Iris* 1890-91

worship it.   I tell you flatly, I am totally devoid of ideas when I
have nothing to copy, but as soon as I see nature showing me shapes
I find something worth saying—worth developing, even. Sometimes, looking at a model, you think you have found nothing.
Then, all at once, a little bit of nature reveals itself, a strip of flesh
appears, and this shred of truth conveys the whole truth and enables
you to rise, at a single bound, to the absolute principle of things.'[13]

Rodin's methods of 'copying' a model had nothing whatsoever in common with that of contemporary schools of art. Like the modern photographer, who captures a person's natural expression by selecting from several snapshots instead of making his subject pose, Rodin was so anxious to capture life 'on the wing' that he devised all sorts of ways of catching his models in unwonted attitudes. Having sketched them from every angle and in every position, he proceeded to capture their fleeting movements in his preliminary studies by selecting from this abundance of highly animated drawings. What he called simple was really complex in the extreme. Only his retentive eye, natural dexterity and long years of practical experience could have produced those inimitable transfigurations whose strength consisted not only in movement but in the static quality which is the consummation of sculpture. Paul Gsell, in his *Entretiens avec Rodin,* gives the following description :

'His method of work was unusual. Several nude models, male and female, strolled round his studio or relaxed. Rodin paid them to provide him with a continuous image of nude bodies moving with all the freedom of real life. He watched them unceasingly, this being the way in which he had long familiarized himself with the sight of muscles in motion. The nude, an unwonted revelation to the moderns and one which even sculptors tend to regard as no more than a spectacle whose duration is limited to a modelling session, became a habitual sight where Rodin was concerned. The ancient Greeks acquired their routine knowledge of the human body by watching it at exercize in the palaestra, throwing the discus, boxing, running, competing in the pancratium—so much so that their artists could speak *the language of the nude* naturally. The author of *The Thinker* obtained that knowledge from the constant presence of the unclothed human beings who came and went before his eyes. In this way, he managed to decipher manifestations of feeling in every part of the body. The face is generally considered to be the only mirror of the soul, the mobility of the features seeming to us to be the unique externalization of the inner life. In reality, there is not a muscle of

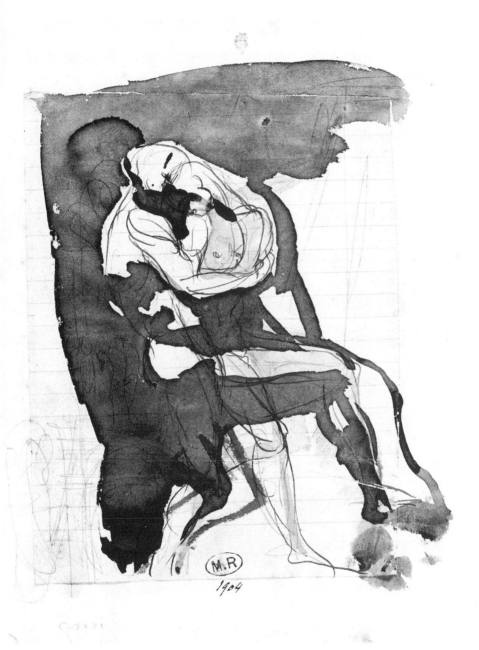

41 *Embrace*

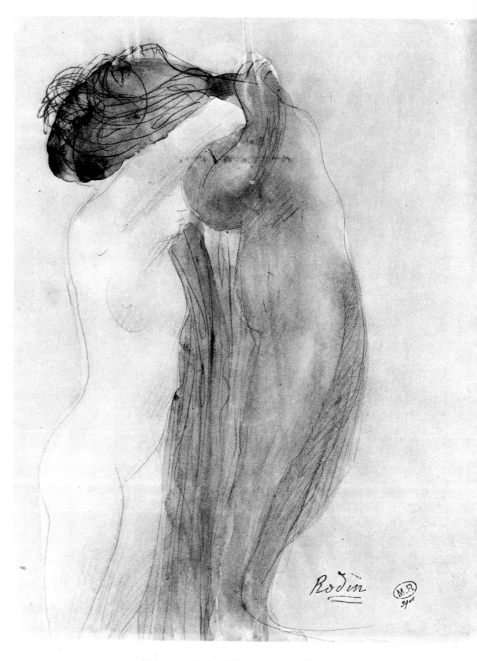

42  *Two nudes, the Black Woman and the White Woman*

the body which does not reflect inward changes of mood.    Everything speaks of joy or despair, rage or serenity, from tautened
arms to a body which relaxes, smiling with as much gentleness as
eyes or lips.    But an ability to interpret all the moods of the
flesh entails the patience and inclination to spell out every page
of that noble volume.    What the artists of the ancient world
were enabled to do by the *mores* of their civilization Rodin did in
our own day by an effort of will.    He followed models with his
gaze, quietly savoured the alluring suppleness of one young woman
as she bent down to pick up a chisel, the delicate grace of another

43 *Breath*

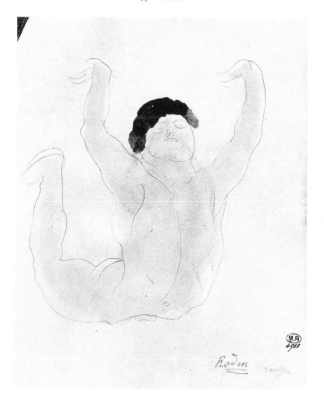

stretching her arms as she swept her golden hair over her head, or the lithe vigour of a man walking—and, when one or the other *gave* a movement which pleased him, asked for the pose to be held.   Quickly, he took his clay, and a maquette was soon in being.   Then, just as swiftly, he passed on to another which he fashioned in the same way. '

Rodin's sculptures gave an impression of movement.  To him, this was just another aspect of his craft.   His models were active, and his sketches captured the development of their attitudes.   To quote his own words: ' Different parts of a sculpture represented at successive moments in time give an illusion of actual motion. '

It should be noted that Rodin's works always involve action of a more or less pronounced kind and are virtual strangers to absolute repose.   As he himself said, he always tried to render inward emotion by muscular mobility.   From *The Bronze Age* to *Balzac* (both of them essentially static), we can always observe, expressed by his modelling, a hint of movement or the violent activity of some inner fire.   The same applies with even greater force to statues such as *Iris*, which portrays the messenger of the gods contorted to the point of improbability and seeming to launch herself into the air like a projectile.

Rodin obtained these results by applying his ' profile ' or outline method.   Far from cloaking this technique in mystery, he expounded it in detail.   However, he charitably warned those who might feel tempted to apply the same method that, since it required strict accuracy of observation and execution, they would have to forgo it unless they were good draughtsmen.

' When I start on a figure I look first at the front, the back, and the two left and right profiles, in other words, I view its outlines from four angles.   Then, with clay, I put the rough mass in place, just as I see it and as accurately as possible.   Next I do the intermediate work, which supplies the profiles seen from a three-quarters angle.   Then, rotating my clay and my model in turn, I make comparisons and refinements.   In a human body, the outline is determined by the point where the body ends, so it is the body which creates the outline.   I place my model so that the light

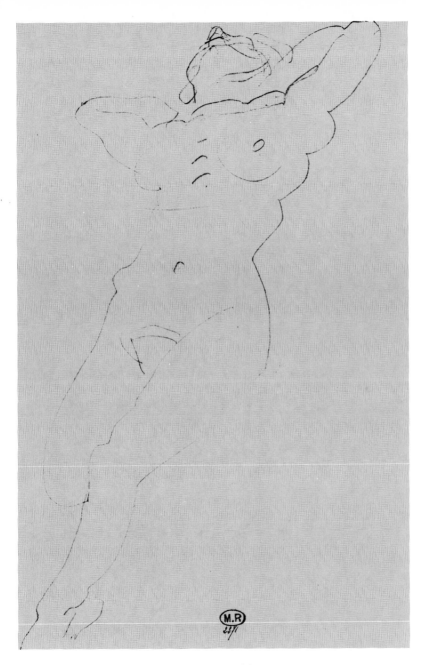

44 *Reclining nude*

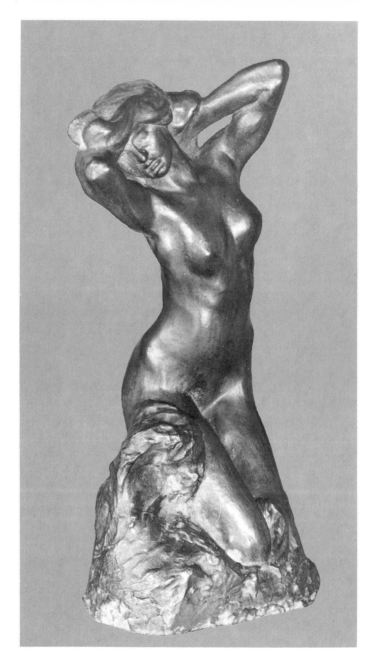

45  *The Toilet of Venus* 1886

shines on the background and illuminates the outline. Having reproduced this, I turn my stand and that of my model so that I see another outline; I turn again, and am thus led, by stages, to make a complete circuit of the body. I begin again, condensing and refining the outlines more and more. Since the human body has an infinite number of outlines, I do as many as I can or consider expedient. Closely observing the model at the moment when he poses exactly in the attitude which I plan to reproduce, I capture his existing outline. I make a point of ensuring that the model always resumes the pose selected by me at the outset, so that he always presents the same outlines. When I turn my stand, areas which were in shadow present themselves to the light in turn. Thus, I see the fresh outline clearly, because I always work in the light—or, at least, as far as I can. To obtain the greatest possible accuracy, I arrange my clay and my model at the same angle and always in the light, so that the outlines of model and clay appear simultaneously and can readily be compared. I then check any discrepancies which may exist between the two outlines and rectify them if necessary. Thus, I place my model in the same outlines as my clay and compare them, or, more often, it is I who follow the model by turning my stand. In fact, I perfect my work by eye rather than with calipers. When my outlines are well drawn there is a chance that they are correct, but I can only be sure of this when they are checked against each other and as a whole. I may have had almost the same outlines in my preliminary rough, but the tighter the drawing of my outlines becomes (by " drawing " I mean plotting in clay) the closer their mutual relationship, for outlines do not blend unless they are very accurately drawn and precisely related to one another. It is important to observe outlines from above and below, from top and bottom, to duck beneath outlines and see them spread out above one—in other words, to ascertain the thickness of the human body. Viewing the skull from above, I see the outlines of temples, zygomas, nose and jaws—the whole of the cranial structure which, seen from below, appears egg-shaped. Then I observe and compare with my clay the outline of the pectorals, scapulae and buttocks; I examine the muscles jutting from the thighs, and, below, the way in which the feet are planted on the ground. When I was working on *The Bronze Age* I got hold of one of those ladders painters use for big canvases. Climbing it, I established as much conformity as I could between the foreshortened views of my model and my clay, and observed my outlines from above. What I did might be called " drawing in depth ", since the procedure I have indicated precludes flat treatment. The linking of correct outlines united by accurate intermediaries gives a faithful reproduction of the model. The geometry may be a little crude, like all actual work, but it gives excellent results. ' [14]

This passage—itself a trifle crude—has been quoted at length because it enables us to understand why Rodin's statues are equally faithful and beautiful when viewed from any angle, why they never disclose the least vestige of dead surface, why life circulates with equal intensity in every part of the body, and why a toe can be as instinct with meaning as any part of the human face.

We should not forget that Rodin started life as a stone-cutter. He knew the exhilaration born of the concentrated effort required to conjure a precise mental image out of an amorphous block. Modelling was easier, but it did not compare with the tussle between man and recalcitrant matter, with the removal of stone which could never be replaced, with the contest between a hand-held tool and an inanimate block from which life was about to spring. Rodin managed to stress this conflict by leaving the less essential parts of his work virtually untouched. Some of his busts (a misnomer) are merely heads which, though treated with infinite delicacy themselves, emerge from blocks of unworked stone resembling natural rocks. Certain pieces, notably *Thought,* owe much of their strength to this contrast. Rodin's visit to the unfinished tombs of San Lorenzo had taught him that to leave some areas unfinished could enhance the impact of others. Where Michelangelo had left marble untouched because time did not permit him to complete his task, Rodin did so deliberately. The delicacy of his modelling benefited by this contrast, which displayed the sculptor's skill to even greater advantage.

46 *Thought* 1886 ▶

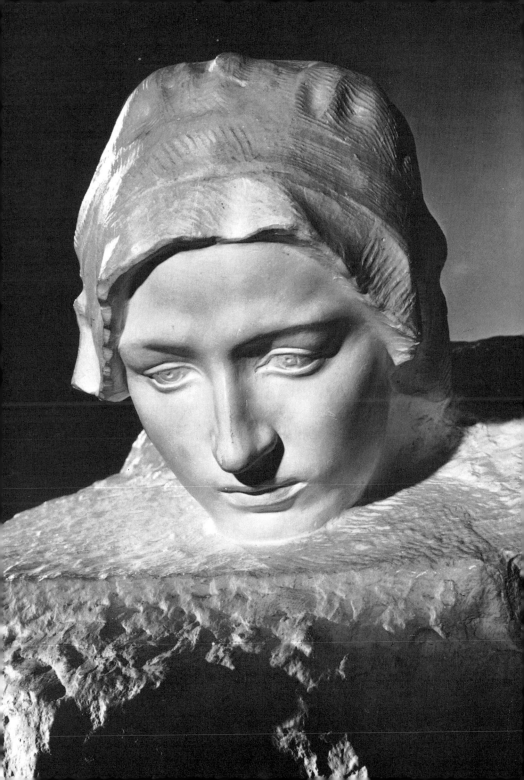

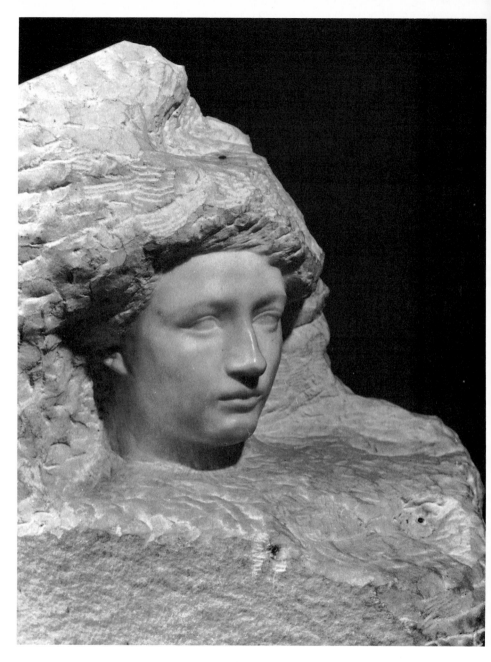

47 *Aurora* 1885

Though possessed of great technical skill himself, Rodin did not care for the word. It was to skill—as defined by him, at least—that he ascribed the ease and panache with which so many sculptors achieved unmerited success. They only saw and reproduced the outer skin of what they saw, and their statues were like empty shells. 'Skill should be distrusted. What people generally mean by the word "skill" is the dexterity with which someone evades a problem by fostering a belief that he has surmounted it instead of tackling it honestly. Myself, I have had an extraordinarily quick hand ever since my youth. I could work quickly if I chose to, but I produce slowly in order to do well. Besides, it never was in my nature to hurry. I ponder things more and I want more. An artist should be patient as well as knowledgeable.' [15]

We may be forgiven for blinking at the words 'I produce slowly'. Rodin's creative rhythm was remarkable and his hand swift in the extreme. The plasters, terra-cottas, bronzes, marbles and innumerable maquettes which fill the museum in the Rue de Varenne, its chapel and garden, as well as the museum at Meudon and galleries elsewhere—not to mention all the lost pieces, unrecorded pieces, and pieces that were broken deliberately or smashed during Rodin's frequent and perilous changes of abode—all bear witness to his bewildering speed of execution.

It is nonetheless true, in another sense, that he did 'produce slowly' in certain cases. His monuments underwent so much study and modification that he seldom if ever completed them within the stipulated time, and this despite his great physical energy and the passion for work which formed the prop and mainstay of his whole existence.

He surrounded himself with assistants of the highest calibre as he waxed in years, wealth, and prestige. His pupils included the finest sculptors of the period—men like Pompon, Maillol, Bourdelle, Despiau, Halou, Dejean and, last but not least, Lucien Schnegg, who gave him faithful and devoted service.

Rodin could not produce a draped figure without first constructing a nude based on a series of studies, and he spared no expense in employing the model who seemed most in harmony with the figure he planned to portray. Finally, he took a wrapper impregnated with plaster and draped it over the nude figure. His numerous studies for *The Burghers of Calais,* and, more especially, for *Balzac,* bear witness to the importance which he attached to experiments in balance and the faithful reproduction of movement and musculature. Although it was the only visible feature, drapery took care of its own arrangement. In short, all construction proceeded from the interior—in the profoundest sense of the word—to the exterior. Clothes were merely an integument which concealed the living form beneath. Rodin apparently took little pleasure in sculpting draped figures, and only did so to conform with the dictates of monumental statuary. It was the nude which constituted almost the whole of his œuvre, and it was the nude which inspired him to the full.

Although consistently true to his methods, Rodin never ceased to develop. As we have already said, he did not do so in spurts or phases of the sort discernible in Van Gogh or Picasso. His art is so prolific that a single year's work can present us with sculptures which would verge on affectation if they were not the products of genius and others which were almost incredibly daring for their period. Yet his work clearly developed along a central line. He began by reproducing his subject with the utmost accuracy, each part of the body being modelled, step by step, with subtle and circumspect skill. That done, he passed on to transpositions in which the exaggeration and distortion of certain areas conveyed the essential movement of the piece or strengthened its impact. He was thus moving towards a spirit of synthesis which became ever more divorced from reproduction and was destined to lead, after his day, to the abstractions of modern art. This was why the very intelligence of his art exposed him to the eternal incomprehension of opponents for whom his simplifications and 'crudity' were marks of ignorance or incompetence. (It ought to have been enough for them to recall, in retrospect, that some people had thought *The Bronze Age* too skilfully modelled and too 'finished' not to have been cast from the life!)

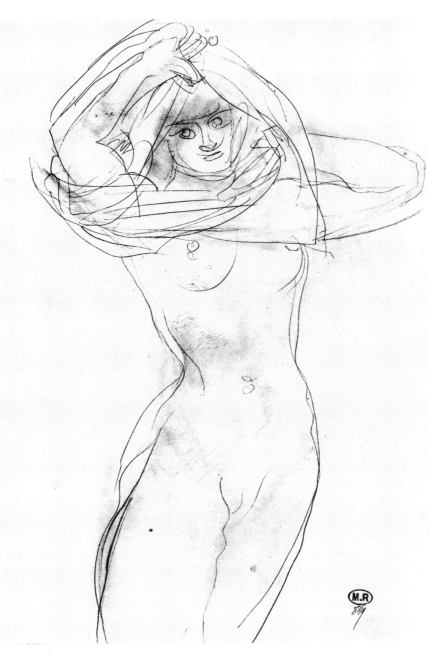

48  *Three-quarter length nude figure, undressing*

Writing at the time of the *Balzac* affair, Mauclair commented on this apparent dualism as follows: ' While M. Rodin, going his way with greater assurance and spurred on by fame and the respect of the élite, ventured to show works directly governed by this simple and unfamiliar principle, he dismissed facile charges of negligence and incompetence by coupling them with small marble groups in his early manner—perfect, masterly and finished, both to the casual observer and the skilled professional. Thus, he arranged *Balzac* opposite *The Kiss,* that fine work which we previously saw as a study and now meet again finished in marble. The aim was to teach public, fellow-artists and critics a discreet and silent lesson, to show them the stage that had been reached, to assure them that in modifying all his working principles in this way, at his age and high level of reputation, the artist acted in obedience to profound motives. The lesson was entirely lost on them, and we all know the result. '

Such is the prerogative of the strong, of those who possess both skill and lyricism. Whether or not Rodin was a seeker after ideal beauty, like the Greeks or the great masters of the Renaissance, he certainly found his true medium in the suggestion of beauty. Victor Hugo, who had recently submitted to dozens of sittings at the insistence of a sculptor of very mediocre talent, only accepted Rodin's proposal on condition that he did not have to pose formally. As we have already said, the admirable bust we know today was executed under working conditions so difficult that few artists could have coped with them. However, these difficulties only vindicated Rodin's normal method of procedure. Describing Rodin at grips with his elusive model, Rainer Maria Rilke tells us that ' ensconced in the angle of a window during at homes, he observed and recorded hundreds upon hundreds of the old man's movements and all the expressions on his mobile features '. Once equipped with an arsenal of preliminary drawings, he went off to work with the clay which stood waiting on a modelling stand at the far end of the gallery. Then, another day, he would make more sketches of his illustrious model as he sat writing at his desk or chatted with visitors.

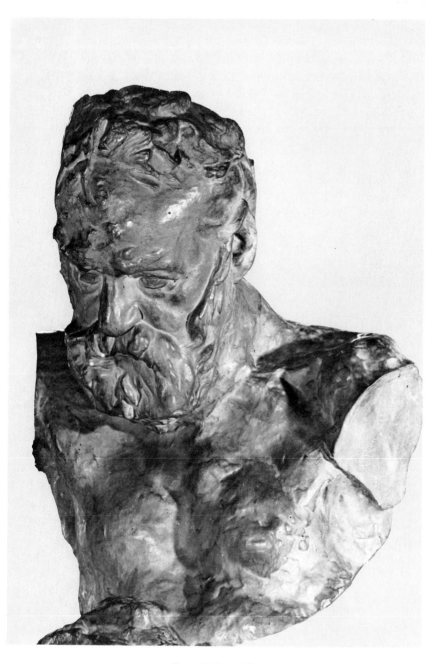

49 *Bust of Victor Hugo* 1897

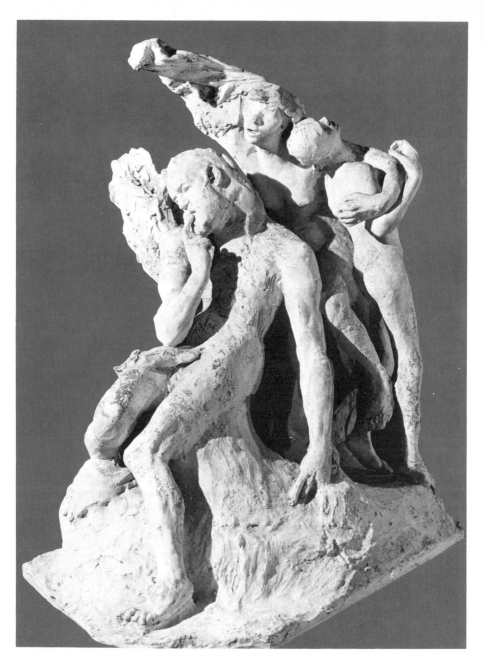

50 *Study for the monument to Victor Hugo* 1886-90

In fact, even when at liberty to sculpt in front of a model, Rodin seldom proceeded otherwise. Single nudes or groups captured in living attitudes—such were the subjects of his numerous studies, and the latter sometimes formed the basis of other drawings or wash-drawings whose *raison d'être* was intrinsic. Although he considered that a good sculpture required numerous preliminary drawings, he also attached importance to his drawings in their own right. He picked out a few of the thousands he produced and displayed them prominently in the room where he received visitors.

Rodin praised the sketch in terms which might be applied to his own drawings: 'How can one fail to admire a lightning sketch in which the artist has recorded the memory of an emotion felt, of an action seen or comprehended; a sketch whose expressive impact has been rendered with absolute sincerity, without attenuation, exaggeration or reserve; a sketch in which sensation is entire and the notation of effect as valid and complete as in a picture? The artist has succeeded—almost effortlessly—in expressing his thoughts. A rough suggestion has conveyed the spirit of the work, and imprecision, in its flexibility, enables the beholder's imagination to make additions, thus completing what the artist has been searching for.'

An evolutionary gulf separates Rodin's first painstaking nudes from drawings as he understood and intended them in later years. He renounced the academic theory which decreed that an object should be encompassed by a line obtained by a process of refinement, so as to crystallize its rigid and schematic unity. He used his unrivalled keenness of perception to convey movement by capturing fleeting images. His eyes never left the model as he recorded these 'snapshots' in pencil on loose sheets, swiftly, unhesitatingly, and without a second thought.

His sketches seem to have been the product of a manual reflex activated by his sudden vision of the essential movement. He covered his shapes with a flat watery tint, sometimes slightly gradated, sometimes done in a flat sienna wash, occasionally inserting an accent or adding a light and rapid suggestion of

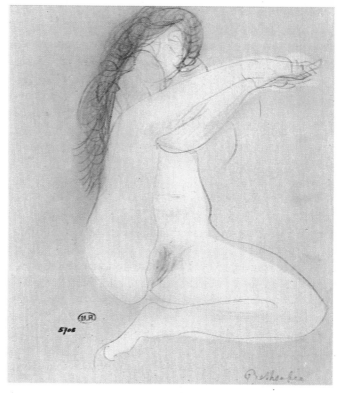

51 *Bathsheba*

modelling with a scrap of chalk or grimy thumb. He became so expert at this ' game' that he joyously filled page after page with drawings which seemed to mirror the transparency of the sky.

The spontaneous wielding of pencil or brush gave even freer rein to his imagination than the manipulation of clay. His bodies swayed, merged, reared up, disintegrated, became entwined or straddled one another with a joy so intense that it acquired majesty and pathos.

Despite their fluidity, these drawings carried such authority that they alarmed the pedagogues whose teaching they put to scorn. Some were genuinely blind, while others affected not to see that these ' impressions ' were truly great art, and that they used the fleeting moment to capture something eternal.

For all that, a few enlightened spirits did pore over Rodin's sketches, initially out of curiosity but later with mounting wonder and admiration. In 1897 the great art-lover Fenaille financed the publication of a volume of 147 drawings, full-size reproductions whose perfection did credit to the new printing process known as photogravure. The volume was adorned with a portrait of the master ' engraved on wood by A. Léveillé after the bust by Mademoiselle Claudel '. Published in an edition of 125 copies and priced at 500 francs, which barely covered the sum advanced, it sold out fairly rapidly. It may be added that Rodin took advantage of mounting public interest to sell his drawings at good prices and put a brake on their casual dissemination.

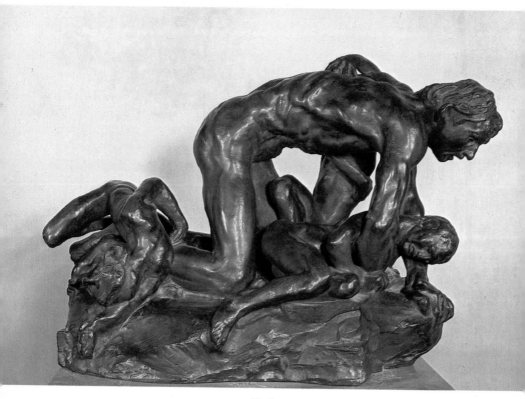

52 *Ugolino* 1882

# CHAPTER SIX

# The Divine Comedy

Rodin was still grappling with *The Gates of Hell,* his mighty dream-turned-nightmare. As his maquettes accumulated, he heaped them up, at the foot of the awe-inspiring architectural frame, which consisted of two sixteen-foot-high panels enclosed by pilasters and a lintel. In his eagerness to charge them with every passion known to man, he allowed himself to be borne away on the swirling tide of his imagination.

He had just turned fifty. Judith Cladel describes him sitting on the terrace of her father's villa at Sèvres, ' slightly aloof from the talkative circle, bulky and taciturn, stroking the strands of a long red beard which was becoming dusted with silver... ' He gave an impression of extreme shyness, of a slow and deliberate mind. His fresh complexion crimsoned at the slightest emotion, and his mouth, invisible beneath the tangled beard, seldom uttered more than a few diffident words. It was hard to tell exactly what he was thinking, but his grey-blue eyes, sometimes narrowed in a faint smile, sometimes alight with curiosity, bespoke the perception and something of the guile of a wild animal. The shape of the skull and the slope of the fine brow, surmounted by greying hair which he wore close-cropped at this period, expressed vigour and stubborn determination. The casual observer might have taken him for a shrewd peasant who kept his thoughts to himself and shunned words on principle. And yet, to those with eyes to see, there was great subtlety and discernment beneath the somewhat lumpish exterior of this sturdy man with the rare and ponderous gestures—great charm, too, born of serenity and a strange gentleness. A letter from Judith Cladel's father once addressed him as ' You great big gentle man with the terrifying beard '.

He was awkward in society, except when alone with a woman. Photographers were always encouraged to take him three-quarter-face or from the side because he was fully aware of the angle which best displayed the purity of his profile. His eye could glint with mischief on occasions. Reserved as he was in public, he spoke freely—and exclusively—of his art in private conversation, and there was a simple poetry about some of his more felicitous remarks which captivated his listeners.

*The Gates of Hell* formed the basis of a large number of drawn or sculpted studies. Rodin's analysis of the human form never satisfied him, and he always returned to it with a joyous and unfailing sense of discovery. He had achieved a simplified suggestion of movement which seemed like a synthesis of the myriad movements that went to make it up.

We are often told that he rediscovered the spirit of the ' Last Judgements ' which adorn the tympana of cathedral doorways. Nothing could be further from the truth. Rodin and the artists of the Middle Ages were linked by a common power of expression, but they obtained it by entirely different means. Cathedral sculptors obeyed the simple and regular rhythm imposed by their master-mason, whereas Rodin's souls in torment belonged to a realm of chaos and disorder. His subjects were treated individually and are so dissimilar in their dimensions and attitudes that they could never have become merged in a unified composition.

If we must talk of influences, the predominant one seems to be that of Michelangelo, but less that of Michelangelo the sculptor, with his majestic style and powerfully exaggerated musculature, than that of the man who painted the frescoes in the Sistine Chapel, notably the *Last Judgement,* that tempest of *terribilità* which plumbs the very depths of grief and despair.

Rodin's reading of Dante had opened up new spiritual vistas and guided him in the choice of certain subjects (Ugolino, Paolo and

53 *Ugolino. Detail* 1882 ▶

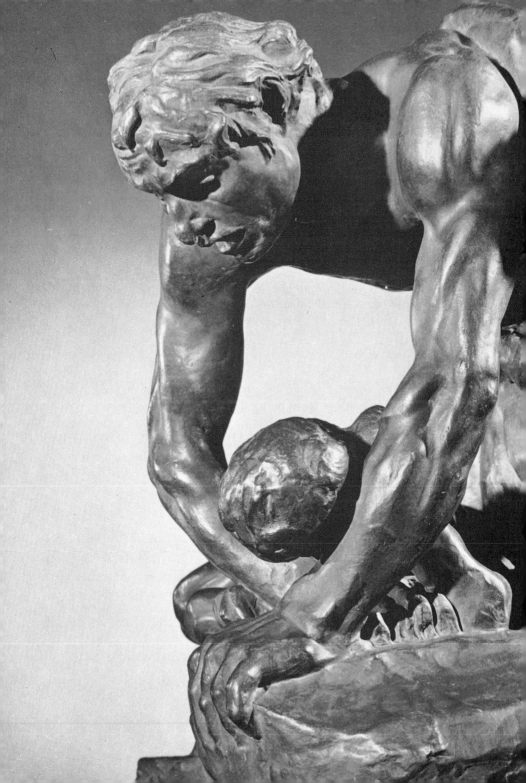

Francesca). However, Dante and Michelangelo lent the Inferno an interpretation which was, in spirit if not in letter, profoundly Christian. Rodin, an unbeliever, conjured up a pagan hell. Michelangelo's damned souls were souls; Rodin's were the bodies of men and women, deprived of celestial light, doomed to inflict mutual suffering, and sucked down into a bottomless void.

Michelangelo's nudes, which Aretino had the incredible effrontery to denounce as obscene, assumed the shape of creatures expelled from an earthly paradise, whereas Rodin's not only writhed with pain but wallowed in an atmosphere of despairing lust. They were their own victims and the propagators of their own misfortunes.

Rodin gave free rein to his imagination. He combined the God of the Bible with the gods of ancient Greece, the heroes of Dante with the doomed women of Baudelaire. In fact, art was his only morality, religion and concept of salvation.

Viewed individually, the pieces intended for *The Gates of Hell* are among his greatest works. Incapable of arranging them, the sculptor split them up, and they became celebrated statues or groups with a life of their own and titles which were given them subsequently.

*The Thinker* is a sort of Hercules in repose, beetle-browed, bull-necked, and brutish of feature. Its strength resides entirely in its redoubtable musculature, but so much concentrated power emanates from the figure that its bowed head suggests meditation. Sculpted in the round and situated above the writhing figures of the damned, which adorn the doors in bas-relief, it seems to ponder on their fate.

Established critics poked fun at the figure when it was shown at the Salon. Gabriel Mourey leapt to its defence by organizing a counter-demonstration in the form of a public subscription. Cast in bronze, which invested it with even greater strength, *The Thinker* was presented to the Municipal Council of Paris and erected in front of the Panthéon. The statue was unveiled with great ceremony in 1906 but transferred to the Hôtel Biron in 1922 on the grounds that it was an obstruction. This is a pity. Its

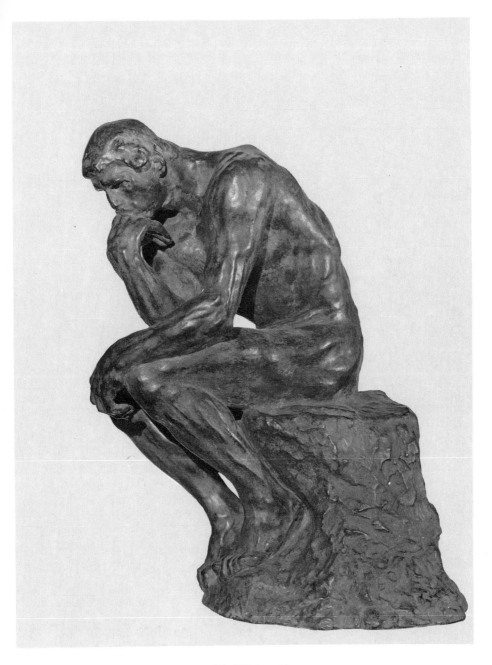

54 *The Thinker* 1880

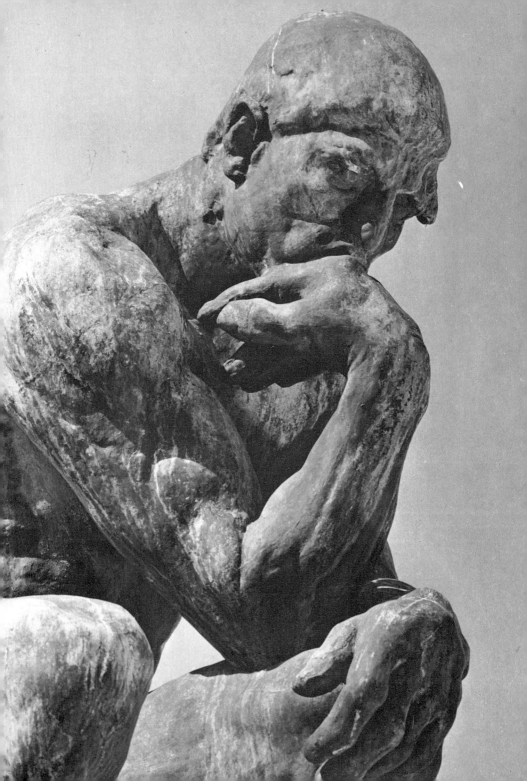

presence conferred majesty on the Place du Panthéon and showed up the conventional mediocrity of Parisian statues. ' *The Thinker* fills the square as though the latter had been made for it, ' wrote Léon Daudet. ' Rodin's works are timeless, and yet seldom depart from the given event. ' Without meaning to, the sculptor had produced his finest public monument.

Many other pieces in the round, formerly also destined for the doors of the Museum of Decorative Arts, acquired their independence and probably gained by it. Each one is alive with its own dramatic intensity: *The Fallen Caryatid Carrying its Stone,* a vision of abject but patient suffering whose strange tenderness and youth contrasts with the sagging, mummified, doom-ridden figure of *She who was once the Helmet-Maker's Beautiful Wife; The Martyr,* a twisted figure sprawling on the ground; *Head of Sorrow,* all the more poignant because its natural beauty has an admixture of suffering; and *The Crouching Woman,* whose mysterious face rests simultaneously on her shoulder and thigh in one of those contorted poses which only Rodin could handle with a complete absence of obscenity and absurdity. There is not a hint of bravura about it, and it gives an impression of harmonious ease.

The jambs of the gate are filled with upward-surging bodies which defy the law of gravity but are laden with doom. On the panels, the souls of the damned plunge headlong into a turbulent abyss pierced by shafts of stormy light. The chaotic medley of nude figures—women with distended breasts, straining rumps and splayed thighs, crushed and battered men, satyrs and centaurs, female couples writhing with lust—represents a gehenna of carnal pleasure and insatiable desire.

The lintel is probably the most muddled section of all. On either side of *The Thinker,* where everything decreed an area of shallow decoration, Rodin created a deep perspective crammed with demented figures. Spilling over the frame on every side and straggling obliquely across the rectangular field, this formless throng gives the lintel the appearance of a cave-mouth choked with jumbled nudes. The figures on the left hover in mid air, while those on the right slump to the ground.

133

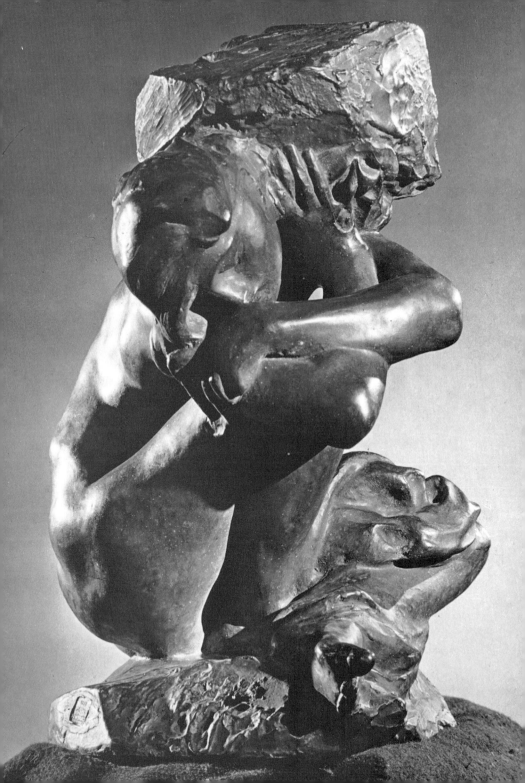

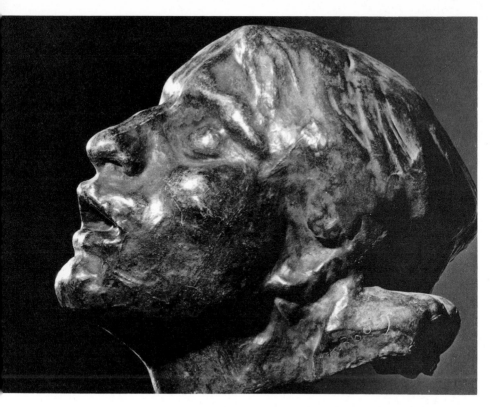

57  *Head of Sorrow* 1882

One group, which was accorded a privileged and isolated position
at the top of the monument, seems to surpass all the rest in aptness
and dignity.  This is the group known as *The Three Shades,*
threefold replicas of the same work arranged at varying angles
which invest each with a personality of its own.  There could be
no stronger corroboration of the ' profile ' theory so dear to their
author's heart.  The unwary eye might mistake them for three
different figures.

Dominating the turmoil of the clustered souls in torment, the
*Shades* introduce a lone element of order.  They belong to the
scene of desolation spread out at their feet.  Heads together and
legs bending under the burden of fate, they support one another,

56  *The Fallen Caryatid Carrying its Stone* 1881

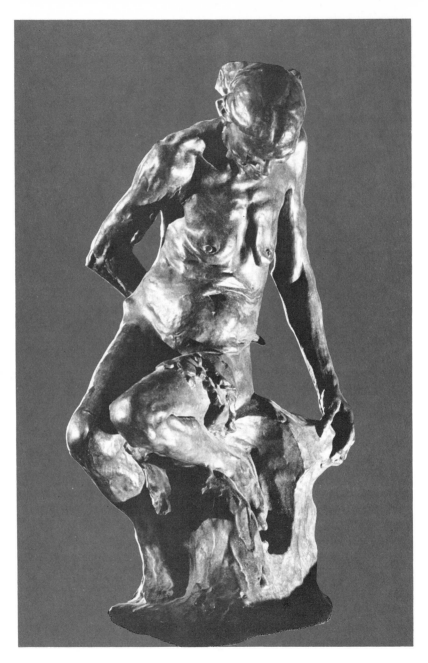

58 *She who was once the Helmet-Maker's Beautiful Wife* 1888

united by common affliction.    The weight of destiny seems even more overwhelming as it crushes the trio and demonstrates the transience of physical strength.    The shades have left the earth, and their mute despair is more terrible than any cry of fear or groan of pain could ever be.    This is Rodin's art at its most daring and most inherently dramatic.    He never ventured further into unreality whilst supposedly ' copying nature '.    The bowed head, neck and shoulder combine to form an almost unbroken horizontal, while the athlete's drooping body is modelled with a knowledge of anatomy far surpassing that of *The Bronze Age,* of which the sculptor himself said, with the simple candour which

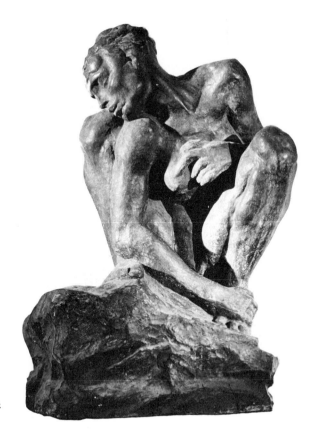

59  *The Crouching Woman* 1882

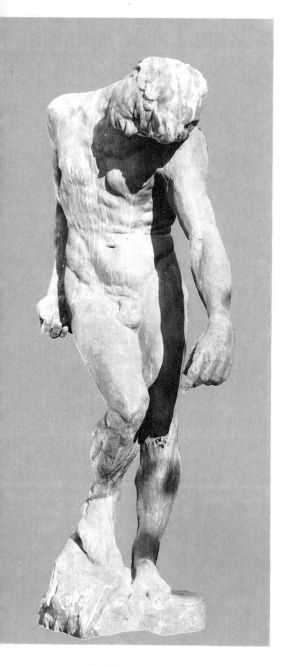

60 *The Shade* 1880

was his artistic conscience: ' I have done better since. ' A magnificently composed group, *The Three Shades* rings out like a solemn hymn to suffering above a hellish region teeming with ghostly flotsam.

The sculptor did not try to inject any symmetry into his multitude of flattened or projecting figures. Two hundred of them have been counted—a difficult task in view of their confusion and, in some cases, fluidity. No preconceived plan can be discerned. It seems that, far from being fortuitous, the ant-like chaos was due to an erratic generative process. One figure engendered the next in accordance with some obscure personal metaphysic and without regard to the law of over-all composition.

Bourdelle, who cherished a lifelong admiration for Rodin despite their numerous misunderstandings, walked into the sculptor's studio one day and hung his hat on one of the projecting features of *The Gates of Hell*. Sacrilege ? Possibly not, but it was an impudent gesture which conveyed a wealth of criticism. Rodin said nothing. He left the hat where it was, but the shaft went home. It was an indictment of his work. He felt that he had squandered himself,

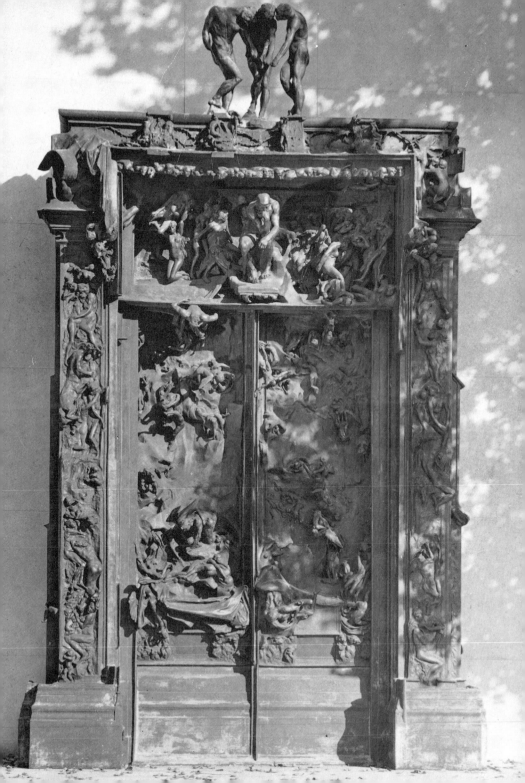

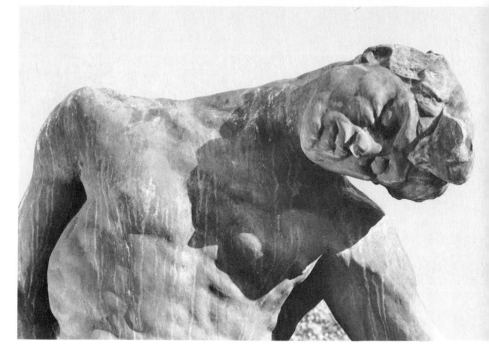

62 *The Shade.  Detail* 1880

day after day, on something which amounted to no more, in essence, than a hat-stand.  Bourdelle never dreamed that his little joke would have such deplorable results.  As for Rodin, he realized that his enthusiasm had led him astray.  He had accepted this commission from the state but lost sight of its true purpose. It had become an outlet for his tormented imagination.  He decided to abandon the project.  Bourdelle, who had helped to design the exterior of Auguste Perret's Théâtre des Champs-Élysées, had a feeling for architecture.  Every one of his monuments betrayed an underlying strength which derived from strong architectural composition, and he thought of all sculpture in structural terms.

Rodin loved architecture.  He was alert to the strong and subtle language of medieval builders and virtually alone among his contemporaries in cherishing old buildings to the extent of wanting

63 *The Three Shades* 1880 ▶

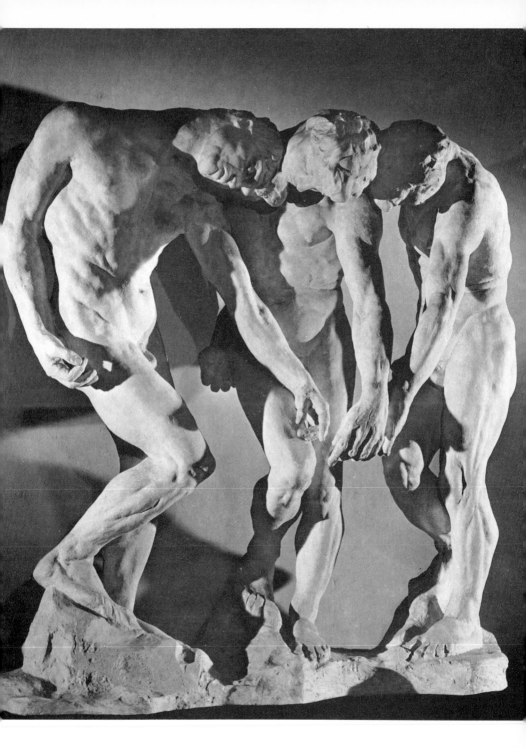

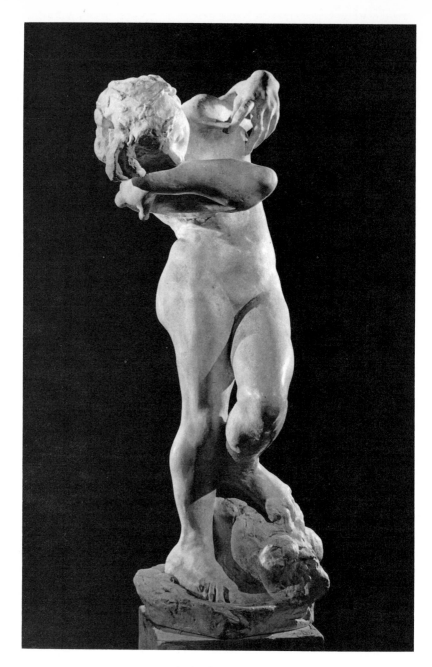

64 *Meditation* 1885

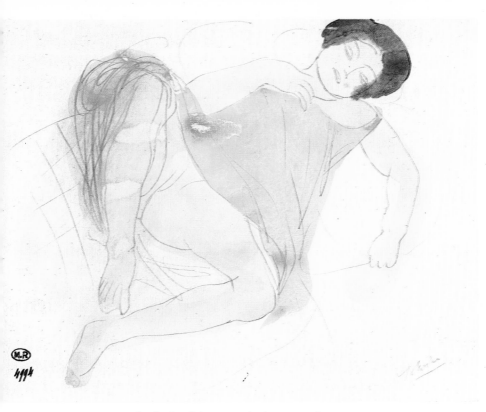

65 *Semi-reclining woman, her legs uncovered*

to buy eighteenth-century houses for his sole delectation. How could such a man have paid so little heed to the principles of the art of construction in his own work?

Regarded individually, Rodin's statues are masterpieces of proportion because he constantly referred to the human body. Confronted by the problem of designing a monument, he was embarrassed by the very superabundance of his sculptural gifts. The six burghers of Calais are six autonomous statues. Despite its plastic qualities, the monument to Claude Lorrain borders on triviality. At one stage, Rodin was taken with the idea of assembling some of his sculptures in groups. For instance, he placed two studies of *The Helmet-Maker's Beautiful Wife* with their bowed heads close together and arranged them beside a sort of grotto to form a piece which he entitled *Sources taries* (Dried-up Springs). He also had the incongruous notion of constructing a vertical group out of *Eve, Meditation* and *The Crouching Woman,* of which the latter, disorientated and on a different scale, seemed to soar ponderously through the air. One could cite many other examples of this defect, which was particularly irksome in an artist of such power. Perhaps the most deplorable was the maquette for a projected *Tower of Labour,* a vast and extravagant tribute to Craftsmanship. The craftsmen, clad in contemporary costume and carrying the tools of their trade, were to appear in bas-relief, spiralling round an immense interior column lit by loggias infelicitously inspired by the staircase at the Château de Blois, the whole to be surmounted by an overhanging group of large winged figures.

The *Gates of Hell* venture was doomed from the outset. It had to fail, not because a subject of such magnitude was beyond Rodin's scope, but because—and this was the obverse of his genius—the Dantesque theme which he had chosen proliferated in his mind like the flames of a fire which it was beyond his power to control.

Rodin ill-advisedly showed *The Gates* (in plaster) at the big retrospective exhibition of 1900. Bourdelle's unspoken criticism rankled so persistently that he had removed some of the projecting sculptures, but this was unwise. The deletions only emphasized the unevenness of the whole. ' But it isn't finished! ' people exclaimed. ' What about cathedrals ? ' he retorted calmly. ' Are they finished ? ' [16]

In 1903, twenty-three years after commissioning the work, the Fine Arts authorities became understandably impatient. In addition to payments on account, they had allocated the sculptor 35,000 francs to cover the cost of casting. They insisted on delivery. However, there was no longer any question of Rodin's putting the work in order. He was sick of it. Besides, he had to concede that his monument bore scant resemblance to what he had been commissioned to produce, to wit, a pair of gates. Under the terms of an agreement reached the following year, he paid back the sums already disbursed and retained possession of his work. Great relief prevailed at the Ministry of Fine Arts.

The gate was later erected in the chapel of the Rue de Varenne museum, where it looked out of scale. Not until 1938 was it done the honour of being cast in bronze and placed against a wall at the entrance to the grounds of the Musée Rodin.

' *The Gates of Hell* is full of masterpieces, ' Bourdelle announced to all and sundry, possibly in atonement for the business with the hat. It was true. Paris argued and debated the subject *ad nauseam*. One thing was certain: public attention had been drawn to an artist whose work resembled nothing that had been seen before. The sculptor's studio was thronged with visitors throughout the afternoons when he held open house.

Rodin's fame had crossed the frontiers of his own land. Foreign

66 *Danaid* 1885

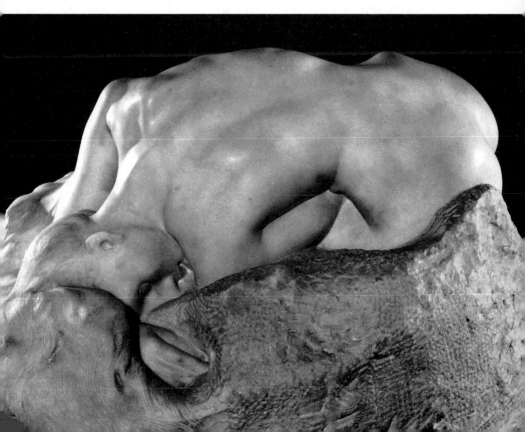

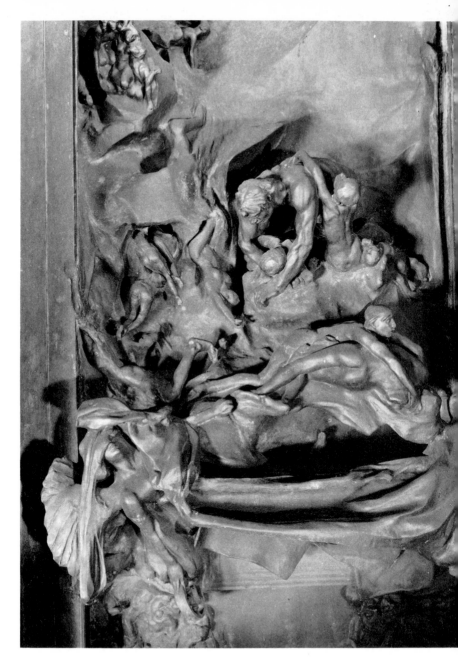

67 *The Gates of Hell.  Detail* 1880-1917

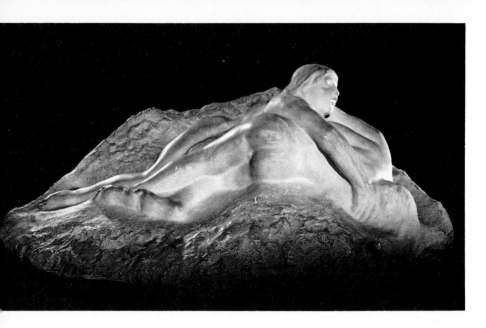

68 *Paolo and Francesca* 1887

museums, their interest aroused by works he had donated to them, were starting to buy now. An exhibition devoted to him and his friends Carrier and Puvis de Chavannes was organized in Geneva, and other shows were held in Germany. Wilhelm II commissioned Rodin to do a bust of him, though this never materialized. Prince Eugene of Sweden and Norway visited the sculptor at his studio and was fired with enthusiasm. When Stockholm's Fine Arts Committee rejected *The Inner Voice (Meditation)*, Swedish artists lodged a protest and the king invested Rodin with the collar of the Royal Order. The acquisition of *Dalou* was rejected by the same committee some time later, but Prince Eugene persuaded the Norwegians to buy it instead. Rodin had to contend with ill will and ill fortune throughout his career.

A group of sculptors and writers met at the Cladel home to organize a major exhibition at the Maison des Arts in Brussels, where Rodin had established useful contacts, some of which went back to his early days there. Camille Claudel's bust of him was surrounded by no less than sixty of his own sculptures. They

147

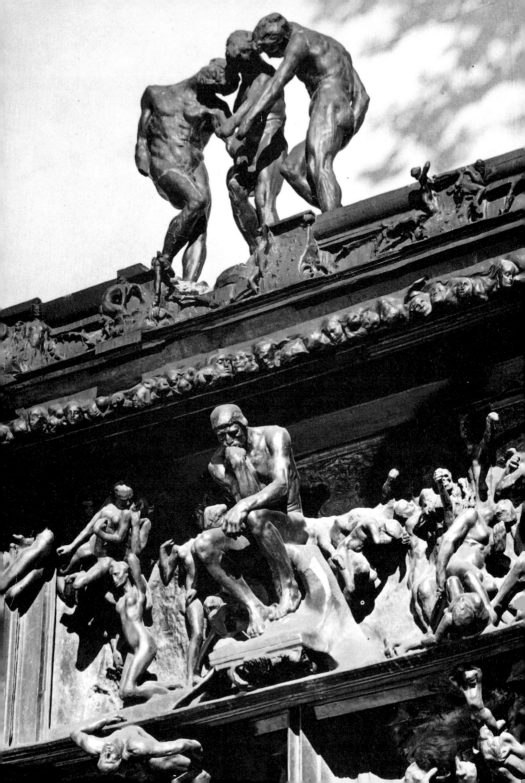

came as a revelation to the city which he had adorned with so many anonymous works. The tone of the press reviews attracted large crowds, some scandalized but almost all overwhelmed by what they saw. Rodin visited Brussels to supervise preparations for the exhibition and make contact with potential clients, but he felt ill at ease. People who expected to hear the great man make scintillating conversation at the receptions held in his honour were disappointed by his silent and impassive demeanour. For his part, he was saddened to see how much mutilation had been inflicted on the old Brussels quarters dear to his youth.

Holland, in its turn, showed itself eager to present works by the celebrated artist. Successive exhibitions were held at Amsterdam (under the patronage of the queen), Rotterdam, and The Hague.

Rodin undoubtedly met with his widest and most spontaneous response in England. He had first visited London to see his former school-friends Dalou and Legros, the latter a friend of Whistler, who had influenced his appointment as teacher of engraving at the Slade. Generous by nature, Legros did his best to plead Rodin's cause and put him in touch with London's art world. His success was due mainly to the support of W. E. Henley, editor of the *Magazine of Art,* and to the novelist Robert Louis Stevenson. Stevenson, who used to spend part of his time in France and was a frequent visitor to Barbizon, used Henley's review to launch an all-out campaign aimed at familiarizing his fellow-countrymen with Rodin's talents. He was aided by yet another ' scandal '. The Royal Academy had opposed the exhibition of a piece of sculpture by Rodin, presumably on the grounds that it might offend English susceptibilities. Stevenson took advantage of this to send *The Times* a resounding letter of protest.

England welcomed Rodin's work far more wholeheartedly than France, and the bond was an enduring one. During the First World War, the Victoria and Albert Museum deemed it an honour to acquire fourteen bronzes by the man who was regarded as the Allies' most famous living artist.

◀ 69 *The Gates of Hell. Detail* 1880-1917

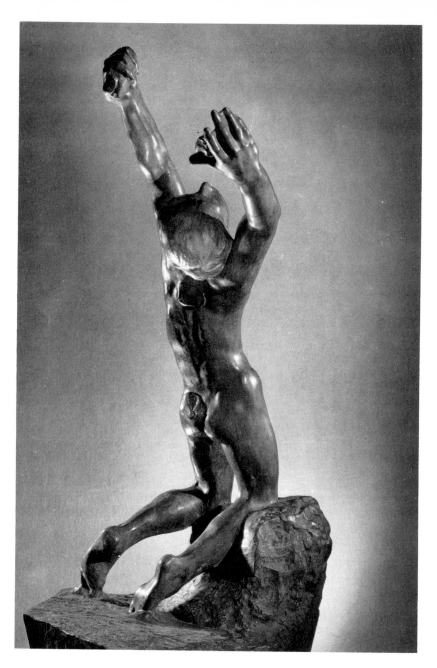

70 *The Prodigal Son* 1889

# Songs of love

The period when Rodin was caught up in the grand passion of his life coincided with the creation of his most impassioned works. Such was his innate vigour, even in decline, that everything which flowed from his hands with such dangerous facility bore the imprint of genius. Songs and sighs of love, cries of pleasure and pain, cries of pain and pleasure mingled, the eternal call of woman, the call of man, the restless summons of the human body—all found expression in his work. No music could be more intoxicating that that of *Orpheus,* who seems to be dying of song, no woman more tense than the one who fights off the embrace of *The Minotaur* when all the time we sense that she is ready to yield.

And, always, drama is conveyed by the movement of bodies. *Fugit Amor*—a girl gliding like a fish beneath the supine body of a youth who tries in vain to hold her back. *The Prodigal Son*— A kneeling boy with head thrown back and arms cast up to heaven, his torso twisted like a long, despairing cry.

It is worth noting that all the sculptures mentioned above are mounted on rocks. They show human beings shackled to the earth and struggling fruitlessly to break free. Rodin liked these contrasts between rough surfaces and the reflected lustre of bronze or polished marble, but he also sculpted ' floating ' figures without bases or even heads. These are simply *woman,* carnal and fleshy, the female animal divorced from everything save its gaping body.

Rodin's passion for work merged with his passion for life. These twin passions met and became fused in his love of the female body, a sensual love which, far from transmuting itself into an aesthetic, remained the basis of his admiration for plastic form. It was a religion. Rodin was receptive to all the marvels of creation when he celebrated nature in his pantheistic shrine, but it was woman whom he placed on his high altar and woman whom he worshipped as he would have worshipped a deity.

Jules Desbois recorded a touching anecdote in this connection. One day, while working on a ladder in the master's studio, he glanced over the top of the screen which cut off the area where Rodin was working with a model stretched out on a couch. The sitting was over but the woman had not yet moved. Heavy-lidded eyes aglow with fervour, Rodin advanced on her and plan-

71 *Fugit Amor* 1885-87

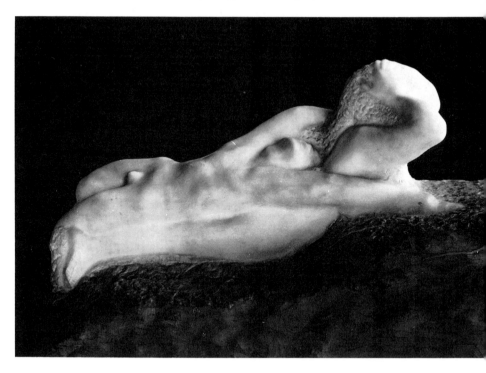

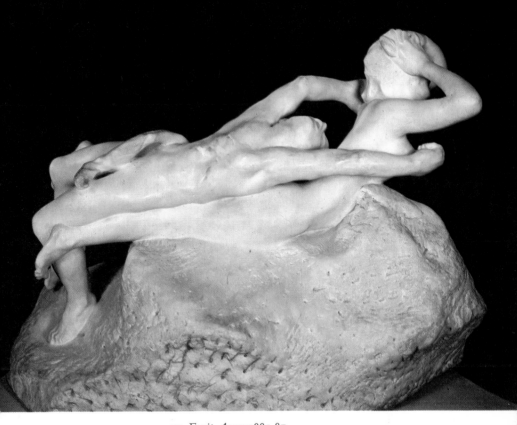

72 *Fugit Amor* 1885-87

ted a reverent kiss on her belly as though in gratitude for her
beauty.

This chaste gesture is echoed in *The Eternal Idol*, which has the
solemnity of a ritual act.  For once, the two bodies do not touch.
Kneeling with his hands behind his back, the man bows his head
with infinite reverence beneath the breasts of the girl, who kneels
above him in an attitude of humility and submission. *Eternal
Idol...*  The words which the sculptor used to describe this group
might well be applied to the bulk of his work—two words which
dwelt in the very depths of his being.

'A woman undressing—what a glorious sight! It is like the sun breaking through the clouds. The first sight of that body —the general impression—comes as a blow, a shock. Momentarily taken aback, the eye darts off again like an arrow. The whole of nature resides in every model, and the eye capable of seeing can discover it there and follow it so far! Above all, it can see what the majority are incapable of seeing: unknown depths and the very substance of life—beyond elegance, grace, and, beyond grace, modelling. But all this transcends words. Modelling has been called soft, but it is powerfully soft. Words fail me... Garlands of shadow hang from shoulder to hip, and from the hip to the jutting bosses of the thigh.' [17]

Glancing through Rodin's notes, we continually come across mental impressions of a like nature. It should be borne in mind that most of them were suggested by statues. This applies, despite appearances, to the remarks quoted above—but then Rodin had the gift of imbuing marble with the warmth of a living creature. Perhaps it is here that we come upon him in the most secret recesses of his genius. The works of the past, classical and Renaissance, were life itself to him, and he viewed them in the same light as his models of flesh and blood. This is what set him apart from other sculptors of his period, who, by studying the technique of earlier works of art as though this were a guarantee of success, lost all awareness of their inherent vitality.

Lovers had not hitherto been a subject for sculpture, at least in the West. Man and woman formed a single group only in scenes of rape and abduction. Alternatively, they were portrayed in death, stretched out side by side on top of a common tomb.

Rodin never modelled a Venus or a Cupid. His representation of Love was the loving couple, a favourite theme to which he constantly returned without ever repeating himself, from the chaste adoration of *The Eternal Idol* to the wildly passionate embraces and sexual frenzy of some of his other pieces. Woman had ceased to be the passive object of male concupiscence and become a sensual being who shared in all the transports of sensual pleasure.

Thus, Rodin's art introduced tremendous innovations. He was the great poet of love, and he expressed it as no one had ever done before him. His admiration for classical sculpture prompted him to retain its lessons concerning structure and modelling, but he portrayed love in living, visual terms, in terms of man and woman, of the kiss, of the embrace of bodies daringly entwined in their craving to become one. Far from giving an episodic impression, his sculptures eternalize the ritual act of an abject humanity which ennobles itself in its quest for self-fulfilment and the flowering of happiness shared.

Even more than his sculptures, Rodin's drawings show that he delighted in picturing the throes and convulsions of physical ecstasy. He was sometimes accused of being obsessed with sex—indeed, charges of obscenity almost stopped the parliamentary bill approving the presentation of his work to the state. It is true that he treated physical love with unwonted freedom. In his admiration for the female form he occasionally grouped women in pairs, as in his *Nymphs* and *Bacchantes* and in numerous drawings.

However, Rodin's work has nothing in common with the laboured eroticism of conventional pornography. With him, passion is so exalted that it purifies the audacity of his lovers. The lovers seem to offer up a sort of pagan prayer which ennobles their physical attitudes, and his sculptural language is wholly alien to eroticism in the modern sense.

We have only to compare Rodin's work with that of certain well-known academic painters of his period in order to see where the real fault lies. Using ' genre ' painting as a pretext, the latter readily subscribed to a genre of painting which was, in essence, smut. Although there was a very specific purpose behind the squirming bodies, seductive smiles and arch glances of their plump damsels, convention had it that these titillating nudes were not only ' seemly ' but medal-worthy. Looking at them, we sense the presence of a model who has just taken off her clothes, whereas the bodies modelled by Rodin have the nakedness of primeval man. His only sin was to restore dignity to the spectacle of male and female obeying the laws of the flesh.

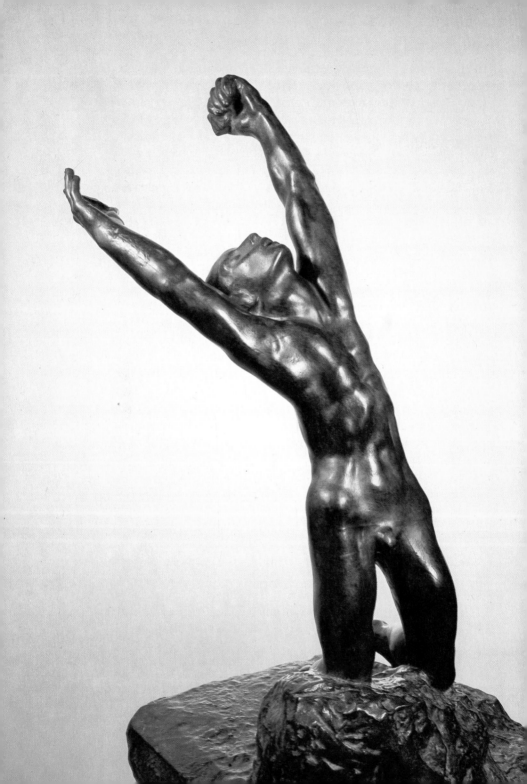

The period 1885-96 produced many of these gravely voluptuous groups, all of which bear the imprint of Rodin's mind. The best-known is *The Kiss,* that luminous symbol of love and of the twofold tenderness of man the protector and woman stirred to the depths of her being. From lips to feet, both figures are pervaded by the same fluidity. Walk round them, and you will not find one angle which detracts from their vitality, one instance where the sculptor's technique failed him. Other groups worthy of note are *Eternal Spring,* handled with youthful enthusiasm, *Paolo and Francesca,* tumbling in the waves, *The Idyll, Daphnis and Lycenium, I am Beautiful,* in which a man carries the folded body of a woman at head height, *L'Emprise* (The Succuba), a female faun clinging to the male like a small predator devouring its prey, and numerous ' entwined women ' and ' nymphs at play ' in which subtly suggested physical forms emerge from the marble and transport us into the mists of an enchanted world come to life.

Rodin was asked to supervise the work of a group of young women who used to meet at a studio in the Rue Notre-Dame-des-Champs. The person responsible for organizing this small association of friends who shared the cost of studio and models was a beautiful girl of twenty-four, a gay and graceful creature with dark blue eyes of startling intensity.

Rodin's attention was drawn to her straight away, and he soon recognized that her talents and imagination set her far above her fellow-students. She was no ordinary young woman. She listened with keen attention to the characteristically terse comments of her new teacher but would take exception to any remark which struck her as unjustified. Although she was a highly disciplined worker, she retained her pride and independence. All her time was devoted to drawing, painting and sculpture. She analysed details and isolated the essential structure of her model with an authority rare among her sex.

The young woman was Camille Claudel, sister of Paul Claudel. Four years older than Paul, she wielded an ascendancy over him which he later described as ' often cruel '. She taught him to despise religion and social conventions, kindled his imagination by

◀ 73 *The Prodigal Son* 1889

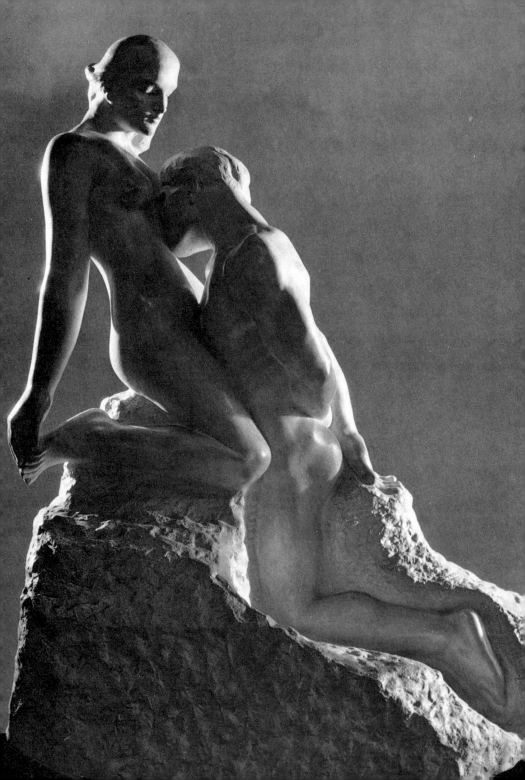

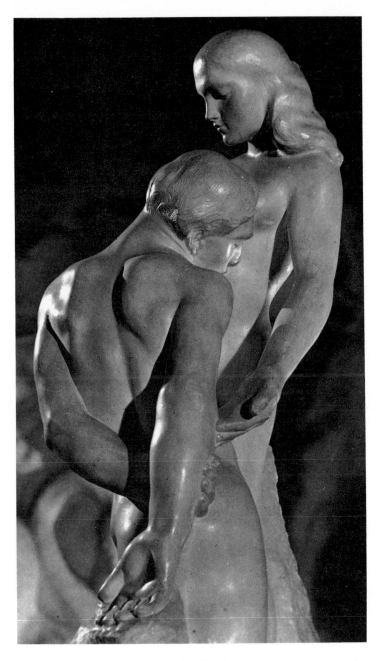

75 *The Eternal Idol. Detail* 1889

◀ 74 *The Eternal Idol* 1889

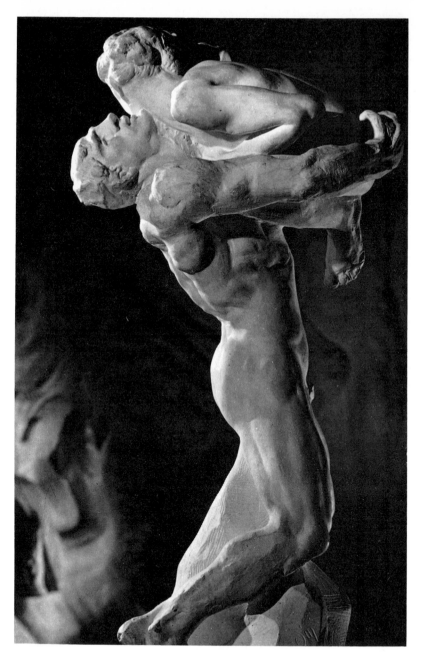

76 *I am Beautiful* 1882

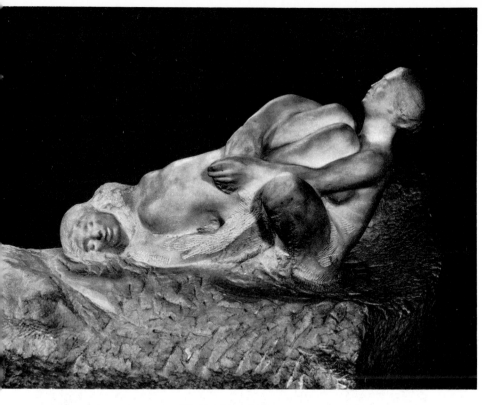

77 *The Bacchantes* before 1910

reading Shakespeare to him, shamed him by modelling in clay without having had a lesson in her life, and initiated him into the splendours of art and human creativity.

Contact with Rodin inevitably released subconscious forces within her. She was dazzled by the genius of the artist and captivated by the quiet strength of the man, but she was too proud to show it.

Camille went to work in Rodin's studio in the Rue de l'Université. His influence over her was complete. She became his secretary and assistant, posed first for busts and then in the nude.

Let Paul Claudel take up the story here. Nothing could convey its drama better than his simple but deeply moving introduction

161

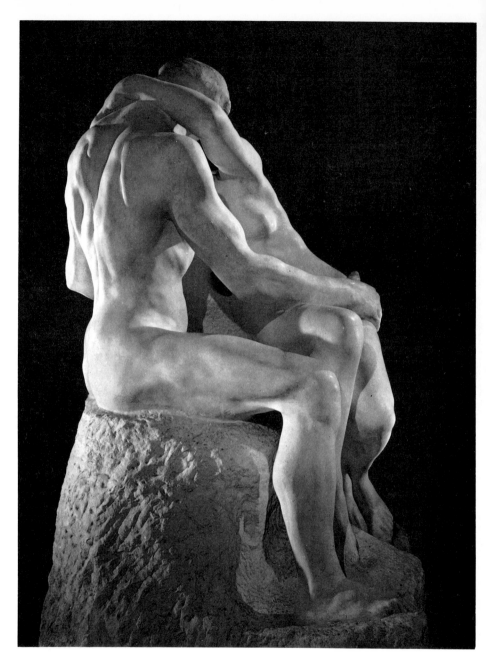

78 *The Kiss* 1886

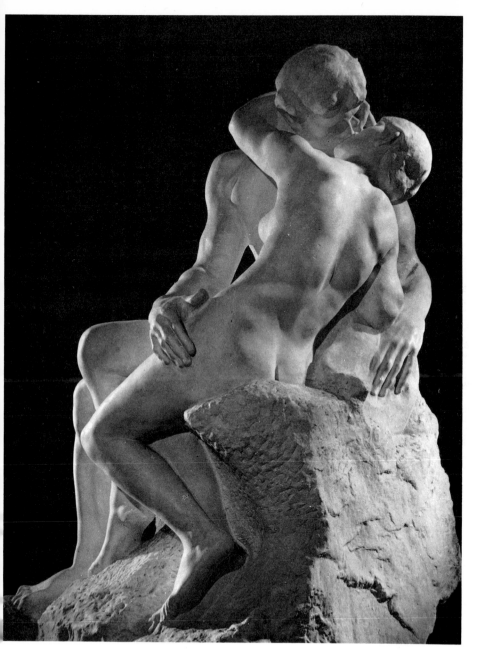

79 *The Kiss* 1886

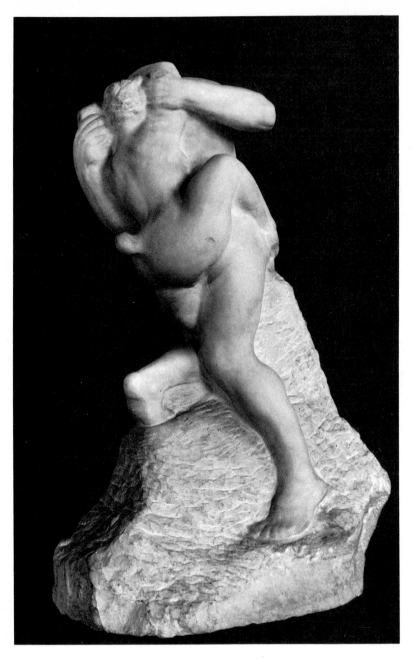

80 *L'Emprise* 1888

to the exhibition of his sister's work at the Musée Rodin in 1951 :

'There was nothing on the pillow of the hospital bed but a skull beneath a shapeless cap, a skull like a deconsecrated building which disclosed its magnificent architecture to my gaze. God was solemnly and finally sloughing off the wrongs of misfortune and old age.

'Camille Claudel... I see her again as she was, a superb young woman, triumphant in her beauty and genius, wielding an often cruel ascendancy over my early years. I see her as she appeared in the César photograph on the frontispiece of the famous issue of *L'Art décoratif* for July 1913, as she was when she had just arrived in Paris from Wassy-sur-Blaise and was attending the courses at the Colarossi studio. Later on, there were the two fine Rodin busts which form part of this exhibition. I see a noble brow surmounting magnificent eyes of the deep blue which is so seldom found outside the pages of a novel, a nose which it later amused her to regard as a legacy of the Virtues, a large mouth, more proud than sensual, and a head of luxuriant chestnut hair—the genuine chestnut known in English as auburn—which fell to her waist. I see again her vivid air of courage, candour, superiority and gaiety—the air of someone who has received much.

'And then—in July 1913!—action had to be taken. The tenants of the old house in the Quai Bourbon were complaining. What was this ground-floor apartment with the permanently closed shutters ? Who was this retiring and emaciated creature who emerged in the mornings merely to collect the makings of her wretched meals ? One fine day, hospital attendants got into the place by a back way and laid hands on its terrified occupant, who had long been waiting for them among dried-up plasters and clays. The dirt and disorder were indescribable, apparently. Pinned to the wall were the fourteen Stations of the Cross, cut with a pair of scissors from the front page of the Rue Bayard newspaper. Outside, the ambulance was waiting. So much for thirty years. Meanwhile, there had been Auguste Rodin.

'I shall not recount the lamentable story which forms part of the mute and unwritten tradition that might be called the Parisian

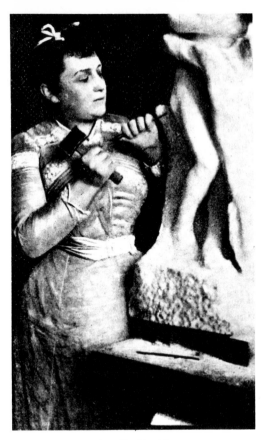

81 *Camille Claudel* 1911

Legend. Let it strike terror into families afflicted by that frightful and most dreaded of all misfortunes, the artistic vocation! In Rodin's day, the smarter members of the academic fraternity used to make do by resorting liberally to the conveniences of casting from the life, which saved both money and talent. As for Camille, she took her vocation quite as seriously as any contemporary of Donatello and Jacopo della Quercia. Rodin's invaluable tuition only alerted her to what she knew herself and helped her to disclose her own originality. The difference between their two temperaments became clear from the outset, however, and the effect of the present exhibition will be to shed light on that difference. Their knowledge of modelling was on a par. My sister acquired hers not only by slaving away relentlessly from the life but by devoting months to anatomical study and dissection. '

Camille lived in Rodin's orbit for nine years. Contact with the master instilled fresh life into her work without destroying its originality. Her bust of Rodin was the only portrait he liked. Conversely, he embodied her in a number of the works dating from his most prolific period. Passion brings joy to the intemperate but it also brings an even greater measure of suffering. Camille may have forgiven Rodin for his passing fancies—they were legion, and involved housemaids as well as society women— but she could not stomach the fact that a man to whom she had given everything still shared part of his life with the woman he returned to at Meudon every evening.

Rodin not only admired Camille. He loved her as he had never loved before and would never love again. She brought him exchanges of ideas which enriched and stimulated his imagination. Rose's innocuous chatter paled into insignificance beside Camille's intellectual fireworks. Rose herself, who was well aware of the other woman's status, suffered torments of jealousy and vented her bitterness in violent outbursts which left her physically exhausted.

Rodin's reunions with Camille were attended by stormy scenes of mounting intensity, manifestations of suffering to which his gentle nature found it impossible to react, emotional crises which rent his heart and sapped him to the point of collapse.

One day Camille left him for good. She went to live in wretched and self-imposed seclusion in her apartment on the Ile Saint-Louis, half-consciously assisting the inexorable deterioration of her own mind. Eventually she was put away. She died in a communal ward at Villeneuve-les-Avignon, a full thirty years after her parting with Rodin.

Paul Claudel never doubted that Rodin was responsible for this appalling tragedy. He handled him roughly, employing all the mordant eloquence at his command. ' Personally, ' he wrote in

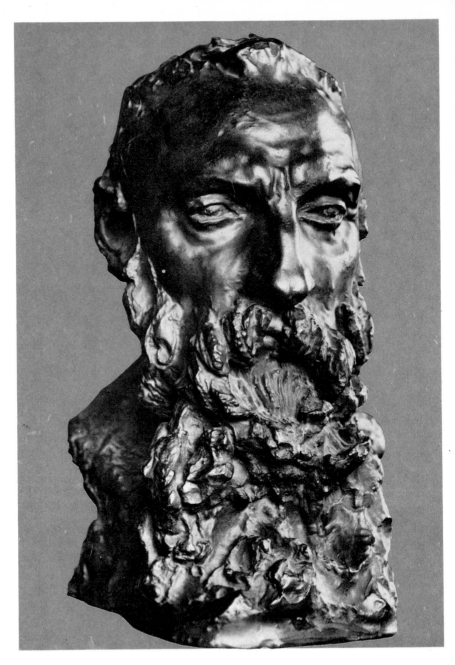

82 Camille Claudel. *Bust of Rodin*

1905, ' I can find nothing in this banquet of buttocks but the work of a myopic man who can see nothing of Nature save what is grossest. ' Claudel shrank from no form of stricture, however unjustified, where Rodin was concerned. ' Irresponsible critics have compared the work of Camille Claudel with that of someone whose name I will not mention. In fact, no one could conceive of a greater or more glaring antithesis. The work of the sculptor in question is heavy and gross in the extreme. Some of his figures cannot even extricate themselves from the lump of clay in which they are embedded. When they are not crawling along, hugging the mud in a sort of erotic frenzy, his interlocked figures look as if they are trying to re-create the original block from which they came. Solid and impenetrable, the group reflects light from every quarter like a boundary-stone. ' However, reverting to the same passage in the 1928 edition, Claudel added the following note: ' Alas! I am nonetheless compelled to acknowledge that Rodin was an artist of genius. ' [18]

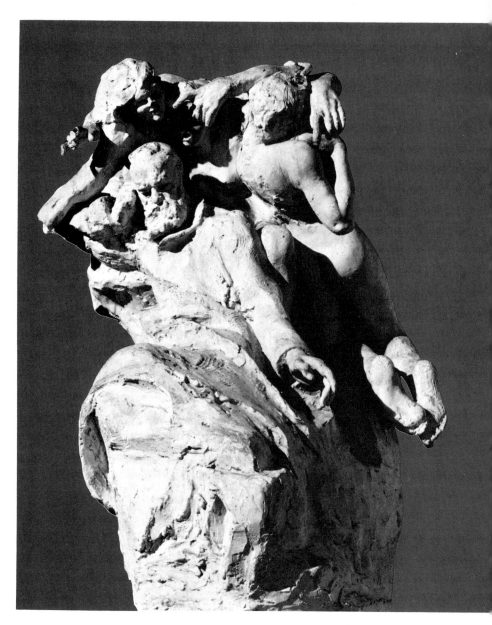

83 *Study for the monument to Victor Hugo* 1886-90

# CHAPTER EIGHT

## La Comédie humaine

Rodin had not abandoned his *Victor Hugo* for the Panthéon. Two years after the initial setback he resumed work, doing his best to obey instructions. The poet would be portrayed standing and fully clothed.

He began with a nude maquette, needless to say, but difficulties arose when the time came to dress it. For allegories, he decided to use three female heads borrowed from the lintel of *The Gates of Hell*. They were extremely beautiful, but, having been designed to fulfil another purpose, they formed a confused jumble behind the poet's head. Rodin dropped the scheme once more.

Yet another commission for a public monument remained unfinished. Some artists need a precise schedule, a definite plan which will keep their ideas in order. Being a former stonemason who had often extolled the virtues of disciplined instruction in the manner of the craftsmen of yore, Rodin was well aware of this. However, he already belonged in spirit to the twentieth century. His ideas had become too free, his imagination too inventive and his hand too adventurous for him to submit to imposed rules.

But there was still the first *Victor Hugo,* the nude figure seated on a rock, which was intended for the Jardin du Luxembourg. Slowly, very slowly, assistants executed it in marble under Rodin's supervision. He modified it, left it in abeyance, and ultimately lightened the effect of the monument by eliminating the Muses, whose expressive strength overshadowed the principal figure and impaired its glory instead of enhancing it.

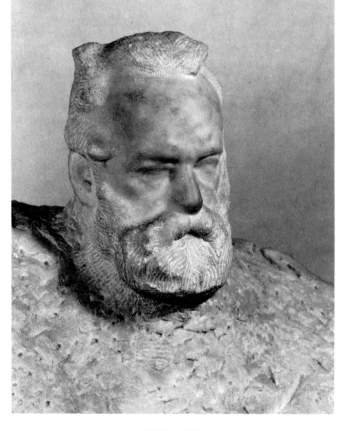

84 *Bust of Victor Hugo* 1910

The Ministry of Fine Arts had once more demonstrated the extent of its forbearance, though it should not be forgotten that the Minister, Dujardin-Beaumetz, was a personal friend of the sculptor. Since the Luxembourg was genuinely overcrowded with statues, this one was erected in the grounds of the Palais-Royal late in 1909, some twenty-seven years after being commissioned.

One day, while strolling through one of his favourite Parisian quarters, Rodin paused in front of a house which was for sale and might, from its appearance, have been on the market for a long

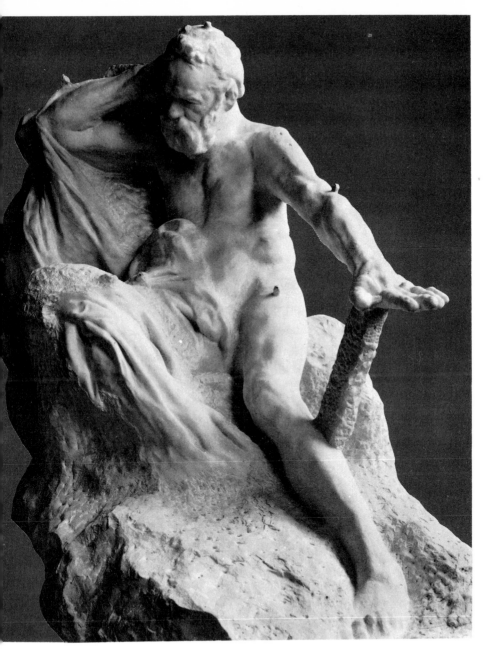

85 *Monument to Victor Hugo* 1886-90

time. Situated in a dark and narrow street, it showed signs of age and neglect, but its simple eighteenth-century exterior enchanted Rodin and its ancient stonework held an appeal which he found it impossible to resist. The house stood in the Rue des Grands-Augustins, not far from the Seine. He bought it and installed Rose there as comfortably as the condition of the place allowed. Meanwhile, he continued to meet Camille at the studio in the Avenue de l'Italie.

Camille's passion for him had become yet more exacting. At its height, while rejecting her imperious demands that he should leave Rose for good, he promised to take her away on a trip. Camille did not care where they went provided she could be with him for as long as possible.

They stayed at a hotel in Tours and spent happy days relaxing beside the Loire and Indre. Rodin was delighted by everything he saw—the great royal châteaux and handsome villages of Touraine, the streets of the old city, the surrounding country-side, the fields and sun-drenched river banks. He immersed himself in Balzac's Touraine novels and dwelt in spirit with the ' *grand bonhomme* ' by reading *Le Curé de Tours* and *Le Lys dans la vallée*. He sketched during the day and made nude studies of Camille in their hotel room at night, working by candlelight. He also made notes: ' I won't have seen any cathedrals this time, but I have seen the very sky pouring out blue happiness... A glorious day. The Loire steely, its entire width like watered silk.

' This morning's stillness extends to the furthest horizon. Everything is at rest. Full effects of slowness and order everywhere. Well-being visible everywhere. The haze tinged and made balmy by good weather. Can the same reassuring and comforting uniformity of air and light be found in any district but here ? The subtle, soft grey of the Loire beneath the clouds, the grey roofs of the town, the grey bridge of old stone...

' There is this little church in the region of Chambord. It has not been restored—not completely, at least. For the choir, which was Romanesque, they consulted an engineer, some bigwig in the sanitation service. He did his job... But the nave, those marvellous reliefs, those smooth columns, those big crisp ribs, divided into several more delicate ribs...'

He was constantly inveighing against latter-day vandals. ' Just wait and see what fine town halls they'll put up for you in the provinces when there are no more Louis XVI châteaux for municipal councils to occupy. '

He had told Rose, before leaving, that he would be away for a few days. He did not return for a month.

Two years after Rodin's trip to Balzac country something happened which was to cause so much controversy that its echoes continued to be heard until the eve of the Second World War. The Société des Gens de Lettres commissioned him to produce a monument to Balzac.

Things were complicated from the outset. The Société's scheme was a revival of one originally put forward by the elder Dumas, who had launched a public fund for the purpose of raising a statue to Balzac shortly after the latter's death. As it turned out, the plan was doomed by the peculiarly sensitive attitude of Balzac's widow, who tried to prohibit the fund by taking legal action. In 1885, thirty-five years after Balzac's death, the Société des Gens de Lettres launched a new fund which raised 36,000 francs. It was decided to entrust the statue to Chapu, the official monument specialist, and erect it in the Galerie d'Orléans at the Palais-Royal, an incongruous show-case which was demolished in 1933.

The choice of site was hotly debated. The architect of the pedestal and the sculptor failed to agree, and the latter died before completing his maquette.

A new sculptor had to be found, especially as the government, the Prefecture of the Seine and the Municipal Council had now agreed on a more worthy site, namely, the Place du Palais-Royal. Among those who put their names forward were Coutant, Antonin Mercié, and Marquet de Vasselot, who fancied his chances because he had done a bust of Balzac twenty years earlier.

We are now in 1891. Rodin's name was known, if not renow-ned, and had been so particularly since the Georges Petit exhibi-tion. A number of writers and artists agitated in favour of entrusting the monument to him. Goeneutte, Champfleury, Arthur Arnould and several others wrote in this vein to Zola, who was president of the Société des Gens de Lettres that year.

Zola agreed. He presented the committee with a short list comprising the names of Marquet de Vasselot and Rodin. At the first ballot, each candidate received nine votes; at the second, Rodin got twelve, mainly because of an impassioned plea on his behalf by Zola. Under the terms of the contract, Rodin was to produce a statue three metres high, pedestal excluded, and deliver it by May 1893—a mere two years hence. The fee was set at 30,000 francs, part payable in advance.

By all accounts, Rodin was fairly quick to see what course to adopt. Only ten months later Roger Marx wrote: ' A maquette exists, very finished and well-defined—superb, in fact. It portrays Balzac draped in a Dominican habit, the shroud which that single-minded and industrious thinker always wore, like the monks of olden times. And, since the capacious secular robe is timeless, thought becomes generalized and the only idea suggested by the costume is that of solitary toil, of labours resumed each daybreak without respite or intermission. ' [19]

Rodin was at grips with a task which was quite new to him and fraught with danger. The method which he had always practised and advocated as the sole road to artistic verity—copying his model—was impossible in this case. And yet, how to re-create the likeness of a man who had died forty-two years before, when photography was in its infancy ?

Curiously enough, iconographic records of the great writer were not only rare but unrelated to the latter part of his life. Rodin went prowling in search of evidence which would give him a grasp of his subject. Devéria had painted Balzac as a young man. The museum at Tours possessed two rather insipid por-traits by Louis Boulanger and Gérard Séguin, a pleasant smiling lithograph by Lasamme, and, finally, the well-known caricature

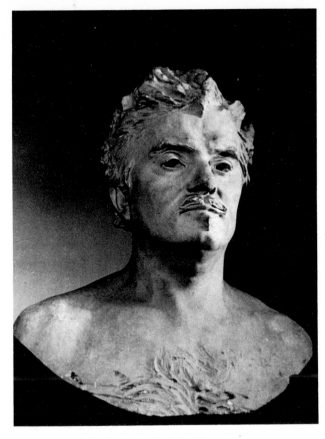

86 *Study for the head of Balzac* 1893-97

from *Charivari,* which showed the novelist clad in a dressing-gown with his enormous face framed by flowing hair. (The latter document may have been the most vivid of all and the one which inspired Rodin, consciously or unconsciously, to transpose its humorous aspect, as work progressed, into the aura of sublime pride which emanated from the finished statue.) Not long afterwards, Nadar's effects yielded a daguerrotype dating from the last pain-racked days of the writer's life. [20]

By August Rodin was in Tours, hoping to find echoes of the author of *La Comédie humaine* in the places that had so entranced

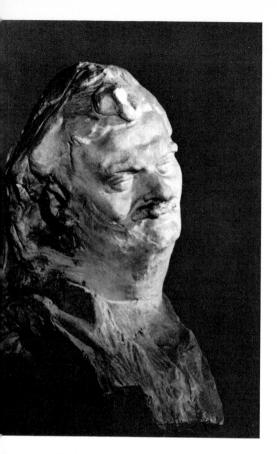

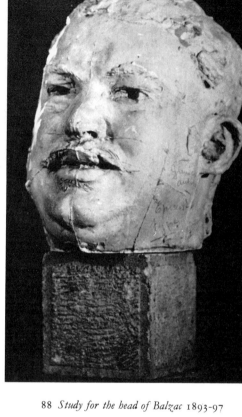

87 *Study for the head of Balzac* 1893-97          88 *Study for the head of Balzac* 1893-97

him on his earlier visit. Although concerned with resemblance, or at least verisimilitude, he was also anxious to make his statue a translation of the writer's gargantuan œuvre. Tours boasted a bust of Balzac by David d'Angers, but he scorned this. Doubtless unaware that Balzac was of Languedoc stock, he set out to find some doubles among the local population. He found some, or so he evidently believed, because he modelled several busts of men from Touraine with his statue in mind.

While not seeking to produce an artist's impression of his subject, Rodin sculpted numerous heads. Comparison of the

178

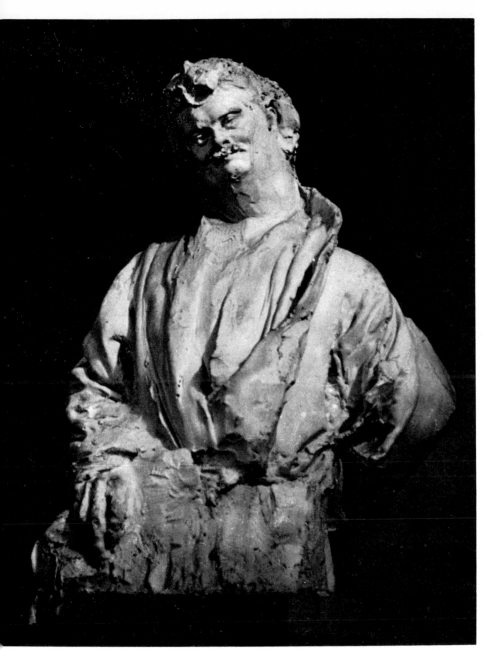

89 *Study for Balzac* 1893-97

twenty studies which survive (he undoubtedly made more) is of great interest.

However, the statue had to portray Balzac standing erect, and this presented an extremely difficult problem to someone who wanted to spiritualize his sculpture without idealizing it in any way. Although he died at fifty-one, Balzac was already misshapen with age. It was as though his body, warped by the years spent behind a desk, had become set in the bloated curves imposed by his sedentary way of life. He had stubby arms and legs, a thick torso, and—according to the Goncourts—a belly with a profile like an ace of spades.

Rodin carefully noted all that had been said or written on the subject. He even looked up Balzac's old tailor, who still had the great man's measurements, and ordered a suit from him. Putting this on a dummy padded with rags, he proceeded to model a study from it.

He had always visualized Balzac in very loose clothing, and several studies portray him thus; but he now adopted the idea which dictated all else: Balzac in his normal working attire, the white Dominican habit which figured in his friends' recollections and the *Charivari* caricature. Although Rodin transformed and stylized the garment, it was this line of approach which ultimately led to the extraordinary draped figure with its bull-neck and massive head.

Rodin began by making some highly realistic nude studies, many with arms crossed like those of a fair-ground wrestler and all with the left leg advanced. Seven of these have survived. It was not, as some have thought, that he ever meant to portray Balzac in the same manner as Victor Hugo. This was simply the way he worked, the method which would enable flesh and blood to be sensed beneath the drapery. He also produced several studies with deliberately accentuated musculature. They were splendidly vigorous but transcended mere humanity and looked more like mythological gods or heroes.

May 1893 arrived. With his customary disregard for contractual obligations, Rodin had been devoting precious little thought to

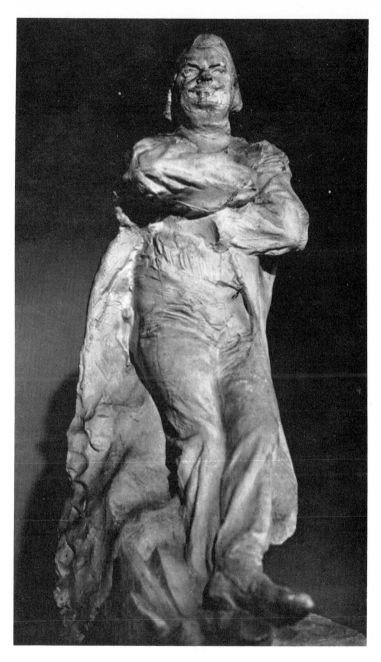

90 *Study for Balzac* 1893-97

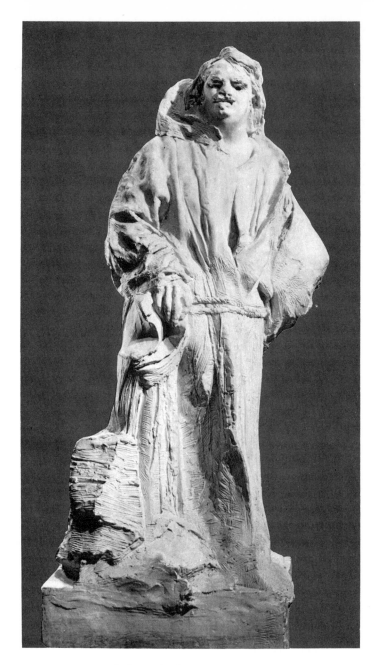

91 *Balzac in his Dressing-Gown* 1893-97

the Société des Gens de Lettres. He was astonished to learn, by contrast, that the Société was extremely worried about him and his monument. 'Don't they realize that art won't adapt itself to delivery times?' he protested, and references to the contract which bore his signature merely elicited smiles and airy waves of the hand. Nevertheless, friends warned him that it was high time to put a stop to the plots which were being hatched against him by members of the Institut. Although Rodin saw red whenever the Institut was mentioned, he agreed to invite the members of the committee to come and inspect his maquette in the studio.

They came. They inspected the maquette under Rodin's polite but silent gaze. One or two of them raised vague objections which remained unanswered. Finally, they took their leave with a sense of dismay which was shared by friend and foe alike.

Things looked thoroughly black. The sculptor's opponents demanded that the Société should institute legal proceedings. Zola went to see Rodin and implored him to state a firm delivery date, pointing out that the Société's elections were due in the following year and that another president might be less accommodating. All he got was vague replies and laconic remarks from which it emerged that the task of completing the maquette, enlarging it and casting the enlargement could not be completed before 1895.

As luck would have it, the next president of the Société was the poet Jean Aicard, a personal friend of Rodin. Zola briefed him on the situation by letter: 'I have left a very thorny problem pending at the Société—the question of the Balzac statue. Between ourselves, it is going to give you a lot of trouble. I am devoted to Rodin—you have heard me doing my utmost for him in committee—but I don't want you to feel bound by my views. The best thing for all concerned would be for you to get in touch with Rodin's friends. Be conciliatory and try to find some common ground. Legal proceedings would only waste the artist's time and bring the Société into disfavour.'

The committee's second visit to Rodin's studio created an even worse impression than the first. There was no discussion at all this time, since the sculptor again barely uttered a word. Back at the Société, on the other hand, words flew thick and fast. It was inconceivable that any public square in Paris should be adorned with such an ' obese monstrosity '. The maquette was further described as a ' shapeless mass ' and a ' colossal fœtus '.

Rodin was going through a particularly difficult time, and his health had suffered in consequence. His relations with Camille Claudel were at their stormiest and most exhausting. Rose had suffered heart attacks and was not recuperating as she should. He had plenty of worries. Finally, high blood-pressure was giving rise to depressive symptoms. His habitual appetite for work had waned. Once more, he refused to stipulate a firm delivery date.

Most of the committee members were furious. Zola's insistence on Rodin had landed them in a hornet's nest. There were fears that the statue would not even be ready in 1899, the year when Balzac's centenary was due to be commemorated by the Société. Just to make matters worse, the sculptor was still battling with *The Gates of Hell* and *Victor Hugo,* neither of which had ever been completed.

None of this was very reassuring. By a unanimous vote, the committee decided to demand delivery of the statue within twenty-four hours. Failing this, Rodin's contract would be cancelled and he would have to refund the 10,000 francs which he had received on account. Graver still was the committee's unequivocal declaration that the monument was ' artistically inadequate '.

Jean Aicard, whose reputation was that of a rather mawkish writer and poet, showed unexpected vigour and diplomatic skill. Trying to temporize, he managed to persuade the committee that it would be highly undesirable to present an artist of Rodin's eminence with an ultimatum of this kind. Besides, there was no guarantee that the Société would obtain judgement if it plunged into litigation. He offered to speak to the artist in person and ask him to relinquish the commission voluntarily, and asked the committee to trust him.

Some weeks later Aicard read the committee a letter from Rodin, skilfully worded and magnanimous in tone. All the evidence suggests that it had been dictated either by Geffroy or by Aicard

184

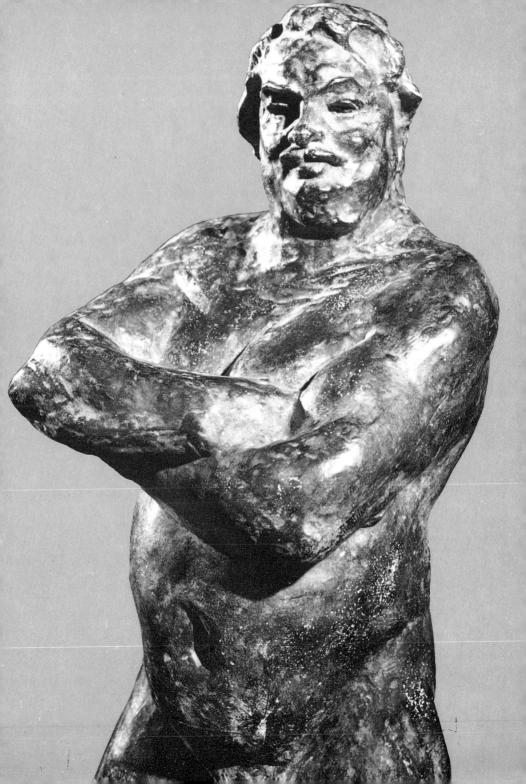

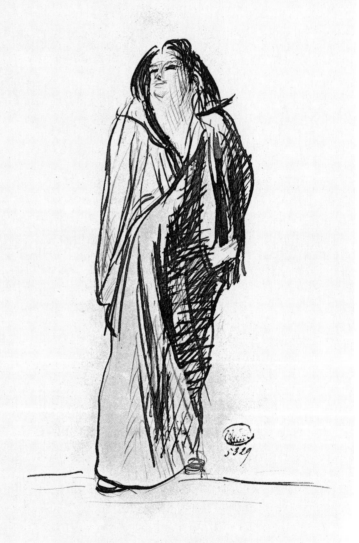

93  *Balzac*

himself: ' A work of art, as all who have wrestled with one will know, demands calm and untrammelled reflection. That is what I should like to see you grant me, so as to enable me to complete my work as promptly as possible. You could and should do so, since these concerns are yours too, as they are those of all creators in the field of art and literature. I have been constantly and keenly aware of my responsibility as an artist, and this is what has occupied my mind since the few weeks' rest which I was compelled to take. I ask you to grant me the opportunity of paying homage, with all my heart and all the resources at my command, to the great man whose example should be an inspiration to us all. I think of his relentless toil, of his difficult life, of the unceasing battle which he had to wage, of his high courage. I should like to express all this. Put your faith and trust in me. '

No one could have taken the offensive against the writer of such a dignified letter, but the question of finance—of the 10,000 francs advance—was raised. Once more acting on good advice, Rodin responded by proposing that he should place the sum on deposit until delivery had been made. He estimated that the monument would be completed within a year.

The committee declared itself satisfied. It agreed to the arrangement, and everything seemed to have sorted itself out.

However, anyone who assumes that the affair was settled can have little conception of the bitterness felt by veteran artists who had been supplanted by this ' anarchist ', or of the often sincere horror which took possession of academic artists at the idea of seeing one of the glories of French literature commemorated in the heart of Paris by Rodin's misshapen, outrageous and obscene silhouette. The statue was an insult to France itself and its whole great tradition. Cabals were organized and campaigns mounted in the press.

The committee took fright and tried to reconsider its decision. However, Aicard surprised the meeting which had been convened to vote on the proposal by reading out a vitriolic statement, announcing his resignation from the presidency, and leaving the hall. Six members of the committee supported him.

This incident caused a sensation. The press took sides for or against Aicard, in other words, for or against Rodin, the ' cons ' being the more rabid of the two parties. Just as there was a Dreyfus affair, then at its height, so there was a Rodin affair which reached beyond the confines of the world of art and letters.

Rodin was deeply affected. The man of granite wavered and the glutton for work abandoned his labours. His will-power, which he had so often demonstrated in the past, faltered. He lost faith in himself, and his attitude seemed to vindicate those who broadcast the rumour that he was finished, artistically impotent, and that his so-called *Balzac* proved this beyond dispute. He was going through a crisis similar to the one that had affected him in his youth, after the death of his sister. But he was fifty-four now and he reacted by venting his sudden fits of anger on those closest to him. Poor Rose, who was the most frequent target of his wrath, now resembled a shrewish old peasant-woman. She nagged Rodin incessantly, reconciled to his fleeting affairs but painfully aware that he was in the throes of a grand passion. Fearful of being banished for good, she was maladroit enough to show her anxiety by indulging in bouts of recrimination.

Camille's transports of jealousy had assumed gigantic dimensions. She refused to share Rodin any longer. Her exasperation became virulent and almost pathological. She even spoke of taking her own life—a threat which, coming from a woman of her calibre, should have been taken seriously. The drama of a broken relationship was ultimately succeeded by the drama of insanity.

Rodin fled Paris in search of oblivion. A spell of relaxation in Switzerland, at St Moritz, did much to restore his equilibrium, and his friends racked their brains for ways of showing their regard for him. An opportunity soon presented itself. A split in the ranks of the Société des Artistes Français, an organization which had often snubbed Rodin in the past, gave birth to the Société Nationale des Beaux-Arts. His fellow-artists nominated him for the presidency of the sculpture section.

At the banquet held to commemorate the seventieth birthday of the sculptor's great friend Puvis de Chavannes, each guest was presented with a small bronze plaque bearing a profile of the painter based on Rodin's earlier bust of him. Rodin presided. He also delivered a postprandial address which had been drafted by Geffroy, ' but nobody heard it because he muttered it timidly into his beard '. [21]

These demonstrations should be regarded not only as marks of friendship but also as a stand in favour of the author of *Balzac*, whose opponents had far from abandoned the struggle. Strong feeling was aroused by satirical and provocative articles in the press. One particularly explosive piece appeared in *Gil Blas*, whose editorial staff included well-known writers. Pregnant with sarcasm, it was signed by the novelist Félicien Champsaur: ' It is forbidden to utter Rodin's name without making obeisance. Critics mount guard round this, the greatest genius of the age— pardon me—" of every age ", to quote the words of one peculiarly sensitive journalist. Without debating their arbitrary judgements, they brandish their pens at anyone who fails to bow low and employ words of artistic esteem to humble the mighty splendour of Michelangelo before the unprolific master whom they acclaim as a means of demonstrating their own originality. The snobs of literature, journalism, the salon and the boulevard have the knack of creating ephemeral gods of varying nuisance value: Mallarmé, prince of poets and literary puppet; and Rodin, principally famed for a *Gates of Hell* which will never be finished— indeed, which no longer exists because it sprang from a magnificent dream only to return there—and now for this statue of Balzac, which is beyond him... Balzac deserves his statue. Thanks to M. Rodin's inertia, however, the man whose immortal right it is to stand erect in the heart of Paris still lies entombed in shapeless marble. He will lie there for a long time to come unless M. Rodin withdraws and someone else is called in '. [22]

Rodin decided to send his *Balzac* to the Salon of 1898. He was advised to offset this daring step by exhibiting it opposite *The Kiss* on the grounds that everyone would be captivated by the latter. As it turned out, the public only had eyes for the statue which had provoked such violent controversy, and critics vied with one another in pouring scorn on it. Bourdelle went angrily from one to another, indicating first *The Kiss* and then *Balzac*. ' That's charming, ' he declared in tones loud enough to be heard by everyone around, ' but that—that's great sculpture! '

Few works of art have unleashed such a fierce and protracted war of words. The repercussions of *Olympia* and Cézanne's other unintentional ' shockers ' had, on the whole, been confined to the rather restricted world of art-lovers. The *Balzac* affair inflamed a vast public, and the fanatical fury which it aroused on both sides extended to the man in the street. The committee members of the Société des Gens de Lettres were delighted by the fuss, confident that it would be impossible to erect the *Balzac* in a public place now that Parisians had reacted so strongly. A military historian named Alfred Duquet, vice-chairman of the committee and the man who had led the fight against Balzac from the outset, submitted the following resolution: ' That the committee of the Société des Gens de Lettres forbid M. Rodin to cast in bronze the plaster statue exhibited at the Palais des Machines, in view of the fact that, having commissioned a statue from him, it declines to accept a work which has no connection with the said statue. '

Some members felt that the resolution was too strongly worded, and the meeting grew stormy. Then Henri Houssaye, president of the Société, made a brilliant suggestion. It should not be too difficult to persuade the Municipal Council to ban the erection of the statue in a public thoroughfare. The committee's legal advisers observed that this altered nothing. A contract was a contract, and Rodin's contract contained no stipulation that it could be broken if his statue did not find favour. The Société would have to accept the monument and remunerate him on the agreed terms. Finally, after a good deal of muddled argument, the committee adopted a face-saving resolution drafted by Henri Lavedan: ' The committee of the Société des Gens de Lettres feels it sadly incumbent upon it to protest at the rough model exhibited at the Salon by M. Rodin, and declines to recognize it as a statue of Balzac. ' The text of this resolution was released to the press.

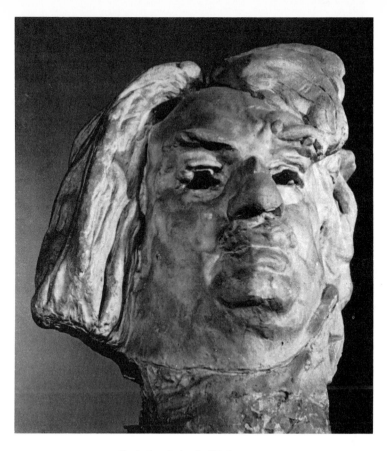

94 *Study for the head of Balzac* 1893-97

A number of artists were infuriated to read this report in the newspapers, and Rodin's closest friends drafted a rebuttal: ' In the belief that the resolution passed by the committee of the Société des Gens de Lettres is unimportant from an artistic point of view, Rodin's friends and admirers urge him in all sincerity to pursue his work without regard to present circumstances. They also express the hope that, in a noble and cultured land such as France, he will never cease to be accorded the public esteem and respect to which his great integrity and exemplary career entitle him. '

After being printed and sent to numerous prominent figures, this declaration was signed by writers and artists of every complexion. Following this success, a fund was launched. Donations, accompanied by letters of support, flooded in from newspapers, reviews, publishers and associations of various kinds. Carpeaux's widow offered to send a terra-cotta bust of one of the figures from *The Dance*.

Nothing boosts an artist's reputation more than a scandal. Rodin had not sought notoriety—it was absolutely foreign to his nature. Clouds of despondency enveloped him. Normally so confident of his ability, he could now be seen staring anxiously at the statue which had provoked such paroxysms of rage. What if his enemies were right ? What if his statue really was the ' monstrosity ' it had been called at a meeting of the Municipal Arts Committee ? After all, his old friend Dalou had refused to associate himself with the declaration of solidarity on the grounds that memories of their former friendship forbade him to participate in ' this new fiasco in which clumsy friends are embroiling him '.

But a new band of champions had arisen, led by *Le Figaro*. Writing in *L'Écho de Paris*, Émile Bergeret castigated those whom he described as ' hawkers of literature ', and journals as reputable as *La Revue des deux mondes* and *La Revue de Paris* published articles brimming with admiration.

At first surprised by this furore, Rodin regained some of his peace of mind. Friends exhorted him to defend his work, insist that the Société fulfil its side of the bargain, take legal action if need be—but no. What he wanted now, most of all, was peace and quiet.

This was easier said than done. Apart from press-cuttings, every post brought messages of solidarity from France and elsewhere. His studio in the Rue de l'Université was invaded by admirers and unabashed sightseers, so much so that he was afraid to go there himself. This was not the sort of fame he had envisaged.

Two letters arrived on the same day. One was signed by Auguste Pellerin, the well-known Cézanne collector, and contained an offer to buy the statue for 20,000 francs. The other came from a group of influential friends in Belgium: ' We sincerely trust that the Société des Gens de Lettres will reject your statue. We therefore beg you to be kind enough to relinquish it to us. Balzac is admired in Brussels, and your work would be erected in one of our squares. '

Meanwhile, the fund had raised the purchase price (30,000 francs, including the pedestal designed by Frantz Jourdain).

Although tempted by these offers, Rodin was justifiably apprehensive about the possible intrusion of politics. Clemenceau, never one to mince words, announced that he was withdrawing his name from the subscription list because he had heard that Rodin was afraid of having too many of Zola's friends on it. Feelings had reached such a pitch of intensity that the pro- and anti-Dreyfus camps were incapable of assessing anything, however far removed from the ' affair ', except in terms of the supposed political opinions of the parties involved. Rodin, to whom art transcended such squabbles, had always tried to dissociate himself from political passions.

Accordingly, he decided to send everyone packing in the politest possible way. To the friends who had conducted the fund-raising campaign he wrote: ' It is my firm wish to retain sole possession of my work. My interrupted labours and my thoughts on the subject all demand that I do so. All I ask of the fund, in token and requital of my efforts, is a list of the generous subscribers. As for you who are still more enthusiastic, old friends of long standing who may have made it possible for me to produce sculpture in the first place, to you I say thanks with a full heart. '

The letter was published, the subscribers got their money back, and Rodin kept his *Balzac*. Finally, since the Salon was still open and some people only went there with the object of making petty and offensive demonstrations, he sent the newspapers a brief letter to announce that he was withdrawing his statue from the Salon and that it would ' not be erected anywhere '.

The Société des Gens de Lettres had won, but all the honours went to its defeated adversary.

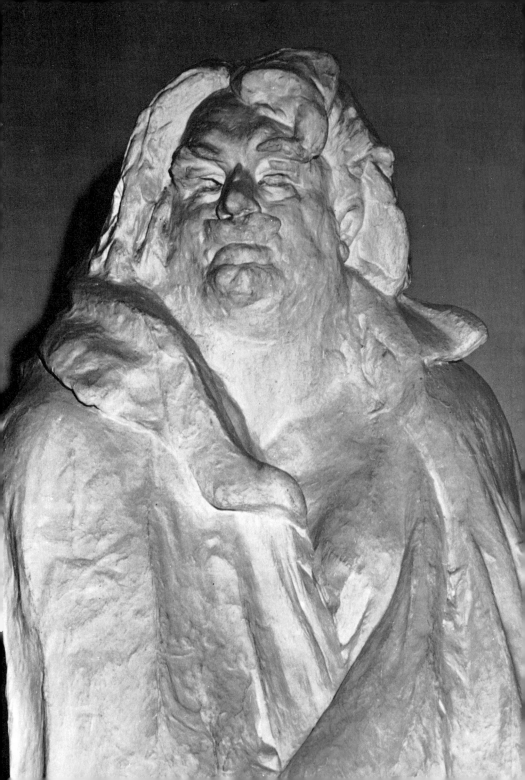

The Société consulted Falguière, who promptly accepted the commission and undertook to complete it in time for the centenary of Balzac's birth, barely ten months away.  Rodin showed no bitterness whatsoever.  Not only did he refuse to bear his fellow-artist a grudge, but their ties of friendship became even closer.  It should be said at once that Falguière was a sterling character and that he did his utmost not to hurt Rodin's feelings.  Knowing that Rodin admired his painting, he sent him a large canvas of nymphs disporting themselves against a rustic background.  Rodin hung it in his drawing-room at Meudon.  To dispel any public doubts about their bonds of friendship, the two men agreed to do busts of each other and exhibit them at the Salon of 1899, where Falguière also showed the maquette of an anecdotal Balzac.

The demonstrations of mutual esteem gratified Rodin and were highly profitable to Falguière.  However, Falguière died before he could complete his monument, the cutting of which was entrusted to Paul Dubois.  The Société des Gens de Lettres seemed to be dogged by misfortune.  The Balzac centenary came and went, but the statue was not unveiled until 1902.  The ceremony, plentifully garnished with rhetoric, developed into a rally in honour of Rodin.

All eyes turned to watch him as he sat there, smiling quietly, and Abel Hermant, president of the Société, presented Falguière's monument to the Municipal Council with the words: ' The work before you is too strong for me to shrink from evoking rival memories here, the name of Falguière too great for me to fear giving offence by uttering the great name of Rodin.  It is my duty to do so, and Falguière, if he could hear me, would never forgive me for failing in that duty.  Silence would be vain—your memory would faithfully repair my omission.  For, even in the presence of the living, tangible *Balzac* we see here, the phantom of the other one persists, haunting, obsessive and unforgettable. ' Hermant's words set his audience alight.  They rose as one man and applauded the sculptor whose statue had been rejected.

Rodin's *Balzac* was banished, but it kept its intense vitality. Standing among the trees and flowers of his garden, it acquired a new and unforeseen dimension. Those who saw it at this period, solitary, mysterious and erect as a menhir with a human face, say that they scarcely recognized it when it was transferred to the noise and bustle of a Paris road junction. Such is the lot of public statuary today. Once conceived as part of a monumental ensemble and the focus of architecture designed to do it honour, urban statuary has become a superficial accessory, flotsam on the fickle tide of fashion, changing ideas and political vicissitudes, haphazardly sited in places where it will not obstruct the traffic too much.

The plaster model and maquettes did appear from time to time, notably in 1908, when Balzac's house in the Rue Berton was opened as a museum. But, even *in absentia,* Rodin's vision of Balzac remained imprinted on the minds of those who had succumbed to its impact. Most of the articles devoted to Rodin placed it in the first rank of his work, and no piece of sculpture ever underwent more frequent or searching analysis.

To quote Rilke: ' The hair reposed on the sturdy neck, and set firmly into the hair was a face gazing and drunk with gazing, a face effervescing with creation: the face of an element. ' Léon Daudet wrote: ' This *Balzac* is at once the Balzac of self-abandonment, of the ailing heart, of *La Comédie humaine.* He takes his place beside Hugo's *Choses vues,* heavy-arteried, head erect, eyes seeking the sun but already invaded by darkness. He has emerged from literary servitude, from marital and emotional stress, and finally entered his dream. He is a dying visionary who looks immortality in the face. It is quite clear, however, that to understand this masterpiece presupposes a knowledge of Balzac's life and work. Rodin spent much time with Balzac enthusiasts, notably my father and Geffroy. He had steeped himself in the conversations about Balzac which recurred in our circle like a refrain of love and admiration. That was why, after many tentative experiments, he created this accurate and extraordinary phantom, whereas the worthy Falguière's version at the end of the Rue Balzac is no more than a portly gentleman of indeterminate appearance. '

The statue was exhibited as a matter of course when the Hôtel Biron museum was opened after the First World War. Georges

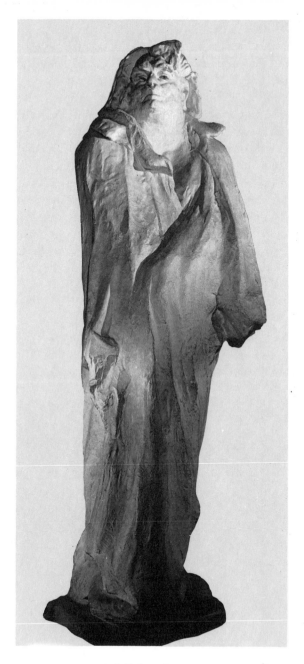

96 *Balzac* 1893-97

Grappe, who became curator in 1926, felt that it was the duty of the state to have it cast in bronze. Two copies were made, one of which was acquired by the Antwerp Museum.

People still toyed with the old idea of erecting the statue in the middle of Paris, especially as it was thought that public opinion had matured sufficiently to accept it. With the same drive and determination that had marked her successful handling of the Hôtel Biron project, Judith Cladel set about forming a committee. Georges Lecomte, a veteran of earlier pro-Rodin campaigns, agreed to take on the chairmanship. After three years of hard work, official wire-pulling and ministerial lobbying (the committee of the Société des Gens de Lettres being by now persuaded that it ought to rectify its predecessors' mistake), it was decided that the *Balzac* should be erected at the intersection of the Boulevard Raspail and the Boulevard Montparnasse.

The official ceremony was a glittering affair. The honour of unveiling the statue went to the two greatest living French sculptors, Maillol and Despiau, who had known Rodin well.

It was 1 July 1939, the eve of the Second World War, and Rodin had been dead for twenty-two years.

# CHAPTER NINE

## The Villa des Brillants

Rose was complaining of ill health, and Rodin had suffered from spells of physical debility himself. They decided to give up their gloomy abode in the Rue des Grands-Augustins and go to live in the country. (The heights of Bellevue were still 'country' in 1894.)

They rented a house in the Chemin Scribe. As yet immune from the passion of modern local authorities for pruning every tree in sight and marshalling houses in orderly rows, the road wound along between acacias and lilacs. The little lattice-work gate was half obscured by honeysuckle and ivy, but the windows on the other side of the house overlooked Mont Valérien and the meadows bordering the Seine.

Rodin went down to the station every day, bound for one or other of his Paris studios but not always for the one where most work awaited him. His aging mistress still quaked at the thought that an interloper might permanently deprive her of the man she had loved so much, for all the heart-ache he had caused her. ' Monsieur Rodin is becoming so difficult, ' she used to tell her friends (she always referred to him as ' Monsieur Rodin '). ' If he ever left me... '

She cross-questioned him sharply in the evenings, but they usually made it up over a plate of good cabbage soup. Rodin had a craze for this national dish. It brought back old memories, and he used to call it the backbone of France. At nightfall he would take Rose by the hand and go for walks in the surrounding

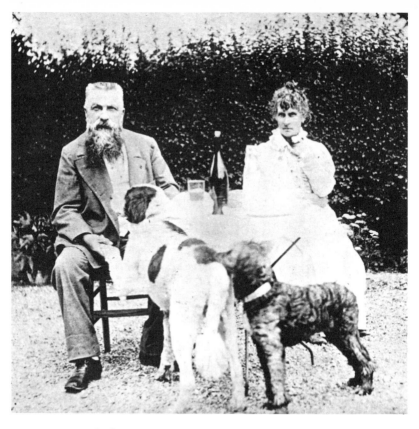

*97 Rodin and Rose Beuret at the Villa des Brillants, Meudon*

country-side. Whatever it was that occupied his thoughts—
whether Victor Hugo, Balzac, or Camille—he seldom spoke.

Since there was not enough room in the charming old house for
a proper studio (he had installed a makeshift one in the loft), he
moved again after only two years. It is hard to tell why he was so
attracted by the ghastly suburban villa which he had discovered on
the hill-side near Meudon, but it was probably because it had a
spacious garden enclosed by orchards and because it, too, overlooked the valley of the Seine. The house was linked with the
main road by a long and almost level avenue of chestnut-trees, but
the garden in front of it fell away steeply. A small pool nestled in

the thick shrubbery. A flight of steps, a drawing-room and dining-room on the ground floor, and two bedrooms—four main rooms of modest size and wholly banal appearance—such was Rodin's Villa des Brillants at the brilliant zenith of his career.

Although nothing was done to beautify the property, it was adorned with works of art and unsystematically enlarged. Shortly after acquiring the place, Rodin added a studio in the form of a large room accessible from the veranda. After the exhibition of 1900, he had his pavilion—a large arcaded hall in mock Louis XVI style—transferred from the Place de l'Alma and re-erected beside the villa.

And then, in the midst of this confusion, Rodin's love of great French architecture asserted itself. The Château d'Issy had, to his horror, fallen prey to a firm of demolition contractors. Rodin succeeded in buying large sections of the façade and had them set up at the bottom of his garden, demolishing the pavilion from the Exposition Universelle at the same time. ' You can't imagine how horrified I was to see the crime being committed, ' he said. ' Tear down that glorious building ? It had the same effect on me as if those criminals had disembowelled a beautiful virgin before my very eyes! ' (Watched over by *The Thinker,* the simple but moving tomb of the sculptor and his wife now lies in front of this façade.)

The interior of the Villa des Brillants and its annexes was a complete jumble. Like many artists, Rodin was extremely sensitive to the quality of his material possessions but had a blind spot where their arrangement was concerned.

The prevailing fashion was for white-enamelled furniture. At Meudon, white furniture jostled period pieces, pedestal tables and show-cases—show-cases of every shape and description. In the drawing-room cum studio the frame of a Renaissance bed served as a protective container for fragile specimens.

Almost all the money Rodin earned went on his collections. He bought judiciously because the presence of beautiful things gave him pleasure. His acquisitions included Egyptian bronzes, Roman marbles, Greek vases, Persian miniatures, statues of

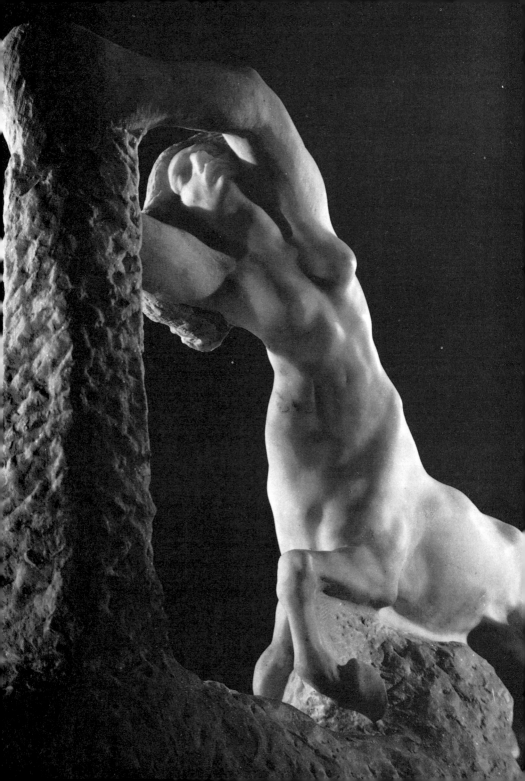

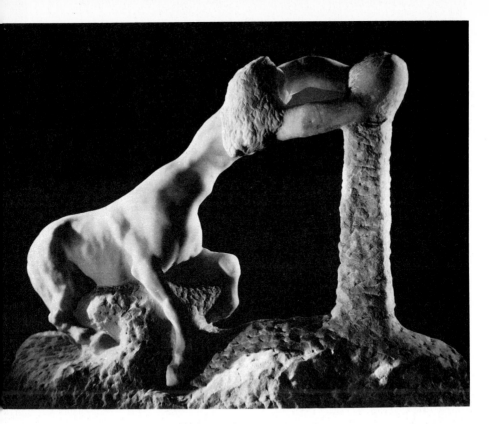

99 *The Centauress* 1889

various periods, contemporary paintings, among them a very
fine Renoir torso and Van Gogh's famous *Père Tanguy,* and a large
Gothic Crucifix which had accompanied him on previous moves.
His curiosity was that of the genuine artist who does not seek to
fathom the secrets of others but rediscovers something of himself
in an authentic work of art and spontaneously communes with it.
His enthusiasm had nothing in common with the craze for carefully selected bric-à-brac which was rife among fashionable artists
of his day.   Eager to appear ' arty ', they draped their furniture in
Italian brocades and Spanish embroidery, covered their floors in
Persian carpets and their walls with kakemonos, sprinkled their
rooms with lamps, pieces of majolica, lecterns, gilded censers,

203

Etruscan vases and hookahs, and displayed Romanesque madonnas cheek by jowl with bazaar monstrosities. It was essential for them to show off their success and originality if they were to keep prices high and create the sort of atmosphere which would soften up prospective purchasers and impress society women.

Rodin's untidiness was anything but premeditated. He invariably did as he pleased without worrying about the wishes or convenience of those around him. With the advent of success and ' pocket money ', he took great delight in surrounding himself with pieces which, like his Roman replica of Praxiteles' *Satyr*, proved a continual source of joy and instruction to him. Although he loved nature and never tired of the sight of a beautiful naked body, he retained his interest in works of art and continued to seek inspiration from them until his life's end. [23]

Rilke has left us his impressions of this ' museum ': ' A highly individual selection of classical statues and fragments... containing

100 *The Illusions* 1895

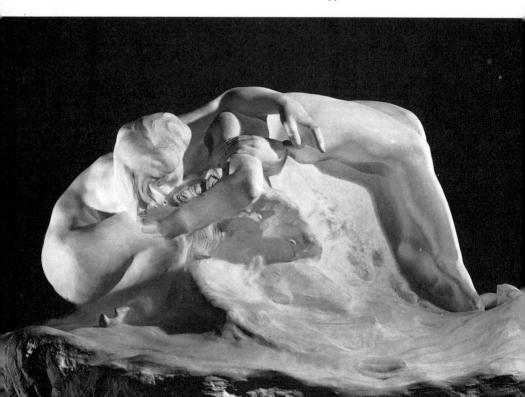

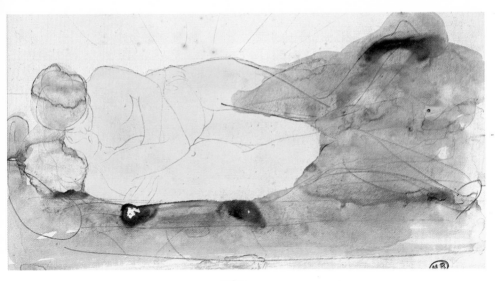

101 *Bilitis*

works of Greek and Egyptian origin, some of which would stand out even in the galleries of the Louvre.   In another room, behind some Attic vases, are pictures which one can identify without consulting the signatures—Ribot, Monet, Carrière, Van Gogh, Zuloaga—and, among other less readily identifiable pictures, a few by Falguière, who was a great painter.   There are plenty of presentation copies, of course.   The books alone form an extensive and peculiarly autonomous library, independent of their owner's choice but not haphazard.   All these pieces are carefully tended and revered, but no one expects them to create a pleasant or comfortable atmosphere.   One almost feels as if one had never seen works of art of very different styles and periods endowed with such individual and undiminished strength as they possess here, where they do not have the pretentious air of a collection and are not forced to contribute their wealth of beauty to a general scheme which bears no relation to them.   Someone once said that they were kept like a beautiful menagerie.   In fact, this is a fair description of Rodin's relationship with the things around him.   He often moves among them at night.   And when he does so—stealthily, as if reluctant to wake them all—and ends by carrying his small candle up to a classical marble which stirs, awakes, and rises abruptly, it is life itself that he has gone in quest of and is admiring—"life, that miracle", as he once wrote.'

Rodin also enjoyed working and supervising assistants in his cluttered studios. However big and crowded they were, human beings were always outnumbered by the teeming products of his imagination—maquettes of all sizes, plaster models, half-finished marbles, and countless sketches, all preserved for the benefit of future art historians. Figures stood in serried ranks everywhere, on the floor, in glass cases, on tables and pedestals. There were fragments of classical sculpture in the garden, but these were arranged with care. Nymphs' torsos gleamed among the foliage, and a plump Buddha at the entrance to the villa studio informed visitors that they were entering the master's sanctum.

The 1900 exhibition, summarizing the achievements of one century and heralding the advent of another, was now in preparation. It not only brought together 22,600 French mayors and the President of the Republic for one of the most colossal banquets of all time but produced an influx of foreign visitors from every quarter of the world, attracted to Paris by French elegance and French novelties. Modern art now enjoyed official recognition. *Olympia* had found its way into the Palais du Luxembourg and the state had accepted the Caillebotte collection. Side by side with earlier masterpieces of French art and works by Salon artists, the innovators (with Impressionists at full strength) were represented at the ' Centennale '. Rodin was naturally allotted a place among them, but it was restricted like all the rest.

Despite the revolutionary nature of his sculpture, Rodin was far from revolutionary in his behaviour. He was born poor and remained so until his fifties, but he never aspired to be a rebel. He loved his country and family, counted his *sous*, and accepted his fate. Although involved in working-class life, he seems to have known little or nothing of the working-class movements and socialist trends of the nineteenth century. An artist first and foremost, he readily submitted to instruction, revered the ancient world, and—in reaction to those of his own period—cherished the sculptors, painters and architects of the eighteenth century. However, when his personality finally asserted itself it did so in opposition to that of his teachers, and he isolated himself so completely that he remains without antecedents or descendants in the history of art. He never dreamed of posing as an original artist. Instinct and personal genius were what conduced to the originality which placed his work above and outside its time.

His solitary status in sculpture was reflected in his status at the Exposition Universelle. He had decided to show the full range of his work. Since it was out of the question to do this within the precincts of the exhibition proper, he had a large pavilion erected outside. Thanks to the intervention of powerful friends, the Municipal Council finally, after much prevarication, granted him permission to build in the Place de l'Alma, on the corner of the Cours-la-Reine and Avenue Montaigne, that is to say, beside the exhibition gates. Three admirers of his work each advanced 20,000 francs towards the cost of building the pavilion which was later re-erected at Meudon, and he made up the difference himself.

In addition to 136 sculptures, Rodin exhibited fourteen rough models so as to bring the total to 150, the figure he wanted to appear in the catalogue. They were retrospective of his artistic career, ranging from *The Man with the Broken Nose* to *Mauvais génies entraînant l'homme* (Evil spirits carrying off man), his most recent work. *Balzac* also figured in the collection, as, for the first time, did *The Gates of Hell,* unfinished, awe-inspiring and almost incomprehensible.

The exhibition devoted less space to industrial inventions and gadgetry than its predecessors. A wave of aestheticism had encouraged the organizers to give pride of place to the decorative and plastic arts. There were curious amalgams (the most interesting but most ephemeral being that of Art Nouveau) born of the urge for innovation and revealing a wide variety of influences: Pre-Raphaelite, Japanese, Baroque of convoluted Louis Quinze descent, bastard allusions to the classical spirit, and the androgynous style, graceful, florid, intricate, and overloaded with

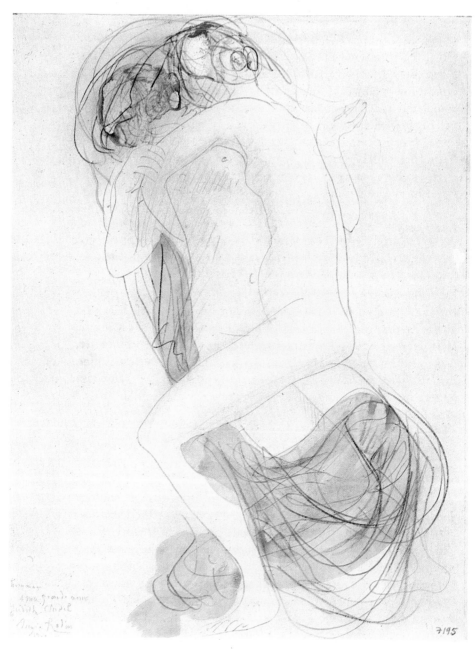

102 *Two women embracing*

ornamentation. Woman, a precious object preciously treated, was celebrated in a sort of secular liturgy. ' La Parisienne ' dominated the arch above the main entrance, and visitors gazed with wonder at Loie Fuller's strange and colourful gyrations and the ritual gestures of Sada Yacco.

Rodin laid a deliberate emphasis on his nudes and his most passionately sensual groups. He showed very few busts on the fair assumption that a surfeit of them would bore people. In fact, visitors to the pavilion avidly scanned them for evidence of emotional ties between the sculptor and his sitters.

It was hardly to be expected that the general public would flock to see an exhibition devoted to a single sculptor, especially as it was situated outside the main grounds and exacted an entrance fee of one franc. Rodin's visitors may have been of high quality, but they did not batter the doors down to gain admittance.

The catalogue, bound in a hazy cover bearing Carrière's signature, was aimed at establishing the reputation of the luckless author of *Balzac* once and for all. A long introduction by Arsène Alexandre, who compared Rodin's sculpture with Wagner's music and condemned the public's failure to understand both these great artists, was preceded by tributes from Carrière, Jean-Paul Laurens, Monet, and Besnard. There followed descriptive notes on the 136 main works.

Rodin, who had been dreading a heavy loss, was not displeased with the final reckoning. ' Few of the entrance fees I was counting on so much, ' he wrote, ' but plenty of purchases. ' A number of museums had acquired major pieces. Copenhagen was devoting a special room to his work. Philadelphia, Hamburg, Dresden and Budapest had all placed commissions, and there would undoubtedly be more to come. He had grossed 200,000 francs of which 60,000 had to be set against the cost of executing works in marble and bronze. That left 140,000. Although his liabilities had by now risen to 150,000, he felt extremely satisfied.

He had been the subject of much comment in recent years, both favourable and unfavourable. From now on, his work was

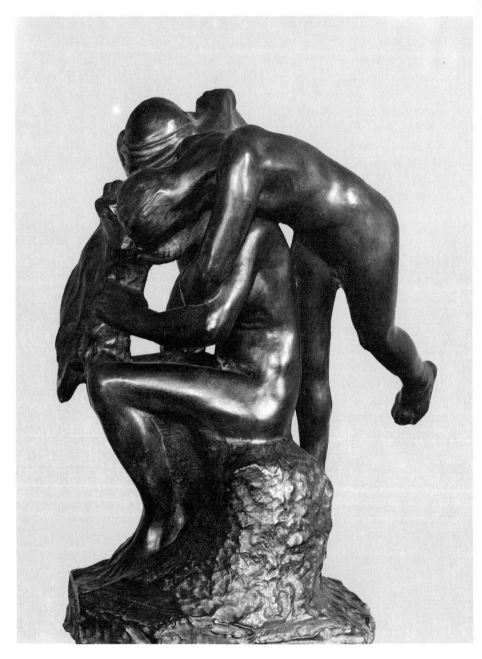

103 *The Evil Genius* 1899

accepted by those who, at this period, had to constitute his public. At the age of sixty, on the threshold of the twentieth century, he was beginning to taste fame and fortune.

The Villa des Brillants became a sort of shrine, both to his disciples and to his steadily increasing circle of admirers. It was a meeting-place which fascinated the Parisian art world and made its influence felt on the other side of the globe. Rodin had achieved the status of an international star.

104 *Grief-Stricken Danaid* 1889

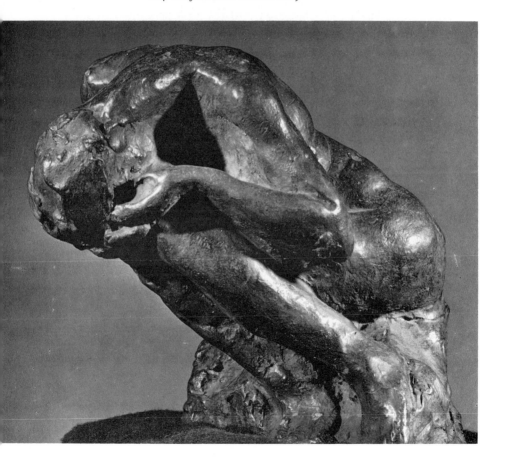

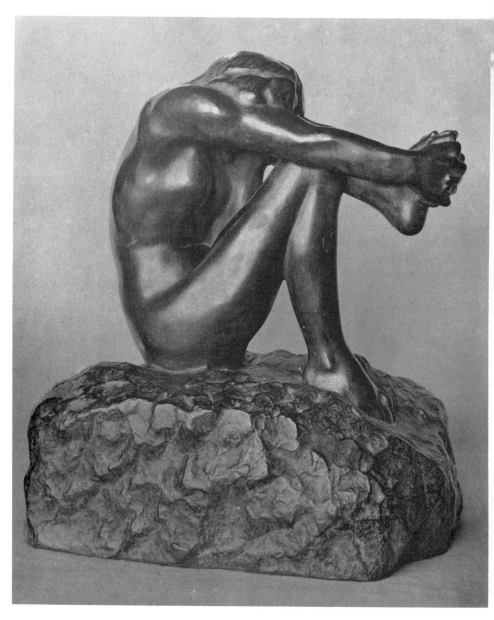

105 *Despair* 1890

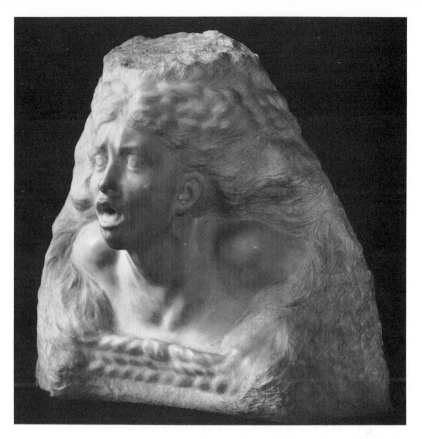

106 *The Storm* 1898

In 1908, in response to a provocative article belatedly accusing him of having practised a deliberate ' hoax ' on the Gens de Lettres, he gave an interview to a reporter from *Matin* and lectured him in lofty terms:

' I have stopped fighting for my sculpture. It has been able to defend itself for a long time now. To say that I scamped my *Balzac* for fun is an insult which would have infuriated me in the old days. Now I just ignore such things and carry on with my work. My life is one long course of study. To scoff at others would be to scoff at myself. If truth is doomed to die, my *Balzac* will be smashed to pieces by generations to come. If truth is

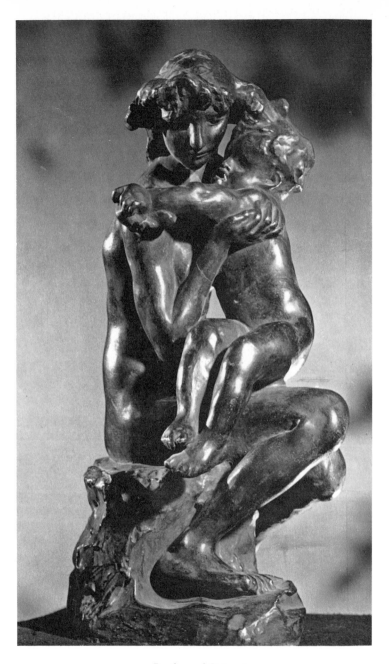

107 *Brother and Sister* 1890

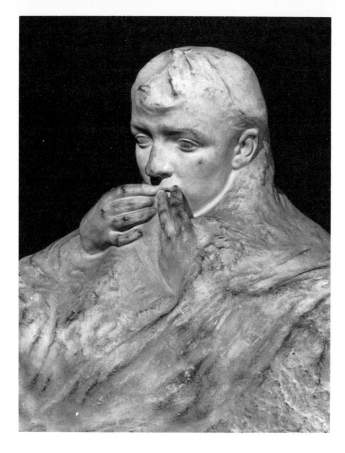

108 *The Farewell* 1892

imperishable, I predict that my statue will make its way in the
world. While we are still on the subject of this malicious
rumour, which will be slow to subside, I should like to say
something. It needs to be said, and said loudly. This work,
which people have laughed at and tried to make fun of because
they cannot destroy it, is the end product of my entire life and the
very hub of my aesthetic. I was a changed man from the day I
first conceived it. I developed along radical lines, forging
links between the great traditions of the past and my own time—
links which grow stronger with every passing day. Some may

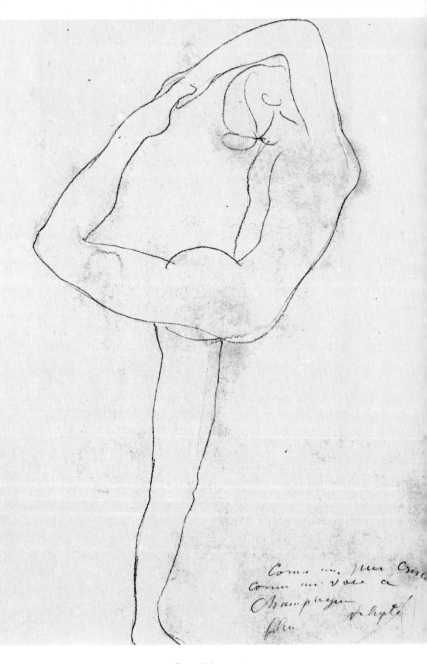

109 *Dance Movement*

laugh at this statement.  I am inured to this and have no fear of sarcasm.  I tell you flatly, the *Balzac* provided me with an inspiring point of departure because its effect is not confined to my own person, because it constitutes a precept and axiom which is still being debated and will continue to be debated for a long time to come.  The battle goes on, as it must do.  *Balzac* is opposed by the exponents of doctrinal aesthetics, the vast majority of the public, and most of the press critics.  No matter; by force or by persuasion it will clear itself a way to the enlightened.  Young sculptors come to see it here and think of it while retracing their steps in the direction prescribed by their ideals. '

This high-flown declaration went further than the truth.  Even though Rodin was amply justified in defending the statue which had made so much ink flow and provoked so many idiotic statements, it was hardly fair of him to call it a point of departure and say that he had developed along radical lines thereafter.  He certainly became a ' changed man ', but this was mainly because the rumours which surrounded his name and contributed to his rise in the world exerted an effect on his personal behaviour.  He remained the same man, but being unsophisticated by nature— even naive in some respects—he was not immune to the clouds of incense that rose around him.  Having scaled the heights, he continued to state his views with the same quiet, smiling, disarming candour that had always marked his pronouncements.

His work had not changed course, but it had become rarefied. He resumed his former studies and pursued them successfully, placing greater reliance than before on his first-class assistants. Admirable sculptures still came out of his studios, but he did not tackle any more large-scale monuments.  He can hardly have been encouraged to do so by memories of his wearisome disputes with government authorities and of all the research he had devoted to projects which came to nothing.  Distinguished writers, politicians and diplomats now descended on Meudon. In 1908 Rodin received a visit from Edward VII, whom he honoured by staging a successful show in his studio (tidied for the occasion).  When visitors asked if they might pay their

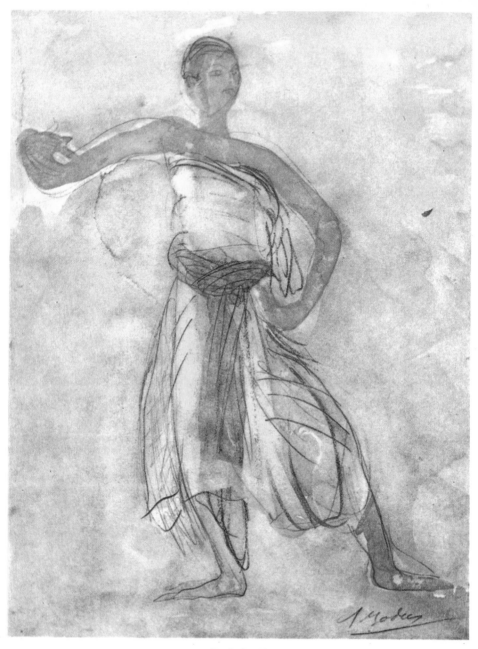

110 *Cambodian Dancer*

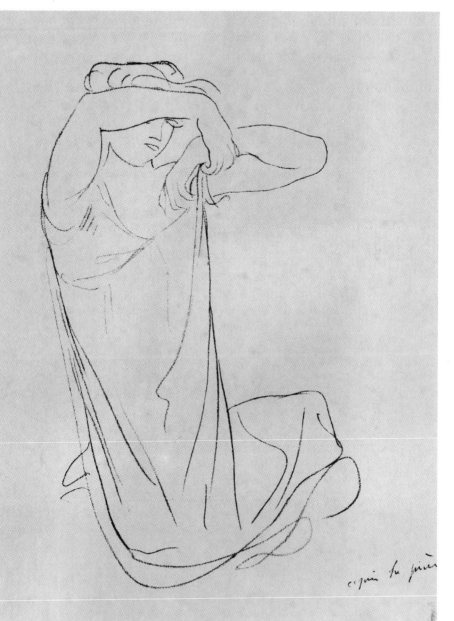

111  *After the Prayer*

respects to ' Madame Rodin ', as they occasionally did out of politeness, Rose would leave her housework and emerge, wiping her hands on a blue apron.

Although Rodin did not go out of his way to solicit tokens of official esteem, he accepted them readily enough. He was not only invited to receptions at the Élysée and big ministerial banquets but accorded all the honours normally reserved for members of the Institut. He swiftly climbed three rungs of the Légion d'honneur ladder and received national awards from almost all the countries which were in contact with him or had exhibited his work.

London fêted him when his *St John the Baptist* was unveiled there, and enthusiasm was so intense that students from the Slade unhitched the horses from his official carriage and hauled him through the streets in triumph. He paid several more visits to London. Guests at banquets expected him to respond to speeches of welcome by saying a few words of thanks, but he was so inept at public speaking that he expressed his gratitude with a mute wave of the hand. He received similar honours from the municipality of Prague, which he had presented with a copy of *The Burghers of Calais*. Although patriotic sentiments had always deterred him from accepting invitations to Germany, he added an honorary doctorate from Jena to the degree previously conferred on him by Oxford. As a self-taught man who had been forced to abandon his primary education, he did not appear to set much store by these academic trappings.

In 1903, some young sculptors and assistants staged a much homelier function in the garden of an inn at Vélizy. Bourdelle, who had erected a scaled-down copy of *The Walking Man* on a pedestal there, delivered an address so moving that Mirbeau was reduced to tears. All Rodin's friends and assistants were there—Maillol, Schnegg, Dejean, Arnold, Pompon—and the fair sex was well represented. Isadora Duncan, fresh from her early successes in Paris, danced in his honour. Rodin and Bourdelle, both of whom regarded her as the very embodiment of the dance, immortalized her in a series of remarkable sketches.

Although he spent most of the day on his feet, working in his various studios or tramping from one to the other, often returning to Meudon in the evening by boat and having to climb the hill to his house, Rodin was so robust that he felt an additional need for country walks. Meudon offered plenty of scope in this respect. Versailles was a favourite haunt of his. To please Rose, who was an indefatigable worker but disliked long walks, he used to drive there with her.

He recorded only a few impressions of the château and gardens of Versailles. Among them is the following note, which was probably jotted down on a scrap of paper or one of his cuffs (his usual method of capturing a sensation at its freshest): ' This part of the garden derives its religious character from the lovely vase in the centre of the flower-bed, and this religious character communicates itself to the trees which cluster round the circular walk. ' Rodin's observations were succinct but all-embracing.

His journeys were almost always undertaken for professional reasons. He liked being at the Villa des Brillants and saw no need to wrestle with the complexities of travel and hotel life. In 1906 he allowed himself to be talked into visiting Andalusia with his friend Zuloaga, the painter. It seems, however, that sumptuous Hispano-Moorish decoration was quite incapable of effacing the impression left on him by the little churches of France.

The same year he travelled to Marseilles, this time aflame with enthusiasm. The object of his visit was to catch another glimpse of the Cambodian dancers whom he had studied so assiduously while they were in Paris. Some of his most entrancing sketches were devoted to them. ' What astounded me most of all, ' he wrote, ' was to rediscover the very principles of classical art in a Far Eastern art which had been unknown to me until then. Confronted by pieces of very ancient sculpture, so ancient that no date can be assigned to them, the mind gropes its way back towards their origins across thousands of years: and then, quite suddenly, living nature appears, and it is as though these ancient stones had come to life once more! The Cambodians gave me all that I used to admire in ancient marbles, supplementing it with the mystery and suppleness of the Far East. How enchanting to find humanity true to itself across time and space! But there is one essential precondition of this constancy: traditional and religious feeling. I have never distinguished between religious art and art. When religion disappears, art disappears too. All Greek and Roman masterpieces—all our own masterpieces—are religious. Sisowath and her daughter Samphondry, the directress of the royal ballet company, have taken great care to maintain the strictest orthodoxy in these dances, which is why they have retained their beauty. After all, it was the same idea, varying only in form, which preserved art in Athens, Chartres, Cambodia—everywhere. Just as I recognized classical beauty in the dances of Cambodia, so I recognized Cambodian beauty at Chartres, shortly after my visit to Marseilles, in the posture of the great Angel, which is not so very far removed from a dance movement.' [24]

# CHAPTER TEN

# The Cathedrals

Rodin's stay in Belgium had been succeeded by a tour of the churches and cathedrals of France. He never tired of studying them. To him, they were sublimely instructive, a pure expression of French genius and a lost link with the ancient world. He was a stubborn traditionalist in this respect. In his view, all the beauty handed down from age to age had disappeared after the eighteenth century because that was when man's understanding of nature disappeared, and because the spirit of simplicity had strayed into the jungle of progress and experimentation.

He resumed his solitary tours as often as he could, watching the interplay of light and shade at different hours of the day and seasons of the year, perpetually stirred by the work of ' these serious artists who worked with a joy perceptible everywhere ' and by ' these great lights and shadows sustained by the only planes necessary, neither thin nor poor because of the predominance of half-tones '. He recognized his own art in the work of these early craftsmen, whom he used to describe as disciples rather than pupils.

His book, *Les Cathédrales de France,* consists of a selection from the countless random jottings in which he recorded his impressions of pilgrimages undertaken over a period of more than thirty years. The original edition, published by Colin in 1914 and illustrated by Rodin himself, was followed by another in 1921.

Although Rodin insisted that the book should be prefaced by ' an introduction to medieval art, ' the reader should not scan it

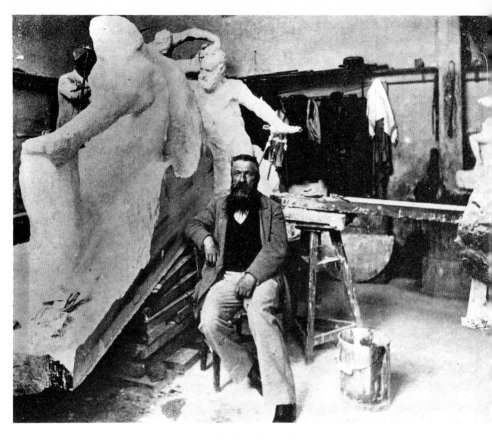

112 *Rodin in his studio* 1905

for too many archaeological particulars. There is no doubt that
he instinctively grasped the great laws of balance which govern
Gothic architecture and invest it with strength and unity. There is
equally little doubt that he sensed the subtle complicity between
sculptural and architectural modelling. However, this is an
enthusiastic and exuberant book, and we moderns are hard to
please.

'To understand these lines, so tenderly modelled, traced and
caressed, one has to be lucky enough to be in love...' Just as
Rodin himself diffused this love of the heart and senses everywhere,
so he sensed it everywhere, in nature, in the landscapes and skies

which shared in the existence of these ancient buildings, and in the women who came to kneel in them. This becomes evident when we hear him speak of mouldings which ' represent and convey the master mason's whole idea ' and which skilled and humble craftsmen ' modelled like a woman's lips '.

He managed to combine his love of feminine and architectural beauty. At Beaugency, there was ' a young French girl whom I saw in church... A little lily of the valley in bloom in a new gown... The lines of her adolescent body were still innocent of passion. What modesty and grace! If that young girl had eyes to see, she would recognize her own portrait in all the portals of our Gothic churches, for she is the embodiment of our style, our art, our native land. Sitting behind her, I could see only the general lines of her body and the velvety pink of her childish-womanly cheek, but she raised her head and turned away from her little book for a moment, disclosing the profile of a young angel. She was the young French provincial girl in all her charm: simplicity, honesty, tenderness, intelligence, and the smiling serenity of true innocence, which spreads like a gentle infection and brings peace to the most troubled heart. '

Nevers prompted him to reflect on the factors common to great architecture of every age, and he related the ancient world to the subtle emotions aroused by Gothic vaults: ' The spirit which created the Parthenon is the same as that which created the Cathedral. Divine beauty! It is simply that there is more refinement here. There is, I venture to say, a luminous mist in which light slumbers evenly, as though in little valleys. People who have visited these naves during the morning hours will understand what I mean. '

Although the Gothic cathedral stirred him more than any other, his admiration embraced all the great ages of church architecture. He had spurned Romanesque art in his youth, but now... ' What amazing beauty of style! I thought it all frightful when I was young. That was because I was short-sighted. I was ignorant like all the rest. Later on, when I saw what people were doing in my own day, I realized who the real barbarians were. '

Again: ' Romanesque is the father of all French styles. Full of restrained power, it gave birth to all our architecture. Posterity will have to pay constant heed to its principles. A new style containing the germ of life, it was perfect from its earliest phase onwards—nor has the horn of plenty run dry. It is inexhaustible. '

His passion for stylistic periods was not indiscriminate. He despised the period which lay between the zenith of thirteenth-century Gothic and the Renaissance, and cherished an even greater contempt for what had been produced after the great decline which he dated in the region of 1820. At a time when the spirit of Viollet-le-Duc reigned supreme, he probably understood the Renaissance better than anyone else. Here is how he extols the doorway of the little church at Monjavoult: ' The divine Renaissance, free from the idolatry of the metropolis, produced as much beauty for peasants as for princes. '

He was also alone, certainly at that time, in sensing the importance of the communion between a building and its district or surroundings: ' At Blois there is a street whose foreshortened view is so pleasing that it has the effect of a building when seen from that angle. It has a discreet charm which caresses the artist's heart and eye, and which I have sampled in many provincial towns. One rediscovers, in views of this kind, the monumental charm which is the crowning glory of the small town. '

Rodin saw all beauty as the handiwork of God. Speaking of cathedral sculpture and architecture, he declared that ' art and religion furnish mankind with all the certainties which it needs to sustain life and which are unheeded by ages imbued with indifference '. He frequented churches as a religious man, however, not as a believer. His remarkable description of the sight and sound of high mass at Limoges shows that, despite the ' well-loved Latin syllables ', he had entirely forgotten his novitiate. He approached the mass as an aesthete. Indeed, the following abrupt comment is indicative of a feeling that it was aimed at him personally: ' The mystery is accomplished and the god sacrificed, as, daily following his example, are the men of genius inspired by him. '

His passion for churches exposed him to deep and painful wounds. He was obsessed with what he called ' the modern crime ', and continually reverted to it. This crime was ' the neglect of cathedrals—worse still, their murder and debasement '. Rodin attacked the thoughtless architects who had failed to grasp the meaning of balance, moderation, humility, and love. He inveighed against insensitive restorers and all those who had forgotten that cathedrals were houses and citadels of the people, and he vented his anger with unusual eloquence:

' I am one of the last witnesses of a dying art. The love which inspired it is spent. The wonders of the past are subsiding into limbo with nothing to take their place, and night will be upon us very soon. The French are hostile to the wealth of beauty which glorifies their race. Without anyone raising a finger to protect these treasures, they smite and smash them out of spite, ignorance and stupidity or defile them on the pretext of restoring them. (Don't reproach me for having said all this before. I would gladly repeat it over and over again for as long as the evil persists!) How ashamed I am of my own time, and how frightened by the future! I wonder, with horror, how much responsibility for this crime rests with each individual. Am I not branded like the rest ? '

He strove to understand how modern man, that privileged individual, could live so close to so many things of beauty without seeing them. ' Our museums present us with Egypt, Assyria, India, Persia, Greece and Rome. Our native soil bears the sublime traces of Gothic and Romanesque, as well as those miracles of charm, our old houses, beautifully proportioned up to and including the First Empire, severely elegant in their bygone style and endowed with a grace which is eloquent in its very restraint and sometimes expresses itself in a simple string course devoid of moulding. All this we have, yet our architects produce the ramshackle stuff you know so well. Casting from the life, that cancerous sore in the side of art, thrives among sculptors. '

He wanted his book on cathedrals—a word which he applied symbolically to churches and ancient monuments in general—to

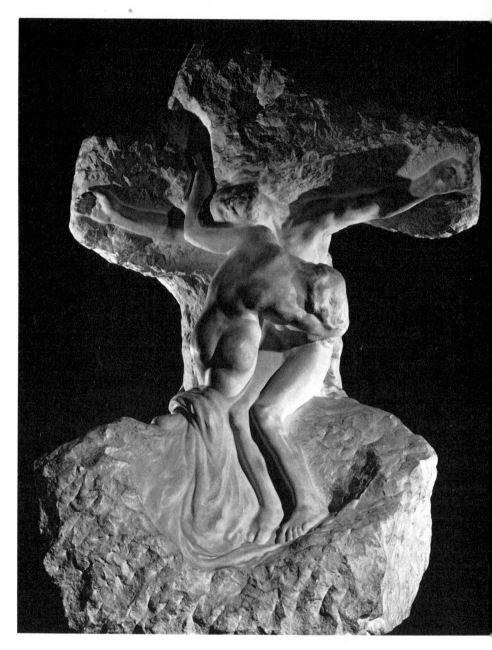

113 *Christ and Mary Magdalene* 1894

be a book of protest and action. He raised his voice in a call for help. ' The country dies when the cathedral dies, struck down and violated by its own offspring. We can no longer pray, in front of these object replacements of our stones. Living stone— destroyed piecemeal—has given way to dead substitutes.' He sang of his love for cathedrals because he wanted to teach the masses to see and be moved by what they saw.

Rheims Cathedral, of which he recorded impressions gathered at all hours of the day and night, was the building which distressed him most, even before it was damaged by fire. ' I think I am more shocked by the restorations here than anywhere else. They are nineteenth century, and remain unconvincing in spite of the patina they have acquired in the fifty years since they were carried out. And these follies of half a century ago aspire to a place among masterpieces! All restorations are copies, which is why they are doomed from the outset. Nothing—let me repeat this with a fervour born of fidelity—should be copied except nature. Copying works of art is forbidden by the very principle of art. Restorations—and I should like to stress this point too—are always soft and hard at the same time. That is how you can recognize them. Skill alone cannot produce beauty. Take the right-hand gable in the façade at Rheims, for instance. It has not been restored. Fragments of torso and drapery—massive and masterly works of art—project from its mighty bulk. Even without understanding it properly, anyone with any sensitivity could recognize the thrill of creation. Although broken in places like the ones in the British Museum, these fragments are, like them, wholly admirable. Now look at the other gable, which has been restored and rebuilt: it has been debased...

' Again, take the restored capitals representing branches and flowers: the colour is uniform, flat and expressionless because the workmen used their tools head-on, at right angles to the surface of the stone. This technique produces a harsh and homogeneous effect—in other words, no effect at all. The secret of the ancients is not unduly complicated, at least on this point, and it would be easy enough to revive their technique. They handled their tools obliquely—the only means of achieving modelled effects and of obtaining oblique surfaces which accentuate and vary the relief. But our contemporaries care nothing for variety. They are oblivious of it. In these capitals, which consist of four tiers of foliage, each tier is as pronounced as the other three. This makes them look like common-or-garden wickerwork baskets. Who says we are making progress? There are times when taste prevails, and there are times like the present...

'Don't replace anything, do you understand? Don't restore anything. The moderns are as incapable of duplicating the smallest Gothic marvel as they are of reproducing the marvels of nature. Another few years' maltreatment of the ailing past by the murderous present, and our loss with be complete and irremediable.'

Rodin knew what he was talking about. Far from trying to imitate, he concentrated exclusively on nature. To him, this was the law from which all other laws derived.

Interest in ancient monuments was far less widespread in Rodin's day than it is in our own. He often noted, on entering a cathedral, that he was the only visitor in sight. The architecture of the past was the province of archaeologists who probed its origins and influences, determined its dates, and analysed it from every angle. They approached it with none of the fervour and sense of poetry which inflamed Rodin, took no interest in the dilapidated condition of such buildings or the butchery inflicted on them by restorers.

Rodin protested against the substitution of copies for originals, copies which in his opinion possessed no more merit than reproductions of antique furniture manufactured in the Faubourg Saint-Antoine. 'A living art does not restore the works of the past,' he proclaimed, 'it continues them.' No one listened to his lone voice or understood what he was saying. It was not until quite recently that people abandoned the falsification of architecture and sculpture. Here, too, Rodin was a precursor.

Though no great scholar, Rodin had a taste for literature—even literature of his own creation. The older he became the greater his urge to record the ideas which surged through his mind. He jotted them down on scraps of paper, couched in disjointed and incomplete phrases, or dictated them to a secretary. One of the ambitions of his latter years was to persuade a big publisher to bring out a miscellany entitled *Pensées,* but his memory was failing and his mind becoming too muddled for such a scheme to materialize.

One of his secretaries was the poet Charles Morice—a curious choice. A friend of Villiers de L'Isle-Adam, Mallarmé and Verlaine, Morice was intimately associated with the Symbolist movement and had become its chief theoretician. Among other things, he decreed that Symbolism must acquire a vocabulary ' which has virtually nothing in common with the ordinary language of the streets or the newspapers '. This attitude of mind scarcely equipped Morice for the task of editing his employer's shrewd but unsystematic observations.

Like most of those who were close to Rodin, Morice cherished an unbounded admiration for him. He was commissioned to prepare *Les Cathédrales* for publication, and did his best to knock it into literary shape. The book was rewritten scores of times, but never to Rodin's satisfaction. He made repetitive additions and accused Morice of cutting his favourite passages. Seeing his manuscripts pruned and embellished with recondite words, he declared that he could not recognize his original train of thought.

The fact was that Rodin could communicate his impressions and demonstrate his keenness of perception in a very few words, however badly strung together. On the other hand, his notes contained too many grammatical blunders and comical schoolboy howlers for them to have made a book without prior editing.

Rodin blithely used members of the Academy, both actual and prospective, as ghost-writers. Two authors of his acquaintance, Gabriel Hanotaux and Louis Gillet, were invited to look over the manuscript of *Les Cathédrales.* Gillet who was a close friend, did the real work. He went to see Rodin every week at the Hôtel Biron and lunched with him at a ' cabbies' eating-house ' in the Rue de Grenelle. Nobody could have been better qualified to edit Rodin's notes than this knowledgeable and sympathetic interpreter of medieval architecture. Above all, he took such delight in the spontaneous freshness of Rodin's remarks that he was careful not to spoil their flavour by injecting too much of his own personality.

Gillet was the current curator of Châalis Abbey, where Rodin stayed with him for several days. In a letter to his friend Romain Rolland, he wrote: ' I am temporarily acting as Rodin's secretary, polishing manuscripts full of divine things. That man writes as he draws—poetry itself. They are only notes and sketches, but enough to turn the Noailles and d'Houvilles green with envy: the charm of a Firdausi floral carpet. ' [25]

# CHAPTER ELEVEN

# Poor little flower of the field

Rodin was a gentleman now. He entertained members of high society. 1901 saw his appointment as chairman of the jury of the Salon de la Société Nationale. It may seem strange that he should have been attracted to the Salons and have lent his name to such an agglomeration of mediocrity, but he knew what he was doing. According to Renoir, who spoke from first-hand experience, there were barely fifteen art-lovers in Paris ' capable of appreciating a painter without the Salon '. How many were capable of appreciating a sculptor whose reputation had not received the same seal of approval ?

Naive as he was in other respects, Rodin took a realistic view of his artistic career. He had always conceded that, however great its defects, a Salon offered the only road to professional success. What was the point of parading one's contempt when the main thing was to win over an uncomprehending public and dispel its incomprehension ? By refusing to exhibit, the Impressionists had burned the bridges which might have kept them in touch with the world of art, and the only effect was to delay the recognition which was their due.

Rodin's persistence did not depend on a mere choice of methods. What mattered was that he never abandoned his principles, never made the smallest concession where his art was concerned. He approached officialdom by the narrow gate—a gate which was often slammed in his face. He presented himself cap in hand, but his freedom of spirit, steadfast attitude and stubborn refusal to compromise, even on details, compelled people to raise their hats to him in turn.

Success inevitably affected his outward behaviour. Taciturn, shy and solitary until his fifties, he now trod the paths of glory with ease, as if it were the most natural thing in the world. Prominent figures clamoured for introductions to him. He was surrounded by a little court composed of society women as well as pupils, assistants and secretaries. His diffidence and inability to converse on any subject save sculpture proved an asset. He shrouded himself in mystery, and his silences were respected as the refusal of genius to squander itself in idle conversation.

The burly physique and brooding gaze, occasionally illuminated by a flash of fire, the Jove-like beard and aristocratic profile—all these attributes combined to give him an air of distinction. Whether working in his studio swathed in a linen smock which fell toga-like to his ankles or impeccably dressed in frock coat and top hat, he always preserved his dignity. He loathed bohemian untidiness and became increasingly dandified as he grew older. A hairdresser visited him every morning. There was nothing in his outward appearance to distinguish him from a banker or politician.

This is not to say that the change in his fortunes made him vain. He was not in the least dazzled by success. Even though he devoted more time to social contacts, and even though the ladies who shuddered at his daring statues paid him attentions which he returned with interest, he remained the hard-working artist he had always been. The main difference was that he now knew that anything which bore his signature would command admiration as a matter of course.

The only fly in the ointment was the presence of Rose Beuret. She, poor woman, had not changed. Long since bereft of the meagre charms of youth, she looked what she was, an uncouth peasant-woman. Not only had she never understood her protector's work, but it is probable that she never even tried to fathom why he applied himself to his peculiar calling with such fervour. She was content to remain the humble housewife, living modestly

234

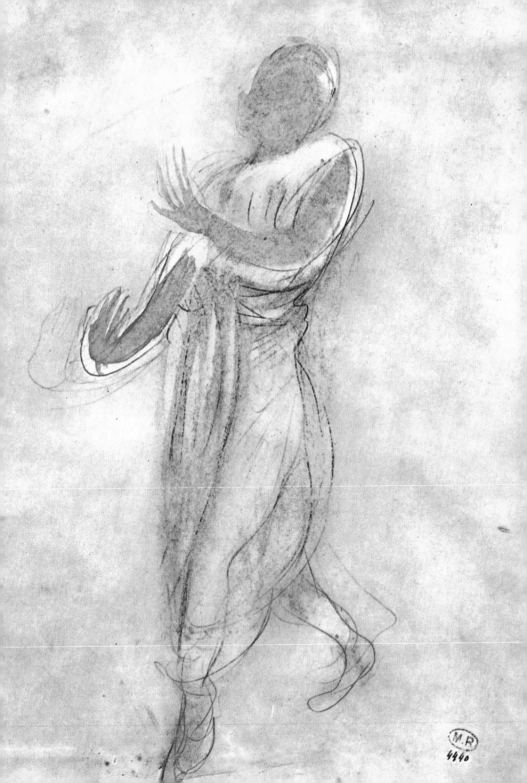

in his shadow and serving him with a devotion which never flagged, however exacting his demands. Rodin never introduced her to anyone. Even when he was working at Sèvres, he surprised his friends by meeting her outside in the road or in the park at Saint-Cloud when she came to fetch him in the evenings, almost as if he were ashamed to produce her.

Now that Rodin was rich, celebrated and lionized, the rift between them widened. The circles he moved in were far from shocked by illicit relationships as long as they were glamorous. If not, it was better to keep them dark.

Rose's demeanour was that of a whipped cur given to sudden fits of rage. She was increasingly gnawed by jealousy, especially when Rodin absented himself without telling her where he was going. One day—the right day, as luck would have it—she had him followed. He caught a train from Montparnasse, bound for yet another visit to Chartres Cathedral. Rose was highly delighted.

Rodin may not have paraded his mistresses, but his mistresses were less discreet. Paris buzzed with stories of his amatory prowess, and lines of suffering furrowed Rose's brow. She confided to one of her few intimates that she only felt really happy when ' Monsieur Rodin ' was confined to bed and unwilling to see visitors. Then she could hover over him, bring him herb tea and stroke his moist forehead, revelling in the rare pleasure of having him to herself.

Despite his reluctance to regularize a situation of such long standing, Rodin was profoundly grateful to the simple creature who had shared his life, nor had he forgotten her devotion to him in less prosperous days. For all his philandering, it never occurred to him to abandon her. His friends suspected that he wanted to feel free and unattached, and that the humble presence of an attentive mistress-cum-housekeeper suited his requirements. He no more wanted to part company with someone for whom he had a genuine regard than he wanted to enter into a marriage which would make him feel tied down. Rose might be irritable, but she could be a model of tact. When friends offered to ask Rodin

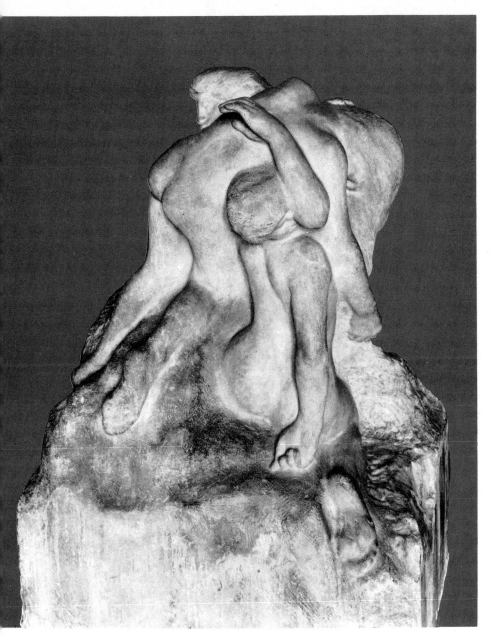

115 *The First Obsequies* 1900

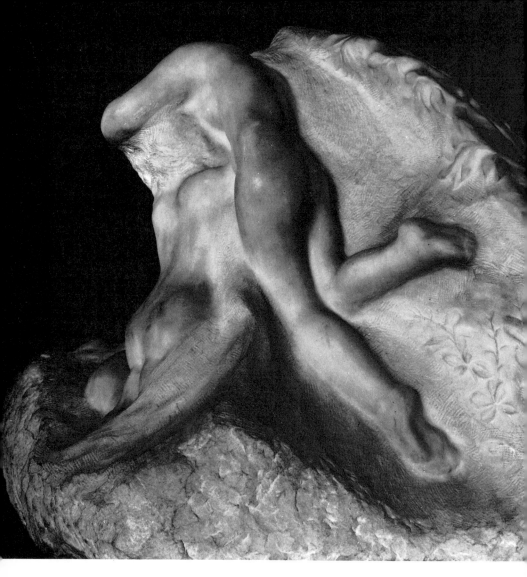

116 *The Oceanids* 1905

to regularize her position, she replied: 'You mustn't bother Monsieur Rodin if that isn't what he wants.'

Then, again, there was Auguste Beuret, the son whom he would have had to legitimize. Auguste was a born failure. Having previously made a determined effort to teach him drawing, his father tried to employ him on minor tasks, but in vain. Auguste lacked both the intelligence and the inclination to do more than enjoy the company of idlers like himself, though he was not fundamentally bad and preserved an enduring affection for his mother. He was always turning up penniless and in rags. His father lost all interest in him and dreaded his unannounced appearances at the Villa des Brillants. Being highly fastidious himself, Rodin no doubt found the sight of his slovenly offspring unendurable. At the age of forty, Auguste secured a job with Renaults and managed to hold it down for three years, but he and his epileptic wife gradually sank into a slough of alcoholism.

Rodin was always having trouble with his secretaries. He picked men of ability, but his treatment of them became more and more impulsive and tyrannical. His first secretary, an Englishman named Ludovici, only stayed with him for a short time. He then came into contact with Rainer Maria Rilke. The young German-speaking poet knew nothing of the sculptor except the few works he had seen in Prague and Germany, but his admiration for Rodin was such that he longed to make his acquaintance. Commissioned by a German publisher to produce a monograph on Rodin, Rilke arrived in Paris in 1902. He requested an interview with the sculptor, met him, and fell under his spell. He paid repeated visits to Meudon, dazzled by the spectacle of Rodin at work in his studio. His monograph, which took the form of a lyrical meditation, was completed in the following year. [26]

Contact with Rodin left a deep impression on Rilke. While pondering on the artist's genius, he took notes for his *Aufzeichnungen des Malte Laurids Brigge*. As Bernard Halde pointed out in his book on Rilke, 'Rodin's teaching set him on a new road'. In 1905 he wrote to Rodin from Germany: ' What moves me, Master, is the need to see you again and feed for a brief while on the glowing vitality of your beautiful works. ' Rodin was flattered and delighted by this token of the poet's respect. He invited him to Meudon and put a small house in the grounds at his disposal.

Although Rilke's knowledge of French was still very sketchy, he was entrusted with the great man's correspondence.

Rilke, who was gentleness and delicacy personified, soon found out what it was like to live at close quarters with a moody and autocratic giant. He took all that Rodin handed out, clinging to the belief that human frailty must be accepted when it is the obverse of genius. Then, one day, Rodin abruptly and arbitrarily dismissed him. Rilke wrote his late employer a letter filled with humility and anguished fervour: ' Here I am, unexpectedly banished like a thieving servant from the little house in which you so generously installed me. I am deeply hurt, but I understand. I realize that the well-ordered structure of your life must at once reject what seems detrimental if its functions are to remain intact, just as the eye rejects anything that impedes its view... I shall not see you again, but for me, as for the Apostles who remained behind, saddened and forlorn, life is beginning anew—a life which will extol your lofty example and find, in you, its consolation, justification, and strength. '

Rilke's successors all suffered much the same fate. We have already mentioned the difficulties that beset Charles Morice. Later, it was the turn of Mario Meunier and the art historian Gustave Coquiot. Much as they tried to make allowances for the notorious temperament of an artist whom they greatly respected and admired, each of them came to realize that daily contact with him was impossible. Age only aggravated his failings. He fell into the hands of spongers who exploited his lack of guile. Advice irritated him, discussion became pointless, and comments went unheeded. The only people who wielded any influence over him at all were women. Judith Cladel could handle him, although even their platonic and beneficent relationship had its ups and downs, and Marcelle Turel—the ' humble employee ', as she termed herself—visited the Villa des Brillants almost daily from 1907 until his death. Despite sporadic rows, her native quick wits and gift of repartee enabled this woman from the Midi, as far as such a thing was possible, to act as Rodin's watch-dog. In view of his growing propensity to thrust aside those who wished

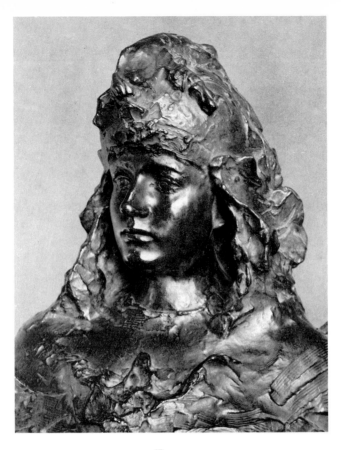

117 *France* 1904

him well and surround himself with knaves and charlatans, he certainly needed one.

The simplicity of Meudon life suited both Rodin and Rose. Rodin liked to hear poultry clucking in the hen-house and see cows grazing in his fields. He always drank a bowl of fresh milk before starting work in the mornings. He was unused to comfort and felt no need of it. The seating arrangements at Meudon were rudimentary and the rooms so ill-heated that he found it quite natural to wear his overcoat and beret at home in the winter. Meanwhile, his art collection grew steadily.

He could have led a peaceful existence at Meudon, tasting the ineffable joys of the country-side, watching the trees at twilight or gazing down at the Seine as it rounded the foot of the hill, but the memory of Camille tormented him. He knew that she was living cooped up in two ground-floor rooms on the Quai de Bourbon, her only furnishings a bed, a few chairs, and her plasters. Aware of her poverty and of her proud refusal to admit it, he tactfully conveyed, via intermediaries, that he would like to help her financially. However, the very idea of accepting a gift from Rodin sent the indomitable young woman into such a fit of rage that she hurled violent accusations at him and furiously showed her visitors out, ordering them never to cross her threshold again. She was obsessed with Rodin's memory and convinced that he meant to make her suffer. Impelled by a mixture of horror and fascination, she lacerated her feelings still further by prowling round the garden of the Villa des Brillants at nightfall and watching Rodin's home-coming from the shelter of the bushes. Rose, who may well have feared for his safety, used to scan the bushes for Camille and call down curses on her rival's head if she sighted her. [27]

Rodin never knew the tragic outcome of Camille's all-consuming passion for him. In the meantime, his life had been invaded by someone as unlike her as it was possible to be, a vain and stupid woman who exerted a baneful influence on him and ultimately covered him with ridicule.

Rodin had got to know the Marquis de Choiseul and was invited to his château in Brittany. The Marquise, an American who had never lost her strong foreign accent, laid siege to the sculptor. It seems almost incredible, in view of her crude blend of flattery, coquetry and enticement, that she should have wormed her way into Rodin's heart, but she did.

His friends were astonished to see her more and more frequently at his side. She held forth when visitors called at his studio and attracted unfavourable attention with her bombastic manner and extravagant hats. She was not ugly, but she tried to enhance her faded charms by plastering her face with make-up. At a period when even the use of rice-powder was confined to women of easy virtue, these daubs of colour were considered not only eccentric but provocative. However, her marriage was a passport to Parisian high society (she had meanwhile become a duchess) and, more especially, to the upper reaches of the American colony.

Rodin's amatory exploits were already legendary when he met the woman who blithely styled herself his ' Muse '. Whether in his studio or elsewhere, he was always to be seen in the company of women—mostly foreign and of all ages—whom he introduced simply as ' my pupils '. His ' pupils ' seldom lasted long. Morice asserted that any woman, whatever her looks, ' sent him into rut '. The models he employed knew what to expect. As for his lady sitters, they knew of his perilous reputation but were not always daunted by it. His powers of seduction were great. Despite the lechery of his latter years, he remained gallantly deferential in the most indelicate situations. Once so shy and reserved, he had come to believe that failure to proposition a woman was the mark of a cad. One day, finding himself alone with a very prim lady of exalted station and feeling no urge to make advances, he thought it necessary to apologize for his omission with the words: ' My doctor has forbidden me to... '

Rodin's expression had changed. The man whom writers had once likened to the god Pan now looked more like a satyr, and his eyes too often shone with unabashed lust. Sem, who entertained Parisians with wickedly accurate caricatures of public figures in animal guise, called his widely publicized caricature of Rodin ' The Sacred Goat '.

Madame Bourdelle recalls that when she was twenty she and some friends watched Rodin leave the Bourdelle house. He set off slowly, then turned and saw the young women watching him. To their amusement he straightened up with a jerk and continued on his way, strutting like a peacock.

Rodin's peccadillos amounted to little as a general rule, but his grand affair with ' the Duchess ' was a regrettable exception. With a cunning which was obvious to everyone in the sculptor's entourage, she played the devoted acolyte, flattered and cajoled him, dressed him and decked him out for excursions into her 'set'. She also promised to dispose of his work at vast profit on the American market. Having ousted his true friends, she replaced them with people whose only aim was to exploit his reputation and financial resources. One day she even refused to admit Maillol, who had always been such a welcome visitor to the Villa des Brillants.

The rapidly aging sculptor had become clay in the hands of a scheming woman. Together, they visited cathedrals, stayed with Gabriel Hanotaux at his villa in Roquebrune, and travelled to Rome, where they were greeted at the Capitol with the honours normally reserved for visiting statesmen.

The Duchess was in the seventh heaven. She became still more arrogant, and behaved insufferably towards models, assistants, servants, and all whose professional duties kept them in contact with the master. As for the latter, part of his precious time was devoted to extolling the love of his 'Muse' in prose-poems of incredible naivety.

The Duchess not only drank—whisky, Chartreuse, wine, and anything else in sight—but tried to interest Rodin in her vice. The spectacle was so distressing that friends braved his anger in an attempt to bring him down to earth, but he cut them short. Articles of value disappeared from the Hôtel Biron, among them dozens of drawings. Stealthy moves were made—stealthy, but nonetheless obvious in intention. The underlying motive was to stake a claim to Rodin's estate by getting rid of Rose for good.

Suddenly, the scales fell from Rodin's eyes. He broke with the Duchess for good, and nothing—neither scenes, threats, nor somewhat peculiar entreaties from the Duke that Rodin should continue to see his wife—shook his rocklike determination to have done with her.

'I've wasted seven years of my life,' he declared. 'That woman was my evil genius... She took me for a fool and people believed her... And I had my wife, too, the poor little flower of the field which I almost crushed.'

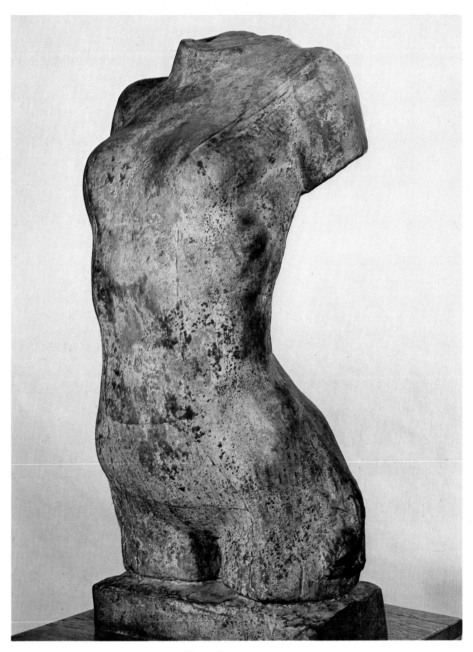

118 *Torso of a young woman* 1909

Eaten up with jealousy, hatred and shame, Rose can have had little left to hope for. Judith Cladel was present when Rodin returned to Meudon. 'He had let her know that he would be coming home after work that evening, as he used to. There was something simple and noble about it. She went to meet her elderly companion at the end of the avenue of chestnut-trees. " Bonsoir, Rose! "—" Bonsoir, mon ami. " Without another word she gave him her arm and led him back to the house. Their life together, with its joys and storms, began afresh. '

# CHAPTER TWELVE

# The Hôtel Biron

The deplorable episode with the Duchess lasted until 1911. Meanwhile, the installation of Rodin's studio in the Hôtel Biron had transformed his life and was to have all kinds of repercussions on his remaining years.

The Hôtel Biron was one of the most majestic mansions in Paris. Built by Gabriel and Aubert in the eighteenth century, it owed its name to a previous occupant, Louis de Gontaut, Duke of Biron and Marshal of France. The property had had a chequered career before being sold, in 1820, to the ladies of the Sacré-Cœur, who turned it into a girls' boarding-school. They built annexes in the main quadrangle and a large neo-Gothic chapel adjoining the Rue de Varenne. After the disestablishment of 1904 they were forced to vacate the property, and it was sequestrated.

The liquidator saw fit to let the available premises at derisory rents to anyone who was interested. Slumbering in the heart of Paris amid the tangled vegetation of a huge neglected garden, the little palace became a haunt of poets and artists, especially foreigners. Isadora Duncan gave dancing lessons in one of the galleries. De Max moved into the chapel and transformed the sacristy into a bathroom. One of the former classrooms served Matisse as a studio. Jean Cocteau records that he wandered in there at the age of eighteen, quite by chance, and rented a large room whose French windows overlooked the silent garden. ' I paid as much in a year as it would have cost to rent a room in a

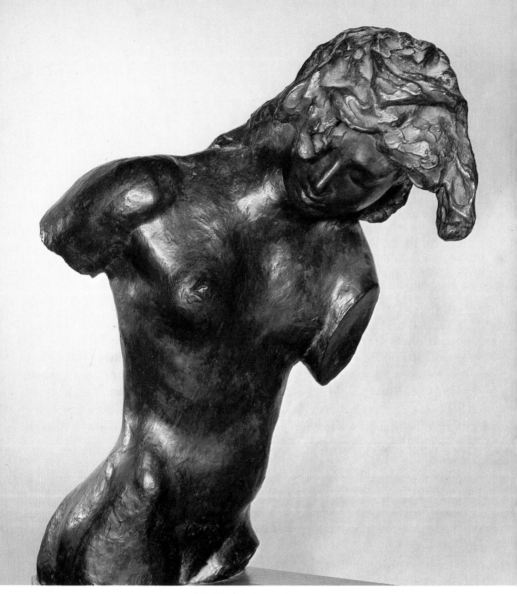

119 *Half-length figure of a woman* 1910

squalid hotel... At night, from my windows, I used to see a lamp burning at the left end of the house, a lamp like a beacon. It was Rilke's lamp.'

Rilke's wife, the sculptress Clara Westhoff, had in fact been one of the Hôtel Biron's first tenants. Rilke himself went to live there in 1908. Forgetting all about his earlier bitterness, he guessed that Rodin would be captivated by the house and invited him to call. Everything about the place was designed to appeal to the sculptor, from the majestic and nobly decorated exterior to the large, well-proportioned rooms and the seemingly limitless expanse of wild and luxuriant vegetation outside. It also happened to be quite near the Dépôt des Marbres.

Within a few days, Rodin had rented the ground-floor rooms facing the garden, two of which retained their period panelling.

He could not have found a finer setting or more ideal place of work. Limiting himself to a few simple pieces of furniture, he hung a large canvas by Carrière near others by Renoir and Van Gogh and distributed a large number of his own watercolours round the walls. The marble sculptures with which he seemed to commune so constantly were everywhere. Looking through the French windows, with their old greenish panes, one could discern a mass of greenery pierced by mossy glades. Everyone who saw Rodin at work here sensed the harmonious relationship between the man and the things he cherished. His new studio lent him even greater stature.

Rodin set off for the ' Biron ' from the Villa des Brillants almost every day. (It goes without saying that Rose was not privileged to cross the threshold.) He liked to sit beneath the trees after work and bask in the stillness.

Unfortunately, an evil fate decreed that his idyll should be disturbed. Barely a year passed before some speculators—the word ' developer ' was not yet in vogue—got their hands on the hundred-acre property and drew up plans for parcelling it up into lots. The house itself was scheduled for demolition.

With her customary enthusiasm, Judith Cladel laid siege to various ministers and gained a temporary stay of execution. In

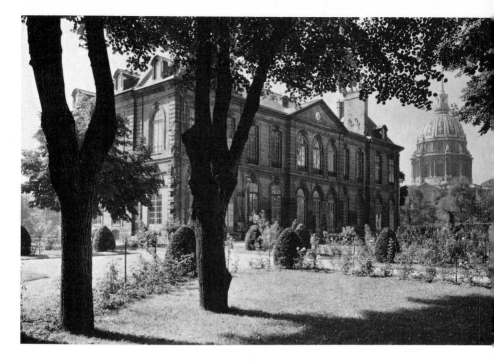

120 *Hôtel Biron*

1911, however, the municipal authorities gave all tenants notice to quit, and she had to start lobbying all over again. Her dream was to turn the Hôtel Biron into a Rodin museum. The sculptor, who dreaded the prospect of leaving, was flattered by this idea and fell in with it. He proposed to bequeath all his works and collections to the state in return for permission to remain at the Hôtel Biron until his death.

This proposal met with an extremely mixed reception. Catholic circles were shocked at the thought of preserving Rodin's ' erotic ' works in a former convent and chapel from which good Catholic nuns had been ousted by government decree. From another angle, it was not the Republic's practice to bestow property of such magnitude on a living artist.

A parliamentary bill proposing the establishment of a Rodin museum was finally tabled at the beginning of 1914, but the mills of government ground slowly. Dalimier, the Minister of Fine Arts, who was eager to lend his name to the project, convened a meeting of government officials and civil servants at the Hôtel Biron on 25 July. After some discussion, the meeting was adjourned until a later date. Within a week, war broke out.

The scheme was revived in 1915 with strong backing from de Monzie. Rodin, as susceptible to the ladies as ever, made them

*121 Rodin in his studio at the Hôtel Biron*

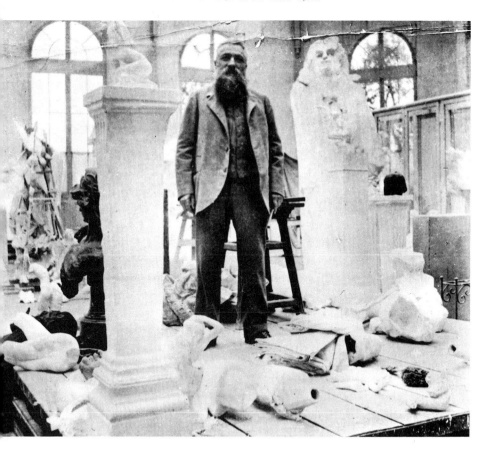

only too welcome in his splendid studio. There were jealous scenes and articles of value started to disappear. More serious still, the ladies took advantage of the sculptor's weakness to get him to alter his will in their favour.

In 1916 Rodin signed a deed of gift embracing ' each and every work of art contained in Rodin's various studios, whether his own work or of any other artistic provenance whatsoever; all his writings, whether printed or in manuscript, published or unpublished, with all the rights of authorship appertaining thereto '.

At the end of the year, despite political opposition and a declaration of protest signed by members of the Institut, the bill was approved by Chamber and Senate.

Rodin's output had declined since the 1890s and more especially since the disruption caused by his affair with the Duchess. Large-scale monuments were a thing of the past but sales abounded. He supervised the casting of his sculptures, checked their patina and finish, resumed work on old studies, had his statues enlarged and cast, assembled groups of figures, continued to turn out drawings and watercolours by the score. In short, since everything that bore his name had acquired value, he exploited the concentrated endeavour of earlier years.

Commissions for busts brought in more than enough to guarantee him a livelihood. He now charged 40,000 francs apiece, having realized that stiff prices only consolidated his reputation and that plenty of people were ready to pay still more for the privilege of adorning their home with a bust sculpted by an artist sufficiently famous to command such fees. [28]

When modelling a bust, Rodin employed methods wholly peculiar to himself. Faithful reproduction of physiognomy was not his sole or primary concern. He began by defining his sitter's bone structure, then modelled the skull down to the lower jaw, viewing it from every angle. After that he tackled the face itself. Far from giving it a single expression, he made it a synthesis of all possible expressions, his aim being to reveal the mystery of inner life.

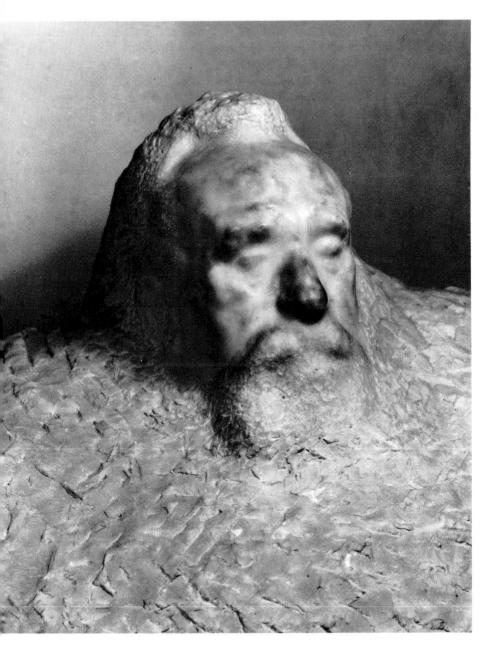

122 *Puvis de Chavannes* 1910

As Rilke clearly saw, Rodin ' preferred to regard a woman's face as part of her beautiful body '. The implication is not far to seek. The sculptor's male portraits generally possessed greater power of expression because he was unimpeded by his devotion to the beauty of the female form. He constructed his heads as he would have constructed a monument, and here his ' outline ' theory found complete fulfilment. One male head was the distillation of a thousand such outlines. Equally, it was the multiplication and continuance of a thousand moments of existence embodied in a single statement which summarized and defined a thousand others.

It must be confessed that most of Rodin's sitters were dissatisfied with their portraits because they did not see themselves as he did and were used to so-called character portraits. Jean-Paul Laurens, a very close friend, criticized his own bust even though its structural splendour made it one of Rodin's finest works, and even though there was not an inch of it which did not vibrate with the life characteristic of all masterpieces. ' It gave me great pleasure to do his bust, ' Rodin said later. ' He reproached me in a friendly way for having portrayed him with his mouth open. I replied that, judging by the shape of his skull, he was very probably descended from the ancient Visigoths of Spain, and that this type was characterized by a protruding lower jaw. I don't know if he acknowledged the truth of this ethnographic observation. ' [29]

Even in their friendlier days, Dalou never expressed any gratitude for the bust which later became so famous, feeling that Rodin could have done better. Puvis de Chavannes made no secret of his disappointment. ' It was one of the bitterest blows of my career that Puvis de Chavannes didn't like my bust. He thought I had caricatured him. Even so, I am satisfied that my sculpture expressed all the warmth and respect I felt for him. ' [30]

Rochefort was another who thought he had been caricatured. As for Clemenceau, he dined out on his experiences in Rodin's studio. Having described how the sculptor climbed a stepladder to make sketches of the top of his head, then squatted down

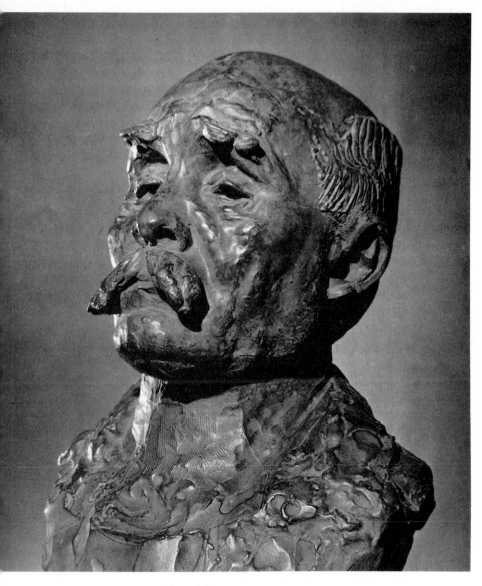

123 *Bust of Clemenceau* 1911

to get a better view of his lower jaw, he added: ' All that, just to
make me look like a Mongolian general! ' The fact was that men

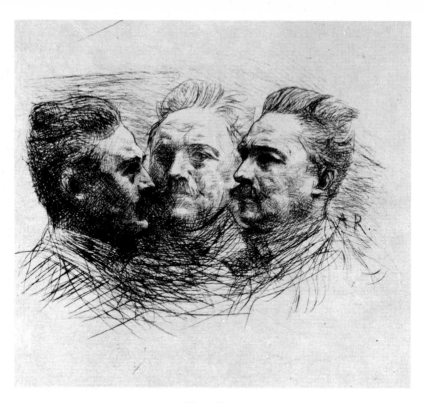

124 *Henry Becque* 1883

preferred to be portrayed as they would have liked to be, not as they were.

The ladies showed greater satisfaction with their finished appearance, which was almost invariably seductive. The only one to suspend sittings before completion was the Comtesse de Noailles, but she was noted for her quirky behaviour. Rodin's other women clients included many foreigners, particularly of American origin. One of these, Loie Fuller, made it her business to foster his reputation in the United States and persuade collectors to buy his work.

Rodin's portrait gallery grew steadily during the last fifteen years of his life. It included women such as Mrs Potter-Palmer, Madame de Goloubeff, Miss Eve Fairfax, Lady Warwick and

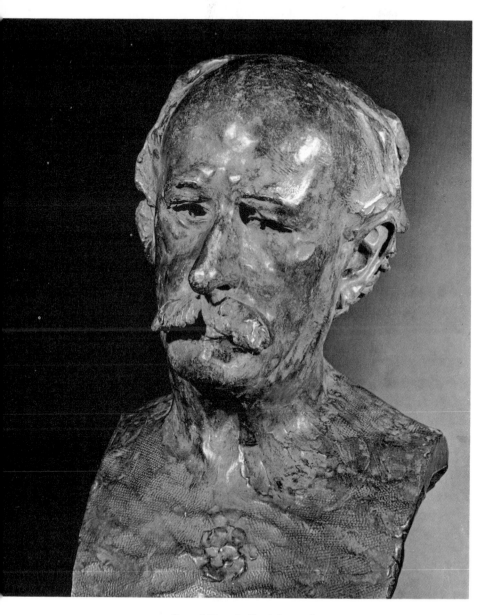

125 *Bust of Marçelin Berthelot* 1906

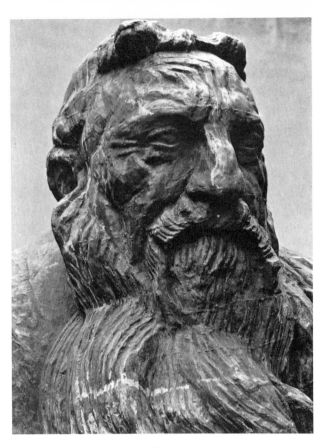

126 Bourdelle. *Rodin* 1910

Lady Sackville-West—not to mention his bust of the Duchesse de Choiseul, a terrible psychological document; writers and artists such as Henry Becque, George Bernard Shaw, Gustav Mahler, René Vivien, Marcelin Berthelot, Gustave Geffroy, Falguière, and Puvis de Chavannes; and politicians such as Georges Leygues, Clemenceau, and Clémentel. To Rodin, there was no such thing as an unrewarding face. He was personally involved in every one of his portraits.

Like his sitters, who did not always appreciate their busts, Rodin was not always pleased with portraits of himself by others,

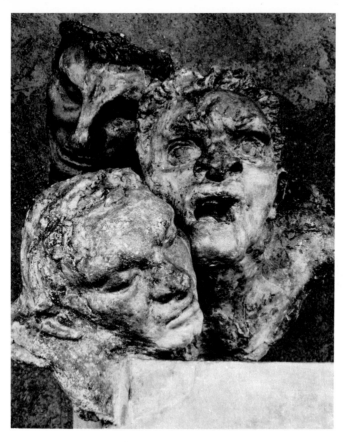

127 Bourdelle. *Howling Figures* 1894-99

like the strong sculpture in which Bourdelle tried, as Michelangelo did with Moses, to turn him into a sort of superman. Although some people regarded it as a caricature, the dedication—' To Rodin, these collected profiles '—was a tribute to artistic mastery. Rodin disliked it intensely when his pupils turned out ' non-Rodin ' work. He coolly declined to go on posing as Bourdelle wished him to. It must have distressed him that his pupils failed, for all their admiration, to follow the road which he had mapped out for them, and his reaction to Bourdelle's *Head of Apollo* was: ' Ah, Bourdelle, you're deserting me! '

We can only guess at what he would have said if he had witnessed the subsequent development of those who used to frequent his studio. What of Maillol, with his smooth, plain, full-bodied figures and total emphasis on the static ? What of Pompon, his former assistant, a late-developer whose aesthetic approach was the reverse of his own ? What of Charles Despiau, the delicate, nervous, morbidly sensitive collaborator of his latter years ? Rodin had been struck by the serene charm of Despiau's bust *Paulette* at an exhibition in 1907. Despiau, then unknown, could hardly believe his eyes when he received the master's invitation to visit him. He became far more than a slavish copyist. Rodin, who liked his spirit of independence and appreciated his talents to the full, entrusted him with the free interpretation of some of his rough models (*e.g.* the bust of Madame Elisseief). Even though traces of Rodin's technical influence can be discerned in the work of this last of the great French portraitists, its decorum, restraint and total lack of animation entirely differentiate it from that of the man who taught him so much but was never, all appearances to the contrary, his master.

A whole generation of sculptors revolved round Rodin, yet none of them continued his work or became his disciple in the true sense. The sculptor who had transformed Romanticism and Naturalism left behind him a generation of ' Classicists ' who saw art as a process of mental elaboration and strove to forge new links with very ancient traditions which included those of Egypt and the Far East as well as Greece. They acknowledged his outstanding greatness, saluted him, and marched on in search of fresh fields to conquer.

Thus, a man whose towering personality had dominated the contemporary scene was succeeded by a generation which took a road contrary to his own—a fate common to the history of art and mankind.

To Rodin, expression did not reside in the face alone but reigned over the whole epidermis and in the depths of the flesh. Similarly, personality was conveyed by the hands. It emanated from the

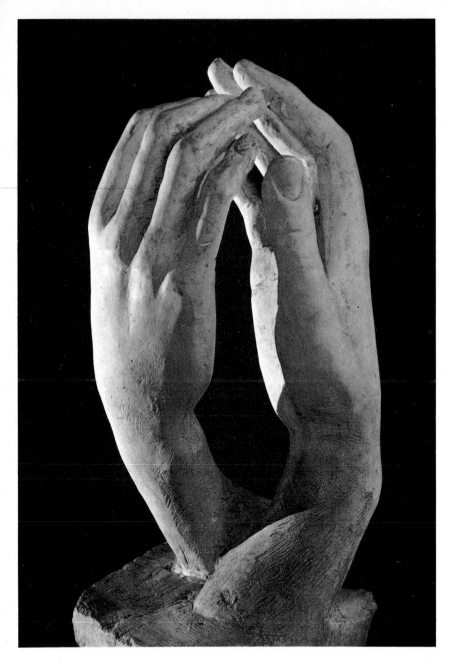

128 *The Cathedral* 1908

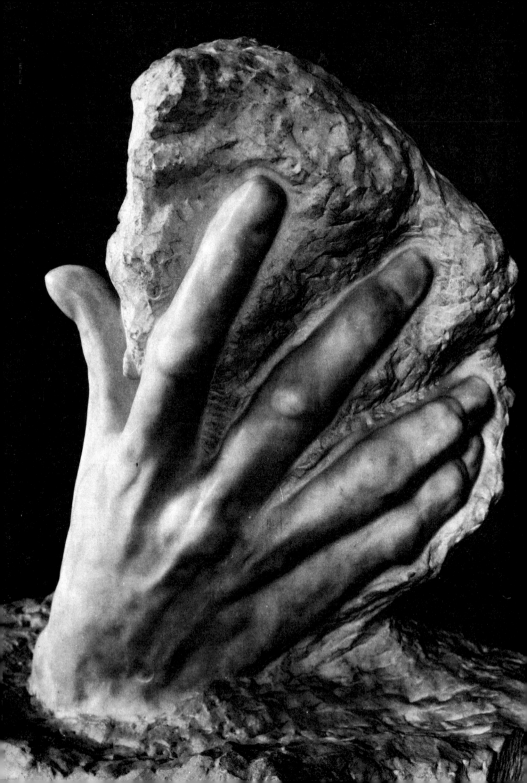

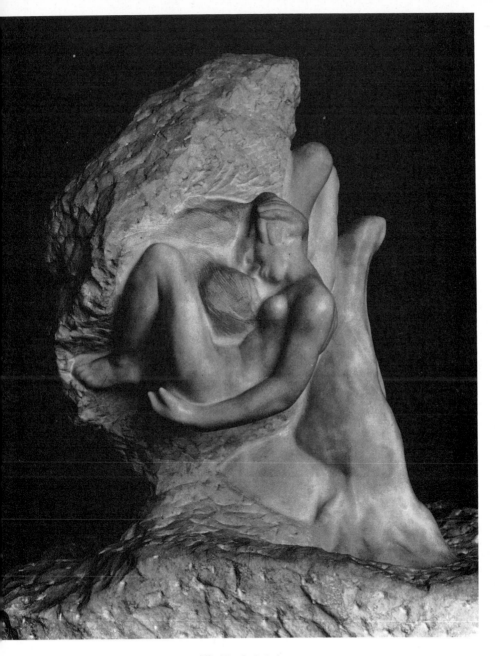

130  *The Hand of God* 1898

◀ 129  *The Hand of God* 1898

softness of a palm, from the flexing of the fingers, from the animation of a gesture. Rodin could invest hands with such vitality
that they defined the person they belonged to. By charging
physical extremities with such energy, he showed that he attached
equal importance to the expressive and artistic qualities of every
part of the human body. The rugged nobility of the enormous
hands in *The Burghers of Calais,* the clenched fists of *The Call to
Arms,* the open palms of *The Prodigal Son,* the gentle hands of
embracing lovers, made for the bestowal of soft caresses, tense
hands, enraged hands, despairing hands, contorted hands straining
at the empty air—Rodin knew the revelatory force of all these. He
cast some of them in bronze and gave them a validity of their own
by divorcing them from the original statue. He also modelled
hands in their own right, raising them to the status of a monument
and endowing them with as much meaning and emotion as if he
had sculpted the entire figure. These include the tremulous,
enigmatic hands entitled *The Secret,* wedded at the base in their
matrix of stone; *The Cathedral,* a pair of devout and tranquil hands
forming an ogee arch; *The Hand Emerging from the Tomb; The
Hand of the Devil; The Hand of God,* gigantic and refulgent, with the
first man and woman taking shape within it; and the *Left Hands*
which are a portrait of his own left hand.

# CHAPTER THIRTEEN

# The great shade

Rodin was passing through a period of physical decline. He was turning into a great big child who needed guidance in everything which affected his every-day life, but he was as autocratic as ever and could still lash out savagely at those around him. Although he put on a show in public, his air of majesty was undiminished and his silences were construed as a sign of godlike superiority.

In January 1914 he decided to go and relax in the south with Rose, who was also in poor health. The old couple spent some weeks in a furnished apartment at Hyères, stayed at Menton, and visited Hanotaux at Roquebrune.

The war came. Rodin, who had grown accustomed to dealing direct with the men at the top, besieged Dalimier in his office—at the height of mobilization fever—and tried to badger him into pressing on with the museum project. He also asked for a travel warrant to the Midi during the German advance on Paris. Then, having learned that Judith Cladel and her mother were leaving for England, he changed his mind at the last minute and decided to go with them accompanied by Rose, who never left his side from now on.

Rodin travelled to London, scene of his first successes and of several earlier visits, but refused to stay there on the grounds that his inability to memorize and pronounce English names might offend the people he would have to meet. (The Duke of Westminster organized a public exhibition of his work at Grosvenor House, but he never saw it.)

Judith Cladel was going to stay with her sister in Cheltenham, so he decided to accompany her. Rose had forwarded some furniture, which arrived after an understandable delay, but she had forgotten to stow any clothes inside. Travelling to England among swarms of fellow-exiles had been a bewildering experience for her.

They put up at a small private hotel. Curiously enough, Rodin seemed to develop a taste for the quiet predictability of this type of life *à l'anglaise*. Accompanied by elderly ladies, he descended punctually for breakfast, lunch and tea, preserving the silence and immobility of a statue. Rose, who showed far more animation, recounted her woes for the benefit of anyone who cared to listen. A peasant and housewife to the marrow, she loathed being waited on and preferred to take personal charge of everything affecting ' Monsieur Rodin '.

In November they returned to Paris, but not for long. Loie Fuller, still a bundle of energy and still globe-trotting in spite of the war, suggested a visit to Rome. Albert Besnard, then director of the Villa Medici, had told her that he was to paint an official portrait of Pope Benedict XV, and there was an idea afoot that Rodin might do a bust in marble.

The Rodin household duly set off for the city which had been such a constant source of joy to the sculptor. Besnard, who was a personal friend, made it his business to find accommodation where Rodin could work. ' It will be delightful to have him with us, ' he wrote. ' The man says such beautiful things about art and nature. ' But the man had changed. ' I think he feels, in his heart of hearts, that people are paying too much attention to the war and not enough to him... He has aged... I found him very taciturn and much withdrawn from the world whose support he still seeks. ' [31]

In fact, Rodin spent long hours in museums and churches. He was greatly moved by a drive along the Appian Way, which evoked memories of Poussin's landscapes. At Besnard's instigation, a bronze cast of *The Walking Man* had been placed in the courtyard of the Palazzo Farnese, but the ambassador Barrère could

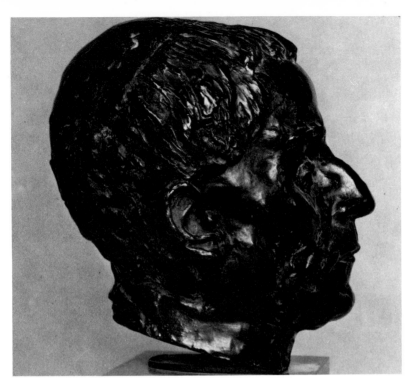

131 *Benedict XV* 1915

not stand the sight of the headless figure. ' The head ? ' retorted Rodin. ' The head is everywhere. '

The Pope, who had already granted Besnard four sittings, postponed the execution of the bust until the following year. Rodin returned to Rome in 1915, this time alone.

Benedict XV was a small man but a great aristocrat and a shrewd diplomat. The war had kindled intense national feeling. As always, the Vatican was accused by both camps of sitting on the fence. The Allies reproached it for not having solemnly condemned the invasion of Belgium, the German States for sympathizing with the Allies.

After the second sitting, Rodin, who was neither aristocrat nor diplomat, boasted of having discussed the war with Benedict and of having 'told him the truth'. Whether for this reason or another, the Pope showed signs of restlessness during the third sitting. Unable to understand why a bust should demand such elaborate preliminaries and unimpressed by an inspection of the rough clay head, he concluded the fourth sitting by informing Rodin that his official duties precluded any further sittings.

Back in Paris during the hard winter of 1916, Rodin persisted in going to the unheated Hôtel Biron every day. He suffered a stroke, and for some weeks life seemed to have ebbed from his face. With a shawl draped round his shoulders, he tottered slowly round the neglected garden, surrounded and supported by the chattering women who had invaded the house. His guile-lessness was strangely mingled with distrust, but gullibility and mental confusion made the ailing old man an easy prey.

All the women in question hoped to profit by their belated devotion to Rodin's welfare. It was not lost on them that neither his old mistress nor his son bore his name. Gifts made on impulse, wills scrapped and redrafted in favour of various women, wills deposited with lawyers and taken back, plans for marriage made and later abandoned—all these gave rise to painful scenes which were rendered even more distressing by the sculptor's periodic bouts of complete mental withdrawal. Mercifully, squabbling between rival parties saved him from the worst.

On the other hand, drawings and small bronzes were still disappearing from the Hôtel Biron. The status of the future museum had yet to be legally confirmed, and there was no form of supervision. Rodin countered his friends' exhortations with impassivity and immured himself in silence.

The situation at Meudon was just as distressing. More exaspe-rated than ever by reports of the 'creatures' who clustered round her lord and master, with his wasted body and feverish eyes, poor Rose was driven almost frantic at times. On other occasions, when they were alone, she would nestle against him and they would sit huddled together in the gathering dusk.

The presence of Rodin's son and the latter's wife in the neighbouring annexe was another disruptive factor. Auguste

Beuret, now a man of fifty, had changed as little as his mother. His wife still drank too much and their home was a complete slum. The servants, who were showered with tips by people anxious to secure friends ' on the inside ', added to the general chaos. Since the household was virtually without a master, its condition was squalid in the extreme. Rodin, who had always been such an orderly person, can never have imagined that he would one day be the victim, if not cause, of such anarchy.

The Minister of Commerce, Clémentel, who was proving an astute friend and doing his best to promote the establishment of a Rodin museum, decided to settle the question of the will once and for all. No one, not even the testator, knew the exact nature of its latest provisions. Rodin was simply persuaded to sign a declaration revoking all previous wills ' other than the one in favour of Rose Beuret, in recognition of fifty years of life together '. [32]

Rose was called in to hear the document read aloud. Judith Cladel then asked Rodin if it would not be appropriate to give Rose his name legally, since he had been introducing her to everyone as his wife for so many years. ' You always have such good ideas, ' Rodin replied. ' Your friends will attend to everything for you, ' she told him. ' The wedding can take place in your garden, in the presence of a few close friends. ' ' It must be like that, ' Rodin replied in his quiet voice.

How to guard the premises was another problem to be faced. Clémentel, Dalimier, Under-Secretary of State at the Ministry of Fine Arts, and Léonce Bénédite, Curator of the Museum of Modern Art, decided to post attendants at the Hôtel Biron and the Villa des Brillants with orders to exclude all who had no right to admittance. Rodin was put in the care of a nurse, but the most difficult thing of all was to protect him from himself. Marcelle Tirel was instructed never to take her eyes off any female visitor whom Rodin's entourage considered to be an intruder— a mission which she undertook with fanatical zeal.

Judith Cladel was given the task of making an inventory of the drawings in the Villa des Brillants. She listed 3,400 of them, and the Hôtel Biron contained at least as many more. Auguste Beuret, who had organized his father's various changes of abode, conducted search parties round various old buildings at Meudon—granaries and barns which were found to contain scores of terra-cottas, moulds, and maquettes, among them an original plaster cast of *Victor Hugo.*

As for listing Rodin's financial assets, this was an almost impossible task. He kept an account and a strong-box at the Crédit Lyonnais (the key of the latter was missing), but he had opened other accounts with banking firms whose names he could no longer recall. He had never discussed money matters with anyone, even though he was on friendly terms with the chairman of the Crédit Lyonnais. When it was finally opened, a chest in the drawing-room disgorged a mass of papers and photographs, as well as several uncashed cheques more than a year old.

The wedding took place on 19 January 1917 in the big drawing-room of the Villa des Brillants, which was decorated with flowers for the occasion. There were a dozen invited guests. Rodin, who seemed quite happy, kept repeating that he had never felt better. He wore a frock coat and a large velvet beret. Rose was soberly dressed and behaved with great dignity in spite of the pains which racked her chest.

Rodin was lost in the contemplation of a Van Gogh when the mayor asked the ritual question, and had to be prompted. ' Yes, ' he replied softly. Rose's response was: ' Yes, monsieur, with all my heart. '

Tired out by the ceremony, Rose retired to bed. Years of sorrow and suffering had reduced her to a shadow, but her last days were serene and happy. She greeted those who came to see her with words of gratitude. Twenty-five days after her wedding she passed away peacefully. She had kissed her husband before he went out for his walk that morning and told him that he had brought her great happiness.

For a long time, Rodin bent over the emaciated body on the big bed and gazed steadily at the waxen face. Death had erased every line of pain. ' How beautiful she is, ' he murmured, ' —beautiful as a statue... '

Lorries arrived at the Villa des Brillants. In accordance with the deed of gift, the sculptor's works were to be concentrated at the Hôtel Biron. All the pieces that held so many memories for him were carted off before his very eyes. One afternoon, removal men came downstairs carrying the big Gothic crucifix which had occupied almost the full height of his bedroom. Inarticulate with rage, the old man tried to restrain them by force. Fortunately, Judith Cladel came to the rescue. Outraged by this display of blundering brutality, she gave orders for the crucifix to be restored to its original place.

Rodin would have liked to draw, but he was not allowed pens and pencils in case he made a new will. His hands were always groping for imaginary clay, but even that had been taken away. Vainly, he ran his fingers over old maquettes. He asked to see the Hôtel Biron again, but was only permitted one visit a fortnight. It is difficult to understand how the authorities could have acted with such harshness and inhumanity towards the broken man who had just made them a gift of his life's work.

Old dreams shed a fitful radiance on the cloudy solitude of his mind. Scraps of accumulated wisdom fell from his lips like the echo of distant gunfire. ' The war is our decadence... People have tried to evade the law of work... The ancients told us everything, but we no longer understand them... Rheims Cathedral is burning. The restorers had already killed it. What are they going to do now? Beauty goes unrecognized everywhere... The architects of Rome cannot see their city any more. They are going to do away with the Via Appia and replace it with their own miserable buildings... '

On 12 November he developed a high temperature and lay there inert with the breath whistling shrilly in his throat. The doctor was summoned and diagnosed pneumonia.

Rodin lapsed into unconsciousness. The whistling in his wind-pipe grew more strident, then gave way to deep, heavy

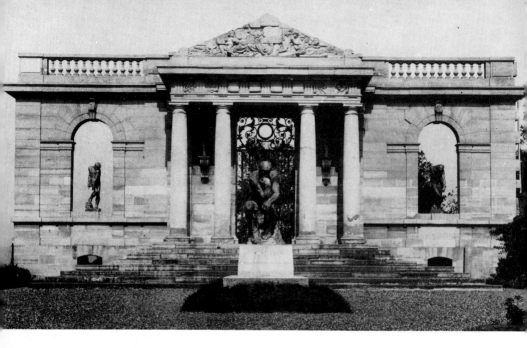

132 *Rodin's tomb*

breathing. From time to time, his sturdy frame emitted a gasp which seemed to fill the whole house. He became restless, waging an unwitting battle against the onset of death. His face worked and hollows appeared in his cheeks. Finally, at four o'clock on the morning of 17 November, the frozen immobility of death descended on him.

His massive head lay heavy on the pillows. His features had relaxed and taken on a new purity, an even greater dignity and solemnity. His white beard flowed over the white woollen robe in which he was to be buried. A maidservant had placed a sprig of consecrated box in a bowl beside him, and relatives had slipped a small crucifix between his fingers. He looked like an effigy on a tomb, hewn in marble by some medieval stonemason.

France was still at war. There was no state funeral, but Rodin's coffin was draped in the national colours.

The procession halted at the bottom of the garden beside the steps of the façade of the Château d'Issy, which Rodin had saved from destruction. The catafalque was dominated by the brooding figure of *The Great Shade*. After an insipid ministerial address the coffin was lowered into the vault at the foot of the steps, where Rodin's wife already lay. In death as in life, he remained united with the woman who had spent her life as plain Mademoiselle Rose Beuret but went to her death bearing the name of Auguste Rodin, the name which bronze and marble were to perpetuate in the memory of mankind.

# CHAPTER FOURTEEN

# Posthumous fame

Rodin's art was hotly debated until almost the end of his life, but time did its work. What had once seemed outrageous gradually faded, to reveal nothing but the radiance of genius. No twentieth-century artist has asserted his authority so completely or with such force. Three museums are devoted to his work—a privilege unique in the annals of art.

The Hôtel Biron museum was established under a law promulgated on 22 December 1916, nine months before Rodin's death, its function being to house the sculptures, drawings and private collections which he had bequeathed to the state. The curators worked hard to turn the handsome house, chapel and garden into a worthy setting for the master's work.

Rodin's presence is most vividly conveyed by the museum in the Villa des Brillants at Meudon, not only because he spent the last twenty years of his life there but also because its numerous sketches, moulds, plasters, maquettes and fragmentary studies show him at work and record the actual development of his sculptures. Nothing could be more fascinating than the successive ' states ' of his large monuments, which bring the beholder face to face with their process of creation. Thanks to the munificence of Mrs Mastbaum, an American, a bright and spacious museum was erected near his tomb in 1930.

Some years earlier, Jules E. Mastbaum decided to found a Rodin Museum in Philadelphia. The façade incorporates a reproduction of the Château d'Issy portico at Meudon. Inside are works representative of every stage in the sculptor's career, including ninety bronzes and marbles, thirty-nine plasters and terracottas, and a large number of drawings. The Philadelphia museum was opened in 1929.

# Notes

(1) The Rue de l'Arbalète was combined with the Cul-de-Sac des Patriarches in 1928, hence the new location of the plaque. Rodin's birthplace was situated near the old École de Pharmacie and the Jardin des Apothicaires, between the Rue Mouffetard and the Rue Neuve-Sainte-Geneviève (now the Rue Lhomond)

(2) Carpeaux, who died in 1875, only knew Rodin as an art student

(3) Dujardin-Beaumetz, *Entretiens avec Rodin*

(4) He earned five francs a day, the most a skilled craftsman could hope for at this period

(5) A professional model

(6) To 268 Rue Saint-Jacques and then to 39 Rue du Faubourg Saint-Jacques, a Public Assistance building which has since been demolished

(7) Renamed Rue Falguière in 1900

(8) Dujardin-Beaumetz, ibid.

(9) The proposed site was the Rond-Point de la Défense

(10) It was placed in the left-hand niche on the façade of the Hôtel de Ville

(11) The Gare and Hôtel d'Orsay were rebuilt on this site in 1898

(12) It was forty-one years before the *Balzac* monument was erected in a public place

(13) Dujardin-Beaumetz, ibid.

(14) Dujardin-Beaumetz, ibid.

(15) Dujardin-Beaumetz, ibid.

(16) Reported by Judith Cladel

(17) Rodin, *Les Cathédrales*

(18) Paul Claudel, *L'œil écoute*

(19) *Le Voltaire*, 23 February 1892

(20) Some extremely interesting documentary material figured in the Balzac and Rodin Exhibition organized by Mme Cécile Goldscheider at the Musée Rodin in 1950

(21) Reported by Judith Cladel

(22) *Gil Blas*, 30 September 1896

(23) At the time of his death in 1917, experts valued Rodin's private collections at four million francs

(24) Rodin, ibid.

(25) Correspondence between Louis Gillet and Romain Rolland, letter dated 31 December 1912

(26) *Rodin*, English edition, Grey Walls Press, London 1946

(27) Reported by Judith Cladel

(28) The annual salary of a civil judge varied between 6,000 and 8,500 francs, according to seniority

(29) Paul Gsell, *Entretiens avec Rodin*

(30) Paul Gsell, ibid.

(31) Albert Besnard, *Sous le ciel de Rome*

(32) About ten handwritten wills of similar content were found after Rodin's death

# List of Illustrations

Page numbers in italics indicate colour plates

ALL PHOTOGRAPHS ARE BY RENÉ-JACQUES EXCEPT WHERE OTHERWISE
INDICATED

284

# Index